The Maquiladora Revolution in Guatemala

The Maquiladora Revolution in Guatemala

KURT PETERSEN

Occasional Paper Series, 2

Orville H. Schell, Jr.
Center for International
Human Rights at
Yale Law School
1992

Designed by Elizabeth Duncan Lyons, Lyons Graphics.
Set in Bembo Oldstyle and Univers 65 on a Macintosh IIcx.

Printed in the United States of America by Yale University Printing Service.

Library of Congress Cataloging-in-Publication Data
Petersen, Kurt, 1965–
The maquiladora revolution in Guatemala / by Kurt Petersen.
p. cm. — (Occasional paper series ; 2)
1. Offshore assembly industry—Guatemala. 2. Offshore assembly industry—Employees—Health and hygiene—Guatemala. 3. Investments, South Korean—Guatemala. I. Title. II. Series: Occasional paper series (Orville H. Schell, Jr. Center for International Human Rights) ; 2.
HD9734.G82P48 1992
338.4'7'00097281—dc20 92–23067
CIP

ISBN 1–881862–00–3

A 1992 graduate of Yale Law School, Kurt Petersen is director of the Farm Worker Democracy Education Center in Granger, Washington, which is affiliated with the United Farm Workers of Washington State.

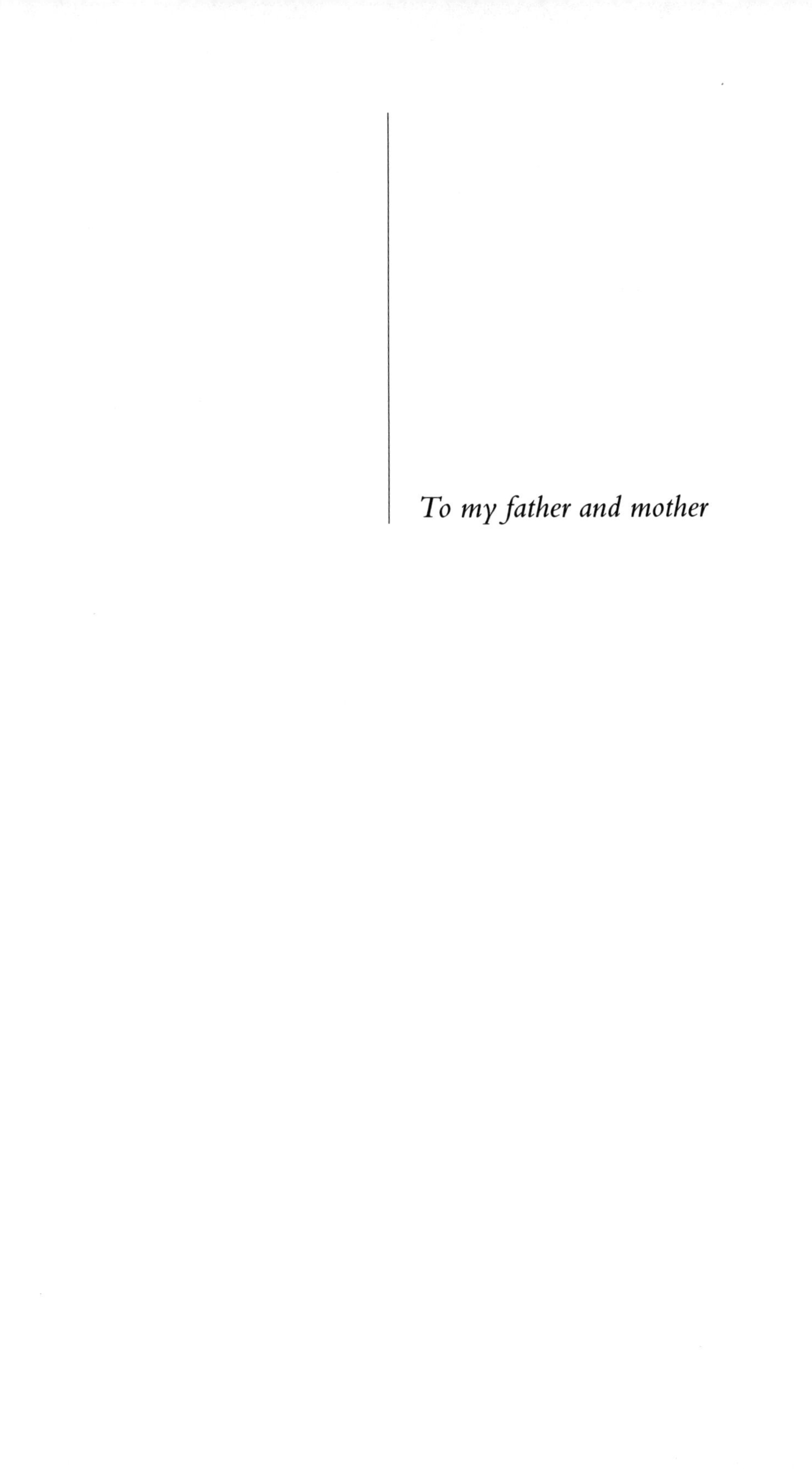

To my father and mother

Contents

Foreword

The Orville H. Schell, Jr. Center is very pleased to present Kurt Petersen's book *The Maquiladora Revolution in Guatemala.* In this first comprehensive study of the garment-assembly industry in Guatemala, Petersen offers a powerful rebuttal to the argument that this industry constitutes the only viable development strategy for countries in the Central American region.

Proponents of the industry view the growth of the maquila as an indispensable step toward the realization of the ladder model of development. They assert that garment-assembly production is the first painful but necessary step toward creating more sophisticated, capital-intensive export-assembly operations, which will usher the country into the much needed phase of industrialization.

This study demonstrates that behind the spectacular growth of the maquila industry (250 factories employing more than 50,000 workers and having revenues of $350 million) lies an industry that prospers by exploiting young women and poor children; an industry that refuses to abide by even the most rudimentary provisions of Guatemala's admittedly outdated, weak, and rarely enforced Labor Code; an industry that has consistently thwarted all legitimate attempts at unionization; finally, an industry that has sustained employee obedience by keeping its work force in a state of permanent insecurity. Needless to say, none of the above would have been possible without the complicity of the Guatemalan government.

Therefore, before we, mesmerized by its impressive statistics, uncritically embrace this new development strategy, we should take a hard look at its hidden costs. To be sure, for the victims of this strategy, the hidden costs constitute part of everyday life. However, for those not familiar with the socioeconomic engineering currently unfolding in Guatemala, Kurt Petersen's excellent study is a reminder of the continuing challenges that face the comprehensive enforcement of human rights norms. The Schell Center welcomes this opportunity to help his findings reach the widest possible audience.

George Andreopoulos

New Haven
June 1992

Preface

The idea for this project surfaced during the visit of a March 1990 delegation of labor lawyers, unionists, and academics to Guatemala. Our purpose was to evaluate the overall quality of labor rights and working conditions being experienced by Guatemalan workers. In our brief stay, numerous persons, from trade-union leaders to representatives of the private sector, spoke of the burgeoning apparel-assembly industry, known in Guatemala as the maquila industry. Opinions about the importance and value of this expanding industrial phenomenon varied tremendously. Some saw it as an economic miracle, providing desperately needed employment and foreign exchange, while others viewed it as the most recent example of abject exploitation of Guatemalan workers. Impressed by the impact and controversy of this industry and concerned about the welfare of the young female workers running the sewing machines, I proposed a project to study the working conditions of Guatemalan maquila workers to The Orville H. Schell, Jr. Center for International Human Rights at Yale Law School in April 1990. The center accepted my proposal, and I left for Guatemala a month later.

It took me only a few days in Guatemala to realize that, because the growth of the maquila industry had been so sudden and rapid, data was scattered and a systematic survey of the industry was nowhere to be found. A few private-business-sector representatives and United States Agency for International Development (AID) personnel were able to list the extraordinary rates of factory output and employment. Union officials were quick to point out insufferable labor conditions. However, no one, when pressed for substantiation, was able to produce documentation for these statistics and anecdotes. As one AID official explained early in my visit, "For the past few years, we have been in the business of producing results, not counting them." Struck by the paucity of formal research, almost immediately I decided to expand the scope of my research to an overall study of the Guatemalan maquila industry.

Almost two years and over three hundred interviews later, this study is ready for public dissemination. In the absence of secondary sources on the Guatemalan maquila industry, interviews and personal visits to more than half the maquila factories form the bulk of my sources. I interviewed a wide spectrum of people with firsthand experience or special knowledge of the industry, including workers, owners and managers, union officials and organizers, government officials, labor inspectors, representatives of the Guatemalan Association of Nontraditional Exporters, AID officials, representatives of the Korean and United States embassies, and assorted other bureaucrats and private individuals. (See page 187 for a description of methodology.)

Chapter 1, "The Maquila Revolution," describes the proliferation of assembly production throughout the developing world that has resulted from the new international division of labor and production. In particular, this section examines the role of Guatemala and its comparative advantage of inexpensive, abundant labor to this new international economy. Chapter 2, "The Construction of an Economic Miracle," provides an economic, political, and historical perspective on the development of the maquila industry in Guatemala. As the most recent form of U.S. economic development assistance, the industry has become the most prosperous and successful sector of the Guatemalan economy in less than five years. This portion ends with an assessment of the maquila revolution's actual contribution to the Guatemalan economy. Chapter 3, "The Market and the Players," describes the policies used by the government to lure investment to the maquila industry, the present propitious investment climate, and the individuals and companies that have taken advantage of these incentives. This chapter also sketches the background and ethnography of the Guatemalan maquila worker, mainly setting up categories and questions for future research.

Chapter 4, "Health and Safety Conditions," documents the deplorable state of health and safety precautions in maquila factories, including an examination of the government's efforts to enforce statutory standards. Chapter 5, "Working Hours, Compensation, and Labor Relations," reports the paltry compensation, long, forced hours of work, and paternalistic, and at times cruel, treatment by employers found in the factories. Both the health and safety conditions and these working conditions exact a heavy toll from workers and place the future of the work force, and probably the industry, in jeopardy. Chapter 6, "Unions and the Maquila Industry: A Battle Against Impunity," analyzes the history and present status of labor unionism in the maquila industry. Despite dozens of formal and informal attempts to unionize, there are no functioning unions in maquila factories. Finally, Chapter 7, "The Korean Model of Development," details the remarkable expansion of Korean maquila production in Guatemala, which represents the largest source of direct foreign investment in the industry. In addition to capital, Korean factory owners also have imported a brutally effective system of labor control that terrorizes workers into obedient, efficient production.

I completed most of the research and writing of this study before my most recent visit to Guatemala in March 1992. Where possible I used information obtained from this trip to update and revise my previous findings. However, several significant changes have occurred which could not be incorporated into the manuscript but nevertheless merit attention. First, prompted by international concern over the industry, the rightist, pro-business administration of President Jorge Serrano Elias, at least on the surface, appears to be to trying to curb labor rights violations in the maquila industry. In fact, labor ministry officials and labor inspectors made it clear that eliminating such violations is their most important priority. Since April 1991, the ministry has been regularly issuing and publicizing reports on the labor violations in the maquila industry as well as lobbying for specific maquila labor legislation. The headlines created by this emerging concern, however, are far more impressive than any concrete improvements taking place in the factories. The factories look the same as they did a year ago, and workers told me repeatedly that they have not noticed any improvement in their working conditions or freedom to associate.

The most poignant example of the administration's superficial concern for the labor conditions in the maquila industry occurred during the visit of Christian Tomuschat, the United Nations Expert on Guatemala, in early 1992. While in Guatemala, the human rights expert accompanied labor ministry officials and media representatives on a "surprise" inspection of a Korean maquila factory. In the much publicized event, Tomuschat witnessed the arrest and sentencing to thirty days in prison of two Korean supervisors who had allegedly beaten workers. Several weeks later, long after the prominent visitor had departed, a judge commuted the Korean defendants' jail term to a fine of Q5, or US$1, a day for thirty days.

The only concrete action undertaken by the new government that may hold some promise of actual improvement is the promulgation of a new minimum wage. Passed during the "honeymoon" period of the Serrano administration, the decree increases the maquila worker's daily wage from Q5.50, or US$1.10, a day to Q11.60, or US$2.32. From my brief visit, I was unable to determine whether factories are actually paying this amount. Some workers told me that many factories, especially the smaller ones, continue to pay the old wage. Workers in Korean factories generally said that they were earning this new amount. Commenting on compliance with the law, one labor inspector said, "Most maquila employers seem to be paying this wage but now overtime [which is a minimum of two hours a day] is never compensated."[1] Widespread compliance with this new wage, however, runs contrary to the general trend found throughout the economy, in which high under- and unemployment have been depressing wages for most jobs, including arguably more skilled positions. In March 1992, for instance, the Labor Ministry posted bilingual secretary positions for Q10 a day and monolingual positions for Q8.25 a day.

Even if employers eventually comply and pay their workers this new scale, which amounts to US$.29 an hour, the wage still falls far below what is necessary to survive in Guatemala. A 1991 study found that a family of four required an average of Q43, or US$8.60, a day to meet a subsistence family basket.[2] In particular, the recent wage hike fails to keep pace with soaring inflation—75 percent in 1991—and cost of living brought on by the government's devaluation of the currency and removal of price controls (see Chapter 3). The fact that the private sector voiced only token resistance to the wage increase indicates that either it does not plan to pay the new wage or it plans to honor the increase because, in the face of the devaluation and inflation, it represents so little in real value.

The other major event occurring in Guatemala is a slowing of, if not an outright end to, the influx of Korean capital into the maquila industry. To some degree, Korean investment has saturated the country, assembling garments in some fifty factories. However, the original Korean investment strategy espoused by the then Korean ambassador, Key-Sung Cho, was to start with the apparel assembly and then move on to electronics and other more sophisticated industries (see Chapter 7). In March 1991, Cho told me that Lucky-Goldstar, a Korean transnational corporation, would soon begin constructing a television factory in the massive Korean free-trade zone in the department of Chimaltenango outside of the capital. A year later, not only has Lucky-Goldstar not broken ground for a factory, but the 90,000-square-meter Korean industrial park is still empty, plowed under land, and Ambassador Cho is in Peru following a hasty, bitter departure from Guatemala in July 1990. According to an AID official, the Serrano government had reneged on the pact made between the preceding Guatemalan administration and the Republic of Korea, in which the latter promised to invest heavily in the maquila industry in exchange for the former's guarantee of trouble-free production—in other words, no unions or meddling labor inspectors.

Unlike his predecessor, the present Korean ambassador, Wung-Sik Kung, is not predicting that Korean capital and experience will lead Guatemala along the road to becoming the next Asian Tiger. Citing "corruption, cultural differences, and U.S. labor unions," the ambassador informed me that Korean capitalists are no longer interested in investing in Guatemala.[3] Instead, he said, these investors are investigating export platforms closer to home, such as Vietnam and Cambodia. Ambassador Kung rejects the view that the maquila industry, with or without Korean capital, is capable of lifting Guatemala into an industrialized state as "pure fantasy." It remains to be seen if U.S. investors, as AID and the U.S. Embassy hope, will take over the foreign leadership of maquila investment in Guatemala.

Lastly, seventy-four maquila workers at Confecciones Unidas S.A., a factory in Guatemala City owned by Israeli investors, have joined the thousands of other maquila workers who have been dismissed for exercising their right to organize and bargain collectively. Soon after these workers initiated the legal process to form a union in November 1991, the company posted a note on the factory door announcing the dismissals as an inevitable consequence of decreased orders. Once it became clear that the workers were going to fight the massive illegal discharge, the owners closed down the operations, transferring production to another factory. Although aware of the illegal dismissals and shutdown, the Labor Ministry has been unwilling to enforce court orders to reinstate the workers. Meanwhile, workers have constructed an encampment outside the factory to protest both the company's actions and the government's inaction. They intend to remain until they can return to their jobs.

The support of The Orville H. Schell, Jr. Center for International Human Rights at the Yale Law School, and particularly of Professor Drew Days, Dr. George Andreopoulos, and Joan Paquette-Sass, was invaluable to this project. I am also grateful to those who took time to read and comment on the various drafts of this manuscript, especially to L. D. Hull, Anne DeWald, Pamela Vossenas, George Ogle, Paul Filson, Steve Coats, Jim Goldston, Keir Jorgenson, and Barbara Folsom. I owe much to Lance Compa, union-side attorney and labor law professor, who introduced me to the Guatemalan people and showed me what it means to be an advocate for workers.

My experience in Guatemala would have been far less productive and manageable without the friendship and advice of Clare and Matthew Creelman, Cindy Forster, Father Greg Schaffer, and Gerald Lamberty. I benefited enormously from the selfless efforts of Brett Wilson, my part-time translator and full-time friend, who spent countless hours accompanying me to barrios throughout Guatemala City and without whom the volume and quality of field research would not have been possible.

Finally, I must thank those hundreds of maquila workers who courageously told me their stories in the hope that their voices and concerns would be heard by those in my country who make the critical decisions that may influence the future of Guatemalan society.

1

The Maquila Revolution

In 1984, few Guatemalans were familiar with the term *maquila*.[1] The Guatemalan Congress had recently passed legislation to lure foreign and domestic investment to this export-assembly industry, also known as outsourcing and drawback assembly production. But only the handful of young, ambitious exporters who fervently lobbied for the bill foresaw that within a decade the maquila industry would be the fastest-growing sector of the Guatemalan economy. When the law was passed, about six factories, all assembling apparel for export, employed fewer than two thousand employees. In a mere eight years, this fledgling industry expanded more than twenty-five times. By 1992, more than two hundred and seventy-five garment maquila factories were employing over fifty thousand workers who assembled nearly $350 million in garments for export to the United States.

The boom in garment-assembly production is thrusting the term *maquila* into the everyday vocabulary of millions of Guatemalans and simultaneously transforming the economic and social history of the country. To most Guatemalans, the maquila industry represents the dozens of converted warehouses where children and young women labor for long, monotonous hours sewing precut pieces of cloth into complete garments, which are then immediately shipped to U.S. department stores. Large signs posted on the sides of these buildings, offering employment and excellent compensation to young women, mark their location. For maquila workers, the labels are the tip-off: non-Spanish-sounding names such as "McKids," "Ralph Lauren," and "Van Heusen" indicate that the clothing is for U.S. consumers. In Zone 12, the major industrial sector of Guatemala City, there are so many of these factories that owners have nicknamed the area The Bermuda Triangle. "When a young woman gets off the bus in Zone 12," a maquila investor explained, "she vanishes into the morass of factories and is often never seen again."[2]

The maquila phenomenon is also changing the face of traditional agricultural villages far removed from the industrialized districts of the capital. Foreign investors, particularly Koreans, are constructing large state-of-the-art apparel-assembly factories in rural areas where labor is less expensive and more abundant. Santo Domingo, Chenacoj, for example, is a town of six thousand indigenous peasants, or *campesinos*, accessible only by a four-mile, winding, hilly road off a highway. For centuries, agriculture has governed the local economy and life in general; harvests from nearby fields and wages from annual migratory treks to enormous coastal plantations, or *fincas*, historically have provided the sole means of sustenance. In 1989 a rival to this traditional way of life arrived in the form of a maquila factory. Today scores of young men and women gather daily at 6 A.M. in the town square. They board old school buses, which transport them to a one-thousand-machine, Korean-owned maquila factory located along the main highway.[3] There, they operate sewing machines and irons, snip dangling threads from assembled garments, and pack the items into boxes for up to seventeen hours a day. When not staying over in the factory, the workers depart well after dusk, reboard the buses, and return to their homes. "Santo Domingo," said one of these workers, "will never be the same. The factory now controls our lives."[4]

Reactions to this disruption of social and economic life have been mixed. Proponents of the maquila industry hail this phenomenon as a viable employment alternative to migratory harvesting and an essential stage of industrial development. Advancing this view, one U.S. development official commented, "The maquila industry is revolutionizing Guatemala in many ways. But, perhaps most important, it is providing poor *campesinos* with a real alternative to [migratory] harvesting."[5] The industry also has its share of critics, who argue that this "employment option" is a contemporary form of servitude in which fourteen-year-old girls work fourteen hours a day for a pittance. Anxious health promoters are calling for health and safety training campaigns to prevent the widespread cumulative trauma disorders endemic to rapid-assembly industries such as this one. All commentators nevertheless agree that the maquila industry's impact on the lives and culture of the Guatemalan people is unprecedented.

In short, the penetration of the maquila into the daily life of hundreds of thousands of Guatemalans has been rapid, massive, and not without significant comment and controversy. It is perhaps the most profound economic event since the attempted land reform of the early 1950s, which a U.S. government-sponsored coup d'état abruptly terminated.

An Uneasy Ambivalence

Since his election in 1991, President Jorge Serrano Elias and his Social Action Movement (MAS) government have embraced the maquila production and other nontraditional exports as the preferred means toward industrialization and economic development for Guatemala. The clearest indication of this policy's prominence was the selection of two of the most important maquila industry promoters to staff the Economy Ministry. President Serrano chose the "Godfather of the Maquila Industry" and foremost maquila consultant, Alvaro Colom, and the former director of "One-Stop-to-Export," the efficient export licensing center, Carlos Tercera, as the vice-economy ministers. "With these appointments," a Guatemalan congressman commented, "he [Serrano] could not have sent a clearer message about where the economic growth of this country will come from—the maquila industry and nontraditional exports."[6]

But not every cabinet member appears to have adopted the maquila industry unconditionally as the long awaited economic miracle. Dissenting from its brethren, the Labor Ministry has made it clear that amelioration of the prevalent labor abuses in maquila factories is its most important priority. Shortly after taking office, the labor minister, Mario Solorzano-Martinez, presented amendments to the Labor Code that provided particular protections for female maquila workers and issued a highly publicized report condemning the deplorable working conditions in the industry.[7] In the same vein, the Guatemalan Congress, as one of the first acts of its 1991 legislative session, formed a commission to study the alleged labor violations in the maquila sector.[8] Most unionists and labor advocates, accustomed to empty promises of past labor ministers and congresspersons, are dubious about the sincerity of these concerns because of the overwhelmingly pro-business bent of the executive branch.

The U.S. State Department also has displayed mixed opinions about the thriving maquila industry. On the one hand, the United States Agency for International Development (AID) is the major financial supporter of and technical advisor for the promotion of the maquila industry. Since the return of a full-time mission in 1986, AID has carefully constructed a political structure to entice, nurture, and protect investors in maquila operations. The early success of these efforts has prompted AID development experts to predict that Guatemala is on the path to industrialization—

that the land of eternal spring has the potential to emulate the remarkable industrial growth of the Republic of Korea and the other Asian Tigers.

On the other hand, support at the U.S. Embassy is far from unequivocal. Ambassador Thomas Stroock pressured the Guatemalan Congress to initiate the commission on labor abuse in the maquila industry, and the embassy's labor attaché persuaded Labor Minister Solorzano to denounce publicly the labor violations. With U.S. government funds facilitating the maquila industry's growth but Korean investors exploiting these efforts, it is unclear whether the U.S. Embassy's ambivalence is due to a genuine concern for the rights of workers or whether it indicates a desire for a greater U.S. share in the profits of the maquila business.

The tension exemplified by U.S. officials, alternating between exuberant praise for the maquila industry as an economic miracle and stern criticism of it as an instance of inhumane exploitation of vulnerable labor, has surfaced throughout Guatemalan society. The press, the populace, and even members of the Serrano cabinet maintain an uneasy ambivalence toward the maquila industry's settlement in Guatemala. Because over three-fourths of the country's population live in extreme poverty and an estimated twenty thousand persons die of hunger-related illnesses every year,[9] any kind of employment is welcomed. Nevertheless, the uninhibited abuse of workers prevalent in maquila factories resonates with the exploitative history of Guatemala since the Spanish conquest.

Even progressive unionists are unsure how to respond to this phenomenon. In the face of massive poverty they are reluctant to condemn the enormous influx of employment; yet they want to expose those managers and investors who memorize the investment code but scorn the labor code. "If they [maquila factories] generate more work, that is fine, but what comes along is disrespect for the law and inhumane conditions," explained Byron Morales, a leader of the progressive labor federation, Trade-Union Unity of Guatemalan Workers (UNSITRAGUA). "In theory this strategy is perhaps a good thing, but in practice it has achieved practically nothing. These are superficial answers, simply generating employment and bringing some foreign exchange into Guatemala but leaving the underlying inequities untouched."[10]

Maquilazation and the New International Division of Labor and Production

For Guatemalan and AID policymakers, the maquila industry represents both a mode of production and a strategy of industrial development. As a mode of production, the maquila industry is a labor-intensive, export-assembly operation. With a burgeoning maquila industry, the host country receives an immediate fix of jobs and foreign exchange with the long-term goal of industrialization. The maquila strategy for industrial development, or "maquilazation," is export-led industrialization constructed through the introduction of increasingly advanced assembly industries and the concurrent development of indigenous inputs for these operations. Over the last three decades, the so-called Asian Tigers—the Republic of Korea, Taiwan, Singapore, and Hong Kong—have pursued variants of this strategy, emerging with remarkable speed as self-sufficient, industrialized nations.

Advocates of maquilazation espouse a "ladder theory" of industrial development. The simplest form of the theory goes as follows. A developing country begins with a low-skill apparel-assembly industry. As the work force matures and increases in skill, more advanced assembly operations—for example, footwear, electronics, and toys—are introduced. In addition to transferring technology to the work force, these assembly operations integrate, or form backward linkages, with the domestic economy. Local industries grow and displace foreign firms as the major source of assembled inputs. For instance, domestic textile and plastics industries expand to supply the cloth and parts for apparel and toy assembly, respectively. The next rung is computers, and so on until the country "climbs" into an industrialized state. The primary examples of this development model can be found in the newly industrialized Southeast Asian countries, which, according to this interpretation, began their development in apparel assembly and then progressed until, in what many term a "miracle," they became industrial powers.

Success, however, has its costs. It is largely contingent on the attractiveness of a country's labor to potential investors. Emphasizing the primacy of labor in the industry, an AID official described the maquila as "the exportation of labor without ever having to send the workers abroad."[11] In essence, a host country, at least in the short term, deliberately chooses to permit exploitation of its cheap, abundant labor force in exchange for foreign currency, employment, and hoped-for industrialization.

Similar efforts of maquilazation have sprouted up throughout the Caribbean and Central America, the most renowned being Mexico's Border Industrial Program and the Dominican Republic's Free Trade Zone programs. The Dominican Republic opened its first free-trade zone in 1969. Costa Rica, Haiti, and Jamaica embarked on maquilazation programs in the early 1980s, contemporaneous with the promulgation of the Caribbean Basin Economic Recovery Act. Thus, Guatemala is a relative latecomer, not launching an earnest attempt to attract this type of industry until the late 1980s. For the most part, persistent internal strife has placed the Guatemalan maquila industry well behind its neighbors in size and maturity.

The maquila industry is a major result of the new international division of labor and production. Since colonial days, the traditional division has dictated that the more developed nations produce and export manufactured goods while the less developed nations produce and export raw materials for manufacture abroad. This division was justified by the theory of comparative advantage, in which nations contribute to the world economy what they do best and most efficiently. In Central America and the Caribbean, climate-sensitive agro-exports like sugar, fruit, and coffee were (and still are, to a great extent) the contribution most desired by the more developed nations, particularly the United States.

Over the last forty years, this traditional division has undergone radical transformation. Exceptional advances in transportation, production technology, and communications, combined with the birth of transnational corporations (TNCs), have made a global division of labor and production economically efficient. This modern international division of production and labor is organized on the separation of a single manufacturing process, which once could only be performed in a single factory or geographic area, into stages of production allocated to different sets of workers around the world.

The paradigmatic model of this new international division of labor and production occurs when workers in a developed country design and manufacture components, these components are exported to a less developed country where workers assemble them into a finished unit, and then the completed good is reexported to the developed nation for marketing and sale. The division of labor and production is simple: the more capital-intensive stages of the design and manufacture of components, requiring sophisticated technology and highly trained and skilled labor, are performed in developed countries; the more labor-intensive stages, primarily assembly, are performed in the less developed countries.

Although the division of labor and production has drastically changed in the last three decades, the theory of comparative advantage continues to provide a rationale for the distinct tasks each country performs. Countries with the comparative advantage of legions of inexpensive labor are entitled to the labor-intensive stages of production; those with the greater technical sophistication and more skilled labor perform the more capital-intensive segments of the production. Most important, TNCs based in the developed countries, powerful enough to control production and develop markets, decide precisely how the production will be separated. The governments willingly facilitate the exchange by suspension or reduction of import and export duties.[12]

The Clothing Maquila

Of all industries, the production of clothing—traditionally one of the least capital-intensive and sophisticated industries—has most efficiently and rapidly adjusted to this new division of labor and production. Hence, Guatemalan workers' initial encounter with this new international division has been with garment maquila factories. As in most other Caribbean and Central American maquila industries, apparel assembly fills Guatemalan maquila factories. In fact, over 95 percent of Guatemalan factories assemble garments for export. Perhaps three or four factories assemble non-garment products. One of the oldest maquilas produces fishing lures.

There are four basic stages in the manufacture of clothing: production initiation, preassembly and cutting, assembly, and finishing. Production initiation comprises the design and engineering of the garment to be produced. It is the most creative function, determines the type of product, and lays the groundwork for the physical production of the garment. Design takes account of the prevailing trends in fashion, consumer tastes, and the overall image of the clothing producer. Engineering determines the approach that is to be taken to construct the garment.

The second stage, preassembly and cutting, consists of grading and marking and then cutting the fabric. Grading extends the designed model to the different sizes, and marking is the making of a guide for the subsequent cutting of the fabric into the various elements that constitute the clothing piece. Cutting, then, is the production of those various elements from the fabric, usually performed on a stack of plies of fabric. In the cutting stage, all operations are relatively sophisticated and generally require a well-trained work force.

Assembly, the third stage, is the joining together, by way of sewing, of the cut components into a piece of clothing. The last stage, finishing, is putting the product into a suitable form for final delivery by pressing, folding, and packaging. Labor skill requirements are comparatively low in these last two operations.

In the new international division of labor, clothing manufacturing is generally separated between the first two stages—production initiation, preassembly and cutting—and the last two stages—assembly and finishing. Predesigned, precut cloth parts are shipped to a less developed country for assembly and finishing. The completed products are then returned to be sold. The Guatemalan maquila industry is typical of this new division. Cloth is manufactured, designed, and cut in either the United States or Southeast Asia; these parts are shipped to Guatemalan maquila factories where workers sew them together and pack the finished garments; and then this ready-for-sale apparel is sent to the U.S. market. Thus, Guatemalan workers perform the repetitive, unimaginative tasks. The label "Made in Guatemala" found in clothing can assure the customer that the garment was sewn together at a maquila factory. This tag, however, is misleading, for it is likely that only the labor is of Guatemalan origin.

The Global Factory

A consequence of this new international division of labor and production is that the world more and more resembles a "global factory."[13] To begin with, the combinations of nationalities in this division of labor and production have become intricate and complex. For example, one of the first Guatemalan maquila factories was owned by U.S. citizens, managed by Israelis, supervised by Filipinos, and operated by Guatemalans, who assembled cloth that was manufactured in Asian and Colombian textile mills. In some cases such combinations foster cultural harmony and understanding. In Guatemalan maquila plants, the mixture of nationalities more often reinforces biases and furthers discord, as those with greater bargaining power are prone to exploit the relationship. In the above-described factory, the Filipino male supervisors were notorious for physically and sexually abusing the Guatemalan female operators. More recently, the boom of Korean factories in Guatemala has set off a wave of racist sentiment among both Guatemalan workers and business leaders.

Another consequence of this division is that the countries with the abundant, low-cost labor have become more involved, willingly or unwillingly, in industrial production of more developed countries. The role of the less developed countries has shifted from mere supplier of raw materials to playing "a vital part in the productive process of the more advanced capitalist countries and thus participating in the actual functioning of these economic systems."[14] In one sense, as an essential cog in the production process, these countries might be thought to gain a greater say in how the production process should be allocated and performed. This hope, however, is rarely realized. In most instances, the less developed countries compete ferociously with one another to entice labor-intensive operations to their soil. The "winner" of this competition is the nation that offers investors the least expensive labor with the fewest economic and political conditions. Because their economic and social woes are so intractable, many countries compromise their peoples' dignity and rights in order to make their nation more attractive to foreign investment.

Therefore, these countries remain dependent on the markets of the wealthy nations that dictate the type and volume of production. Control over production and distribution is frequently sacrificed to the tastes of wealthy consumers and to investments of foreign entrepreneurs and TNCs. In sum, the workers in poorer countries continue to "produce what [they] do not consume, and consume what [they] do not produce," leading many observers to conclude that this new division is simply another permutation of historic economic exploitation and dependence.[15]

Guatemala's Historic Comparative Advantage of Free Labor

Since the Spanish conquest and settlement, from the perspective of the Western capitalist market, Indian labor has been Guatemala's comparative advantage. The manipulation of this labor has determined the fate of the nation. The conquistadors and their descendants carefully cultivated systems for efficiently extracting low-cost labor from the natives. Due to their efforts, the Guatemalan economy has been dependent for centuries on the production of one or two cash export crops grown on vast estates and harvested by forced labor. The receipts from the sale of these crops in Western European and, more recently, U.S. markets have formed the nucleus of a tiny internal economy and market. This economy has reaped substantial benefits for the landed elite, the large transnational agriculture corporations, and the middlemen of the developed world's markets. In contrast, the workers, who represent the vast majority of the Guatemalan population, have suffered from continual deprivation.

The Spanish conquistadors understood that "whatever wealth the New World offered, whether it be in the form of precious metals or agricultural exports, was of little worth if not accompanied by access to Indian labor."[16] The subsequent failure to discover immense treasures of gold in colonial Guatemala disappointed but also nudged these treasure seekers to the next best alternative—agriculture.[17] Abundant fertile land and a temperate climate ensured that the invaders, and others like them in years to come, would become enamored of the land's wealth-creating potential. Realizing that arable land without dependable labor is worthless, the conquerors forced those "fortunate" survivors[18] of the repressive and deadly conquest to work in the fields. Thus began the tradition of forced labor still prevalent today. Soon after the conquest, the formula for fortune-making became clear: controlled labor, combined with huge estates of land known as *haciendas*, equaled enormous financial rewards.

Although slavery was eventually outlawed, the Spanish government formalized by decree the control of indigenous labor for the colonial plantations. The New Laws of 1541 formulated a system of forced labor called *repartimiento*: at any moment colonial authorities could seize up to one-fourth of the inhabitants of any highland village to work in the huge *fincas* on the southern coast. After independence from Spain in 1821, the national government continued this oppressive tradition, enacting legislation to satisfy the needs of the landed elite. Not until 1945 was the last forced labor law officially revoked.

Despite prohibition of forced labor, by most objective standards the practice continues today. Every year tens of thousands of *campesinos* pack into trucks (one or two crash en route each year) that transport them from their highland villages to the southern coast to harvest on the coffee and sugar *fincas*. Often leaving their families behind, the men earn less than two dollars a day (minus expenses) which after several months comprises most of their annual income. While at the *fincas* workers live in slavelike accommodations and endure harsh treatment. Thousands live and sleep together on dirt floors in large open-air warehouses. Most work more than ten hours a day, six days a week, to meet their quota of harvest.

From the perspective of the ruling landed elite, the control and manipulation of labor have been a stunning success. A combination of oppressive law and regimes and sanctioned repression by private business has preserved the most dramatic maldistribution of land and wealth in the Western hemisphere. In 1990, less than 5 percent of the largest landowners possessed more than 65 percent of the arable land, while 10 percent of the smallest owners possess .5 percent of the land. Yet over half of the population still earn their livelihood from agriculture. The participation of most of these people has been limited to the toiling in the fields, not the riches of the barter. As a result, nearly three-quarters of the population live in a "state of extreme poverty," meaning they "do not possess the most essential means for subsistence, including access to production factors."[19]

Labor Alone

The present nontraditional export crusade highlights once again the vital importance of labor in an economy dependent on satisfying the needs of foreign consumers. During the first three centuries of conquest, the main crops in the settlers' fields were cocoa, indigo, and cochineal (red dye). By 1870, when Western palates had acquired a taste for coffee, workers were trained to grow and harvest the delicate bean. Today, with the new international division of labor, foreign consumers are demanding jeans and dresses as well as nontraditional specialty crops such as cauliflower and strawberries. In response to these new Western needs, Guatemalan workers are being recruited and trained to harvest berries and assemble apparel.

The push for nontraditional agro-exports is the most recent articulation of the traditional economic scheme: fertile land worked by inexpensive labor produces bountiful profits for the few proprietors. In contrast, nontraditional manufacturing, or maquila production, bares a new equation in which labor alone, without land or local prime materials, is the supreme commodity. The new international division of labor and production and the ensuing saturation of less developed countries with the assembly phase of this division have created this labor-centered development strategy. For Guatemala, this massive-scale utilization of its comparative advantage of cheap, abundant labor, separated from its fertile land, signals a new stage in its economic history.

While the maquila suggests a new, unknown path in the economic history of Guatemala, successful development arguably depends more on the quality and supply of labor than ever before. Other factors—such as managerial skill, market fluctuations, and political harmony—have an impact upon the maquila industry's expansion; but without an economical and ample labor force the industry will stall. In light of the predominant role of labor in the maquila revolution, a central focus of this study is how workers will fare in this new mode of economic development. Will the expansion of the maquila increase the disparity in income and quality of life between investors and workers so evident in the centuries-old agro-export economy? Or will the maquila industry develop as an unprecedented source of economic and social equality between worker and owner? More fundamentally, will the tradition of forced labor carry over to the maquila sector, only in a more sophisticated form? Or will the advent of the maquila enable workers to achieve a measurable level of self-determination?

2

The Construction of an Economic Miracle

Since the CIA-directed 1954 coup d'état, Guatemalan central governments have had a nominal impact on economic growth. Although these unstable regimes have frequently published plans for economic development, the private business sector has retained de facto control over virtually every significant economic enterprise or decision in the last three decades. Responsible for more than 90 percent of economic activity, the private sector determines whether an economic proposal will be realized. The maquila strategy presents a rare moment of consensus between the private sector and the government over an economic strategy: both view the maquila as a necessary (and profitable) stage in the industrial development of Guatemala.

This government-private sector consensus has generated a clear division of labor in the promotion of the maquila industry: the government promulgates maquila incentive laws and formulates monetary policy; the private sector implements the law and exploits the policies. Left alone, this arrangement might have fostered modest industrial growth. However, the underlying cause for the remarkable explosion of the maquila industry has been the highly influential and supportive United States Agency for International Development (AID), the development arm of the U.S. State Department. As in the rest of the region, the AID Guatemalan mission champions nontraditional exports as the primary development program. With indispensable financial support and technical expertise, AID has judiciously directed the rise of the Guatemalan maquila industry.

AID's selection of nontraditional exports as Guatemala's path to economic prosperity, however, was not made on the basis of a methodical search for the most appropriate, effective economic development strategy. Rather, in the early 1970s the U.S. State Department chose nontraditional exports, including the maquila industry, by default. After numerous efforts to lessen the disparity in wealth and political power failed, promotion of the maquila industry surfaced as a possible alternative, nonredistributive development model. At that time, the State Department faced a dilemma: unable to achieve significant economic reforms yet unwilling to cut off economic assistance for fear of weakening the government, the department surrendered its policy of conditioning economic aid on reform. In the end, AID continued to administer economic assistance, but its objectives shifted from the modest efforts to redistribute resources to promotion of economic initiatives that would not disturb the long-standing economic and political disparity between the landed oligarchy and the impoverished majority.

Thus, AID elected to promote the maquila industry precisely because it was inoffensive and nonthreatening to the landed oligarchy. However, rising political unrest, an unprepared AID staff, and finally, the reduction of U.S. economic and official military assistance to Guatemala in 1977 for human rights abuses stunted full-scale implementation of the maquila strategy. It was nearly a decade later, in 1986, when AID's mission returned to Guatemala, that a systematic campaign to champion the maquila industry was launched.

Democracy and the Maquila

When President Vinicio Cerezo and his Christian Democrat party assumed power in 1986, enormous social and economic problems greeted their arrival. For more than thirty years a corrupt and cruel military had governed Guatemala and brutalized the population into submission. Some independent observers estimated that 45,000 persons had disappeared, 100,000 had died, and over a million had been displaced in that period. In particular, during the five years previous to Cerezo's election, the military had waged a ruthlessly effective "pacification" campaign against an armed guerrilla insurgency and against grass-roots progressive movements that included labor unions, student groups, and peasant organizations. The destruction was immense. The well-documented, daily human rights violations attributed to the military provoked the outrage of human rights organizations.[1] Repeated abuses eventually led to Guatemala's partial isolation from the international community, sparked largely by President Carter's unprecedented termination of official military aid in 1977.

By 1986, the Guatemalan people longed for relief from the decades of violent repression—and from hunger as well.[2] Cerezo and his administration inherited an economy deeply submerged in a severe recession, in large part brought on by the political turmoil. Between 1980 and 1985 half of the economic growth of the previous thirty years was squandered. Five consecutive annual declines of the gross domestic product and per capita consumption, unprecedented inflation, unemployment—over half the economically active population lacked full-time jobs—and the plummeting of real wages demonstrated the collapse of the economy. In 1984–85, 3,300 businesses closed.[3] Industrial production fell in all sectors.[4] One prominent Guatemalan news agency called the drop in purchasing power in the forty months preceding September 1986, "a fall in family income without comparison in modern Guatemalan history."[5] As a last straw, direct investment from foreign and domestic sources decreased dramatically during this period. Many analysts felt that this decline in investment may well have subverted any chance for economic recovery.

The National Social and Economic Reordering Plan: The Call for a Neoliberal Economic Revolution

Confronted with this state of political and economic chaos, in June 1986, President Cerezo and his staff published the National Social and Economic Reordering Plan (PRES), a treatise calling for a neoliberal economic revolution. PRES, like previous Guatemalan central planning attempts, was overly ambitious and unattainable without the support of the private business community and U.S. financing. Nevertheless, PRES was important because it outlined the economic policies of the first democratically elected civilian government in more than thirty years.

PRES expounded two basic themes: monetary, or "structural," reform and vigorous promotion of nontraditional exports. The objective of the strategy was to cap the fiscal deficit and free foreign-exchange controls while simultaneously wooing back private investment to boost export earnings and employment. An additional, unannounced prong of the government's economic revitalization was to secure large amounts of foreign aid to alleviate the growing balance of payments crisis. Although prevalent in preelection campaign promises, tax and agrarian reforms were two "structural changes" absent in PRES. Opinions on the merit of the government's vision differed. The powerful business community initially welcomed the proposal;[6] grass-roots labor and peasant organizations apprehensively awaited the fruits of this economic revolution.

With PRES the government formally announced the abandonment of all vestiges of the 1960s and 1970s import substitution model of development, in which high tariffs stimulated and protected domestic capital-intensive industry. The planners considered tariffs and dollar parity baneful to the new economy that was to be founded on exporting to the world market. Instead of protected industry, PRES called for an openness to the free market and enthusiastically invited low-capital, high-return maquila operations to exploit the surplus of low-wage labor.

The promotion and export of nontraditional products, both agricultural and manufactured, represented the core of this economic development strategy. According to one economy vice-minister, "The primary economic policy of this democratically elected government, quite simply, is the promotion of nontraditional exports of agriculture and manufacturing goods."[7] On the agricultural side, all produce except for beef, bananas, cotton, sugar, and coffee qualified as nontraditional. Leaving behind the call for capital-intensive, highly skilled industry, PRES mandated the labor-intensive, low-skill maquila industry to lead the industrialization phase of this development.

Nontraditional export development was to occur in two stages. During the first two years of the plan, policies would foster much needed jobs and create the conditions necessary for long-term growth. PRES emphasized the need to increase small-property ownership, optimize resource use, and ensure adequate market supplies. In the ensuing two years, efforts would shift to the expansion of the internal and external markets. In the end, nontraditional products grown on Guatemalan land or prepared with Guatemalan labor would be commonplace throughout the world.

The overriding goal of this nontraditional promotion policy was to "create the conditions that will permit the emergence of a new set of owners, which will modify and diversify the productive structure and widen national and international markets."[8] The planners conceded that the government could not lead this economic revolution, but that it could create a propitious atmosphere for the rise of a new class of entrepreneurs. Once the government unburdened the market of price controls, foreign-exchange constraints, and tariffs, domestic entrepreneurial skill and foreign currency would guide the nation to material prosperity. By emphasizing the formation of a new class of entrepreneurs, PRES implicitly excluded the landed oligarchy from meaningful participation in this economic revitalization. This dominant economic force, which had controlled the economy for centuries, was omitted, at least on paper, from the economic future of Guatemala.

Soon after the distribution of PRES, the Christian Democrat government demonstrated its commitment to this neoliberal agenda. In June 1986, it formed the National Export Promotion Council,[9] composed of representatives from both the private and public sector, "to consolidate efforts from both sectors to promote and diversify export."[10] Two months later the government convened the First National Export Congress to address the removal of bureaucratic obstacles to export. Most importantly, within weeks of the plan's publication the government modified the exchange rate for agro-exporters from dollar parity to US$1:Q2.50. These initial efforts fostered an atmosphere of confidence in the Guatemalan business community. Commenting on these early policies and practices of the Cerezo administration, Alvaro Colom stated, "The advent of democracy has facilitated the development of a labor-based, drawback industry in Guatemala."[11]

The Government: Passing Laws and Authority

Since 1966, Guatemalan governments have promulgated five separate statutes to encourage investment in maquila operations.[12] The first three laws failed to bear fruit. But on the eve of free elections in 1984, the Congress passed Decree 24-84, marking the entrance of Guatemala into the modern international division of labor and production. Modeled on other maquila incentive regimes in the region at the time, the legislation offered a ten-year tax holiday and suspension of export and import tariffs on machinery, equipment, raw materials, and semifinished products to any investor, foreign or native, who opened a maquila operation. Notably, the statute prohibited factories from subcontracting, or submaquila-ing, work among each other and from selling any portion of assembled products in the domestic market.

Rather than follow the Dominican Republic's strategy of large, geographically confined, and government-administered free-trade zones, the administration, at the prodding of AID and the World Bank, chose to make every individual factory a free-trade zone. This preference was based on the weak position of the government more than on design. The abject failure of a ten-year-old government free-trade zone on the Caribbean coast, Free Zone of Industry and Commerce (ZOLIC), and a meager public treasury effectively proscribed major government construction projects. Moreover, the private sector enthusiastically welcomed this arrangement, as it further shifted control of production to the individual investor.

In 1989, the civilian Christian Democrat government passed a revised maquila incentive law, Decree 29–89, and a private free-trade-zone scheme, Decree 65–89. The updated incentive decree promised essentially the same benefits as the 1984 law, except that the role of the government was further reduced in two ways. First, the new legislation granted individual maquila owners freedom to share machinery freely and submaquila work among each other without restriction.[13] Second, the statute established more flexible rules for individual factories to expand machinery and production. Decree 65–89 provides a process for private investors to create and administer geographically restricted free-trade zones. Described as "modern, flexible, with clear and simple procedures to obtain benefits," the law exonerates investors in these zones from all taxes and encourages private individuals to invest in and administer Dominican Republic-like, free-trade zones, with one major difference—no government supervision.[14]

One investor noted, "The best thing the government has done is not to do anything."[15] This characterization is only a bit inaccurate. The government's role in maquila promotion concludes when a company submits an application,[16] but the government has contributed an essential component: the legal and economic framework. Somewhat begrudgingly, the government has conceded execution to the more powerful combination of private sector and AID. With much truth, then, the flashy promotional brochure to encourage foreign maquila investment, *Guatemala: A Manufacturing Country by Tradition*, boasts that the new democratic government's policies are "the most export oriented, pro-business" in Latin America.[17]

Civil Servant versus Private Businessman

This division of labor—government as lawmaker and an AID-guided private sector as executor—is primarily the result of the historic battle between the private sector and the central government over control of the country's riches. Even when enmeshed in elaborate bribery schemes, mistrust pervades the relationship between the private and public sectors. As a result, meaningful coordination and consultation between the two sectors are rare. For example, businesses almost never share financial information with the government. Businessmen fear the government will use any submitted data to justify tax increases or will share it with their less honest competitors; the government assumes that the private sector's veil of secrecy proves the extent of its cheating and illegal behavior.

From the perspective of businessmen, government officials are almost inherently corrupt. Guatemalan capitalists expect a bureaucrat to act as self-interested as any other entrepreneur. As easy proof, they point to the rampant corruption that seems to saturate every level of government. The story of a Guatemalan businessman's reaction to the television series "The Lone Ranger" exemplifies this widespread perception. Noticing that the show portrayed the most offensive bandits as those who stole from the government, he said, "In Guatemala it is repugnant only when one fails to use his government position for his own benefit."[18]

Government officials counter allegations of corruption with their own charges that the private sector is equally, if not more, culpable of widespread disregard of the law. Commented an official in the Economy Ministry, "The private business sector lacks all respect for the law. They refuse to follow the spirit, much less the letter, of the law. We lack the resources to police every transaction, so they [the businessmen] violate the law whenever they wish."[19] Bureaucrats who acknowledge the existence of government corruption are quick to point to the low salaries and overwhelming responsibilities that make officials vulnerable to the enticements of unscrupulous businessmen.

Time and time again the private sector has emerged victorious from this struggle with the government for control of the economy. As a consequence, the private sector dominates the economic production of the nation. The government, in contrast, is small and ineffectual. Moreover, since the private sector controls the economy and unconditionally spurns tax increases and distrusts government spending, the government's impotence is perpetuated.

The public sector's influence on the economy, therefore, is nominal unless its policy finds substantial support in the private sector. Virtually all central governments since the 1954 coup have been insignificant players in economic development, bowing before the private sector, the military, and the U.S. State Department. Writing in 1968, a scholar said of the government: "Guatemala's economic growth is influenced less by Government policies than by private investment. The Government seems to prefer letting private investment, which is relatively free from controls, lead the way to economic growth."[20] Whether there is a deliberate "preference" to surrender control is debatable, but the fact is that for most of the last thirty-five years the government has been incapable of planning, much less executing, a course of development. The power and protective tendencies of the landed elite have been, and continue to be, impregnable. And unless the aims of the elite or AID or the military coincide with the government, it is unlikely the last will come away with even a compromise.

Cerezo's Threat to Private-Sector Hegemony

For a brief moment in 1986, it appeared that the central government might assert more than nominal authority over the nontraditional export development strategy. The Cerezo administration contracted a Swiss company, Société Générale de Surveillance S.A. (SGS), to reduce the pervasive tariff evasion by exporters which, by government estimates, had reached hundreds of millions of dollars annually. Since every newly recovered penny meant a loss for a private exporter, the business sector responded vigorously to this "unnecessary government intrusion." Full-page ads appeared almost daily in newspapers alleging that SGS would cripple an already slow and inefficient export control system; television stations aired irate exporters screaming that businesses would go to countries "where the government programs stimulate production."[21]

Eventually, the private exporters wore down the government's bid for control. In September 1987, the SGS contract was discontinued. Although it displayed impressive fortitude, the government could not withstand the onslaught of the private sector's clout. This event affirmed the respective functions of the government and the private sector in the export production. For the remainder of the Cerezo administration, though the rhetoric of a government in command remained forceful and a new maquila incentive law was passed, the private sector and AID exercised control over the development of the nontraditional export production.[22]

AID and the Maquila Industry

Today, many government, private-sector, and AID representatives speak of the recent boom of maquila production as if the strategy had been recently introduced into Guatemala. The concept of maquila as the vehicle for industrial development, however, is far from new in Guatemala. As mentioned, the Guatemalan Congress in 1966 passed the first statute aimed specifically at stimulating the growth of export assembly industries.[23] This law included the normal enticements: suspension of tariffs, unlimited profit repatriation, and lengthy tax holidays. In part, the government promulgated the legislation to take advantage of the potential employment engendered by the emerging globalization of production; but the more pressing motive behind the legislation was the realization that the economic and democratic revolution promised by the Alliance for Progress (Alliance), the U.S. government's massive economic development program to Latin America in the 1960s, was doomed in Guatemala.[24]

On March 13, 1961, President Kennedy announced the Alliance, a ten-point, ten-year program with the ultimate objective of eliminating poverty in Latin America and the Caribbean. On the scope of this program, Jerome Levinson and Juan de Onis have commented:

> The Alliance, as originally conceived, represented a new theory of development which stressed social reform and democratic political processes as much as economic growth. The emphasis on deliberate policy measures to speed up the process of income redistribution and redress social injustices gave the Alliance its revolutionary impact and uniqueness. Without this democratic and reformist orientation, it became just another AID program.[25]

The Alliance was unprecedented not only in its objectives—to use aid for the peaceful achievement of modest structural reforms and to encourage democracy—but in its structure; for the first time, a U.S. aid program was to be applied by a network of development experts following a rational plan. Grants and loans were to be conditional on recipient government promises of reform, particularly fiscal and land reform.[26]

In 1967–68—the same period when Guatemala's first maquila law was enacted—AID made a final appeal to the Guatemalan government and private sector for structural economic reform, specifically tax reform. Convincing the recently installed and underfunded government of Julio Cesar Mendez Montenegro (considered a liberal reformist relative to his conservative counterparts and predecessors) that an increase in tax revenue was necessary for development was easy. The Mendez administration and AID officials understood that the resistance to any tax increase would come from the powerful private business sector, which was extraordinarily reluctant to part with its wealth. Just three years earlier, this stubbornness had been temporarily overcome when Guatemala adopted its first income tax schedule, becoming the last country in the Americas to institute one. Known more for its symbolic importance, this initial schedule affected less than 1 percent of the population and contained the lowest rates in the hemisphere.[27] Both the Mendez government and AID knew that more was needed; the door had been opened, but not nearly far enough. Hence, AID offered the carrot—millions of dollars of aid—conditional on matching government funds, which could only be obtained through increased taxes.

In 1966 and again in 1967, property and sales tax reform packages were presented before the Guatemalan Congress. At the time, a *New York Times* reporter wrote:

> The tax bill has . . . become a question of fundamental principle for many people here. If it cannot be passed or if it is emasculated, then it will mean that nothing really basic can be done in Guatemala—that those who have wealth will not yield something to those who have nothing. If it loses its fight, it is felt, the Government will be doomed to ineffectuality.[28]

Neither bill succeeded. The first, proposing a modest property tax, was thwarted before even reaching a vote, when influential businessmen denounced it as reflecting "the philosophy of the *Communist Manifesto*."[29] The Congress passed the second bill, a progressive sales tax, but within the first few weeks of implementation protest from the private sector threatened the stability of the government; without warning the measure was repealed amid rumors of an impending coup. And the Mendez regime completed its tenure more reliant on U.S. loans and aid than when it had begun.[30]

Frustrated by the intractable opposition to tax and land reform by the landed elites and foreign investors, AID finally succumbed and withdrew support from these reforms. Fearing that a cutoff in aid might contribute to the fall of the government and encourage the armed insurgency movement, U.S. officials decided once and for all against conditioning aid on tax reform, or any other redistributive measure.[31] This rejection of using aid as leverage to obtain reforms in favor of political expediency marked the end of AID's attempts to restructure the economy through mass reallocation of resources and power. The hope of peacefully separating the landed oligarchy from a portion of their riches was forsaken; inevitably, efforts were directed toward finding a way to create more wealth, rather than redistributing the resources at hand. In place of serious reforms, the policy objectives began to accept status quo economic inequities and focus on locating means of economic development that would not disturb the underlying maldistributions.[32] Thus, the first maquila incentive legislation, initiated at the prodding of AID, signaled the surrender of a crucial development goal of the Alliance for Progress.

A "Hodgepodge" Development Strategy by Default

By the 1970s U.S. policy analysts in Central America had admitted the demise of the Alliance for Progress. The need for a new economic development strategy rapidly surfaced. The chosen route was a hodgepodge of schemes that did not require serious economic restructuring or interstate institution building. In Guatemala, nontraditional exports, tourism, and extractive mining led the new list of important development projects, because "these private sector 'productive' activities were not tied to the growth of a domestic consumer market in Central America, but rather used the region as a base for operations oriented toward world markets; hence, they required no serious domestic reforms."[33] The official rationale for the post-Alliance strategy mirrored the goals of the current government and AID policy: foreign exchange, employment, and long-term industrialization.[34]

The hodgepodge strategy of the early 1970s differed enormously from Alliance for Progress in both scale and planning. Massive influxes of capital in the form of loans, direct aid, and investment; introduction of major region-wide institutions such as the Central American Common Market; and attempts to eradicate structural barriers to democracy and development marked the Alliance strategy. In contrast, this new hodgepodge strategy emerged more as an ad hoc scramble to fill the void left by the crumbling of a decade-long plan, as opposed to a deliberate departure on an innovative path toward development.

Soon after a 1968 visit by President Johnson, the Regional Office of AID for Central America and Panama (ROCAP) and local AID missions formed an administrative structure to support this new development strategy in Guatemala. Development experts were sent, local institutions created, and specific projects promoted. In 1970, ROCAP made a $30 million loan to the Central American Bank for Economic Integration, to be used for loans to private, nontraditional export, and tourist ventures.[35]

By the end of 1974, a legislative and administrative structure was in place to conceive and nurture nontraditional export promotion. The Guatemalan Congress had promulgated new legislation enhancing incentives for nontraditional exports. Further, AID established a private-sector, export promotion center, National Center for the Promotion of Exports, or GUATEXPRO, in January 1972. The explicit purpose of this organization was "to stimulate an increase in the production and exportation of nontraditional products" to countries outside of Central America.[36] Financed by AID, GUATEXPRO was commissioned to execute the incentive legislation, and until 1982 the organization coordinated promotion of the sputtering nontraditional export business. In 1973, in perhaps the most significant manifestation of this new strategy, the government constructed one of the first free-trade zones in the region, ZOLIC, near the port of Santo Tomas de Castillo on the Atlantic coast.

AID's main objective of this strategy was to cultivate a new class of entrepreneurs to lead and manage the growth of a prosperous nontraditional sector. To achieve this end, private-sector development experts were imported to stock the local mission, and the decision-making authority of GUATEXPRO was placed securely in the hands of young Guatemalan businessmen. After the recent tax-reform debacles, U.S. development officials viewed the public sector as a burden on development, which had to be minimized. In essence, the business community's defeat of proposed structural reforms induced AID to approach those with the de facto power to bring about economic change. An AID memo from the period made the new principle explicit: "It is the private sector which exports, the government which provides the umbrella of incentives and facilitation."[37] Two decades later, AID continues to view the private sector as the primary actor in economic development and the government as the "umbrella."

In its original form, the hodgepodge strategy, and the maquila portion in particular, never gained significant support from foreign investors or from the Guatemalan private sector, remaining for more than a decade in an embryonic state. The new class of entrepreneurs called to undertake the initiative never surfaced. Inexperienced and disillusioned U.S. development personnel, combined with heightened political strife caused in part by a resurgent guerrilla movement, discouraged potential foreign tourists and investors. When President Carter reduced economic aid in 1977, U.S. and other direct foreign investment halted to a trickle for nearly a decade.

In particular, the maquila industry during the 1970s dawdled along without noticeable growth. The Guatemalan government passed three variations of a maquila incentive law between 1966 and 1984, but less than thirty companies registered to receive these benefits. ZOLIC foundered; its empty warehouses overrun with weeds resembled a ghost town. In comparison, almost two hundred applications have been received under the regimes provided for in 1984 and 1989 maquila incentive legislation. Since the essential incentives of cheap labor and tax-free production did not change over time, the sudden success of the maquila in the late 1980s can be attributed to the return of U.S. financial assistance and a well-staffed, more experienced AID mission.

The Caribbean Basin Economic Recovery Act's Resurrection of the Hodgepodge Strategy

The U.S. Congress ratified the hodgepodge development strategy more than a decade after its inception with the Caribbean Basin Economic Recovery Act (CBERA). (The act is more commonly known as the Caribbean Basin Initiative, or CBI, which actually refers to the ongoing U.S. trade and economic initiatives in the region.) On February 24, 1982, in an address before the Organization of American States, President Reagan, promising to do whatever was necessary to prevent the overthrow of the region's "democratic" governments, announced a broad plan of trade and investment incentives. "The program," he explained, "is an integrated program that helps our neighbors help themselves, a program that will create conditions under which creativity and private entrepreneurship and self-help can flourish."[38]

The bill, which ultimately became U.S. law on August 5, 1983, contained two basic components: trade and development assistance. As for trade, the act gave the president the power to exempt from tariffs certain goods imported from specified beneficiary countries of the Caribbean Basin, which includes all non-Communist countries in the region, for up to twelve years. The act also provided $350 million in supplemental development assistance to "key" countries in the region for balance of payment shortfalls or emergency aid.

The CBI, as an official region-wide development program, and the Alliance for Progress shared identical ends—the stability of the region and the protection and promotion of U.S. business interests—but the two differed notably in means. Just as the Alliance was aimed at preventing another Fidel Castro, so the CBI countered the Nicaraguan revolution of 1979 and the ongoing guerrilla struggles in Guatemala and El Salvador. Unlike the Alliance's call for democracy and peaceful social and economic revolutions, however, the CBI envisions expanding nontraditional export production by itself generating economic development. Duty-free trade channels and private investment, preferably from U.S. entrepreneurs and TNCs, were the key ingredients to this growth. As nontraditional production increases, proponents argue, development will follow. This logic has been bitterly contested by those who doubt that increased trade will magically trickle down to the majority of the population; on the other hand, the scheme has been commended by those who view the market as the best means of economic development. With its emphasis on trade and markets, however, most agree that the CBI reads more like "a plan for the establishment of bilateral relationships with particular individual nations within the Caribbean region" than a traditional development assistance plan.[39]

For Guatemala, the CBI's ratification of the hodgepodge strategy denotes the return, after nearly a decade-long hiatus, of U.S. development expertise, financial assistance, and foreign and domestic investment. Most significant, the CBI reaffirms the option chosen by AID in the late 1960s to forego reform of underlying inequities, pushing instead for the more cosmetic, market-opening formulas of development.

A Rejuvenated AID with Vision—and a Plan

Compared to the confused and desperate U.S. development program of the 1970s, the AID mission in Guatemala of the 1990s is brimming with confidence in its strategy, tactics, and pupils. Evoking the early Alliance days, the enthusiastic director of maquila development called Guatemala "our pet project."[40] A staff rich in experience with private-sector and nontraditional export development in the region has been installed. A change in jargon has accompanied the change in spirit. "Government projects," "agrarian reform," and "tax reform" have been replaced by "free enterprise," "the market," "streamlined bureaucracy," "deal-making," and "privatization." Another AID official scoffed at the notion of land reform, saying, "That is such an Ivy League, liberal idea, totally removed from reality. Can't we move on to something new, something that is actually possible?"[41] That "something new" begins with a large-scale assault on all "anti-export bias" inherited from the import substitution legacy, along with a positive surge of private entrepreneurship and foreign investment aimed to spark an explosion of nontraditional exports.

Since the renewal of U.S. aid to Guatemala in 1986, AID has conceived grand plans for nontraditional exports in Guatemala. Within three years U.S. official assistance totaled more than $800 million, doubling the total of all U.S. assistance to Guatemala in the preceding forty years.[42] Coordinating the monetary injection, an AID report, "National Export Plan for Guatemala: *Guatemala Billions*" (Plan), outlines the agency's long-term plan to refuel the Guatemala economy with nontraditional exports.[43] The philosophy of the Plan is straightforward: economic development is predicated on nontraditional export production. As its title hints, the Plan's primary aim is to increase nontraditional exports to $1 billion by 1995—a goal to which AID officials and their Guatemalan proteges constantly refer.

Detailing forty-five specific policy recommendations aimed at achieving this dramatic rise in production, the Plan resembles a recipe book. In the short term (1989–92), the report calls for several programs, including special credit lines for exporters, privately administered free-trade-zone programs, reduction in costly bureaucratic procedures, and infrastructure improvements to counteract the restraining effects of current policies and economic institutions. In the medium (1993–96) and long (1997–2000) terms, the Plan emphasizes the importance of maintaining a stable, outward-oriented macroeconomic framework, including a complete abatement of protective tariffs. All of these efforts are intended to bring Guatemalan products into the world market.

Groom the Entrepreneur, Restrain the Civil Servant

AID has implemented two complementary practices to promote the maquila industry. First, it is carefully grooming "progressive" young businessmen to exploit the government's pro-export policies. Rather than seeking the partnership of the landed oligarchy, U.S. development officials consider English-speaking recent college graduates, many of whom are sons of the oligarchs, as ideal candidates for this leadership role.[44] Second, AID is aggressively reducing the government's role to that of a pure lawmaker, minimizing both its input in policy-making and its cumbersome bureaucratic hoops. In several years of intense pursuit of these aims, AID has created an efficient legislative, administrative, and political framework to promote and service nontraditional exports and private entrepreneurial initiatives. Similar to the GUATEXPRO era of the 1970s, the government now plays the pro forma role of promulgating prepared legislation; meanwhile, the private sector, prudently guided by AID, works to erect and maintain an administrative and political vehicle to execute the law.

AID's most successful creation in the development of a new class of entrepreneurs is the Nontraditional Products Exporters Association, or GEXPRONT, a private trade association which promotes and advocates for investors in nontraditional export production.[45] Founded in 1982 by a handful of young exporters of nontraditional products, GEXPRONT remained small and ineffectual until AID adopted it in the mid-1980s. Since 1985, AID has provided most of the funding and vital technical assistance to sustain the trade association. In 1990, AID funded over four-fifths of its budget—Q9 million out of a budget of Q14 million.[46] In addition to financial sustenance, AID personnel have nurtured strong personal ties with the leaders of GEXPRONT, who are often appointed to these posts on their recommendation. On the organization's long-standing dependence on AID, former GEXPRONT president, Edgar Sperisen, commented: "We would not be anywhere close to where we are today without the support of AID. From the beginning they gave us vital and essential assistance. Indeed, the growth of nontraditional exports would be at least four times less without AID funds and supervision."[47]

"Export or Die!" the title of a 1990 GEXPRONT seminar, sums up the association's mission. The organization, which has grown to over fifty full-time officials, promotes and assists more than eight hundred companies producing and servicing nontraditional exports. To service these clients, GEXPRONT maintains two floors and a library in the Chamber of Industry building, as well as an office in Quetzaltenango. The trade association's director, Fanny Estrada, explained the agency's single-minded purpose: "We have two types of work. On the macrolevel, we work with political issues—how to improve the infrastructure and formulate strategies for export. On the microlevel, we service individual companies, conduct seminars and conferences, and disseminate information."[48]

The Apparel Manufacturers Exporters Commission, known as VESTEX, is the advocate for the maquila sector within GEXPRONT. Consisting of five full-time staff persons, an elected board, and over three hundred dues-paying members, VESTEX is specifically responsible for supporting and promoting investment in apparel-assembly operations. For maquila owners, VESTEX lobbies the Guatemalan Congress, intercedes with government agencies, and provides essential information and business contacts to its members. Further, VESTEX has an educational component, regularly conducting seminars on effective management techniques and production strategies. For the prospective investor, the commission produces glossy brochures explaining the financial benefits of a maquila factory in Guatemala and conducts personal tours for those with more serious intentions.

AID officials consider the "creation of a deal-making environment" by bringing together U.S. buyers and contractors and Guatemalan maquila owners essential to their task of cultivating entrepreneurs.[49] To this end, GEXPRONT regularly provides fledgling investors with information on how to contact U.S. companies and arrange business deals.[50] Larger Guatemalan exporters are advised on how to set up new operations and to locate new markets and contacts abroad. AID officials solicit and serve as guides to representatives from U.S. TNCs who are interested in contracting work or investing directly in Guatemala. AID has even contracted a former embassy official to work full time for GEXPRONT whose explicit mandate is to encourage deal-making between Guatemalan entrepreneurs and U.S. labels. The culmination of these efforts occurred in February 1991, when Guatemalan maquila exporters and U.S. importers gathered at Guatemala's First Annual Apparel Outsourcing Convention in Guatemala City.[51]

In addition to GEXPRONT, AID sponsors several other programs designed to modernize the maquila industry and attract budding capitalists. AID-funded institutions contract U.S. management experts and retired executives to share their experiences and wisdom with Guatemalan entrepreneurs and managers. Since 1989, AID and a private Guatemalan university have been collaborating on the creation of an apparel engineering curriculum. In preparation for this area of study, professors from Florida International University regularly teach apparel management and production classes to university professors. The objective of these projects, says AID's director of maquila promotion, is "to get as many young [Guatemalan] investors as possible into the nontraditional export game."[52]

AID efforts to mold the private sector into an effective and efficient vehicle of nontraditional export promotion have paid off handsomely. GEXPRONT, by most accounts, is a professional, accomplished promotional organization, dispensing impressive rhetoric and attractive brochures as well as producing concrete results. Indeed, one commentator asserted that GEXPRONT "is generally recognized as one of the most effective private sector promotion agencies in the Caribbean Basin region."[53]

Rigorous attempts to minimize the role of the government in export promotion and production to that of a mere facilitator complements AID's private-sector training programs. "An intrusive government will ruin export production," summed up the director of AID's Private Sector Development. "Our job is to eliminate all vestiges of the previous protectionist policy and effectively remove the government from export production. The private sector is much more able and willing to lead this country on this path to economic development."[54]

AID attempts to reduce government presence in export promotion focus mainly on the reorganization and professionalization of necessary government functions such as customs and export licensing. For those agencies directly involved in the nontraditional export sector, particularly the Customs Office and the Economy Ministry, AID personnel provide extensive training and technical assistance. According to the AID director of maquila development, the goal of this training is "to make these agencies more technically efficient and to keep them less meddlesome in the process."[55] Along with directly assisting government agencies, AID has assumed a vital role in the formulation of legislation and policy. AID-contracted experts, for example, helped draft maquila incentives and the private free-trade-zone laws.

The most widely heralded success of this streamlining enterprise was the creation of "One-Stop-to-Export," the one-stop export licensing center in the Economy Ministry. This office administers all the paperwork necessary to export a shipment. Prior to "One Stop," an exporter was required to find, complete, and submit some twenty-five forms at up to ten different offices for every shipment—a process that often took a week or more to obtain a valid license. The creation of a one-stop export center consolidated this process to one visit. Perhaps more important for AID's aims, the process is not only more efficient but less political. Technocrats, rather than policy analysts and political appointees, now facilitate the export of goods.

Encouraging privatization of government-run services is perhaps the most effective weapon in AID's campaign against government intervention. Some AID officials believe that privatization is the panacea for Guatemala's reputation as an inefficient trading nation. This recurrent theme also indicates the U.S. government's supreme confidence in the private sector. "The only way this system will operate efficiently is to eliminate government involvement," said one AID official.[56] Specifically, many officials argue that the government's administration of customs should be dismantled and replaced by a private company because corruption and inefficiency are stifling export production. "Put all of the present customs officials in a giant warehouse. Pay them to do nothing. Let the private sector operate and manage the real operation," confided an AID expert.[57] Another object of privatization is ZOLIC, the centerpiece of the 1970s hodgepodge strategy. "ZOLIC is a financial disaster," said an AID official. "The only viable solution is to privatize. Give it to some young entrepreneurs at cost and let them run with it."[58] The solution to inefficient export production, according to AID, is to move as many functions as possible out of the hands of the government and into those of the private sector.

An Economic Miracle?

Many AID, GEXPRONT, and Guatemalan government representatives proclaim that the explosion of maquila production is an economic "miracle." The proliferation of assembly factories and the rise of exports has accelerated to rates far exceeding those in any other sector of the modern Guatemalan economy. Since 1986 the maquila industry has been growing at a rate of at least 75 percent a year, growth that would be considered sensational even in a thriving economy. But in this beleaguered one—with a greater than 20 percent inflation rate, an under- and unemployment rate exceeding 50 percent, and the most unequal distribution of land in the hemisphere—any spurt of jobs or economic production may be reasonably heralded as miraculous.

Moreover, this expansion comes at a time when the industrial sector as a whole is suffering its first decline in production in more than two decades, with a 3.5 percent decrease in 1988.[59] Perhaps most spectacular has been the meteoric rise in gross value of exported apparel to the United States. In 1983, Guatemala exported US$6 million worth of assembled garments to U.S. markets; by 1991, apparel exports exceeded $349 million.

This section will examine three facets of this growth: the gross value of exported apparel to the United States; employment in the maquila industry; and the backward and forward linkages that the industry has forged with other sectors of the Guatemalan economy. Unfortunately, precise economic figures are not available. The major obstacles to obtaining reliable data, as in many developing nations, are severe deficiencies in data collection and an extremely secretive business community. In general, the lack of coordinated and centralized professional government agencies generates an array of conflicting and confusing statistics.[60] In light of these limitations, figures should be considered, in most cases, to be well-founded estimates.

Value of Guatemalan Apparel Imports to the United States (in millions)[61]

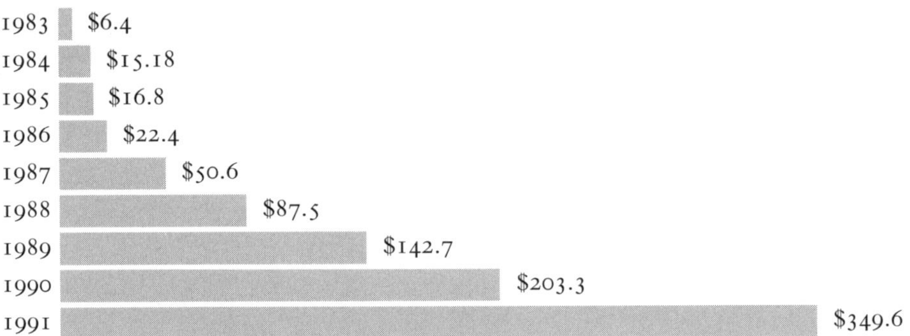

SOURCE: U.S. Department of Commerce.

Since 1984, the Guatemalan maquila industry has undergone a truly extraordinary expansion. Between 1986 (the year AID reestablished a full mission) and 1991, garment exports to the United States have risen almost 1,600 percent.[62] Further, according to industry promoters, the industry will increase 200 percent in the next four years, reaching the $1 billion plateau in 1995. By 1991, the gross value of apparel exports exceeded every other export category, including coffee and sugar.[63] Spearheading the nontraditional export strategy development, the maquila industry accounted for more than one-fourth of the revenue of all these exports in 1991.[64]

The Guatemala maquila industry is rapidly emerging as a major garment exporter in the region. Peter Steele, in his 1988 seminal study on the Caribbean and Central American apparel industry, classified Costa Rica, the Dominican Republic, Jamaica, and Haiti as the "Big Four" exporters of apparel of the region.[65] Guatemala ranked an unimpressive tenth, behind the likes of Belize, St. Lucia, and Barbados.[66] An updated version of Steele's study would unveil a new ranking. Since 1987 the Guatemalan industry has increased its production more than sevenfold and in 1991 accounted for almost 15 percent of the regional production;[67] only the Dominican Republic has doubled its output during that same term.[68] By 1989, Guatemala's production trailed those of the Dominican Republic, Costa Rica, Jamaica, and Haiti. After 1991, only Costa Rica and the Dominican Republic exceeded Guatemalan apparel output.[69] The future for maquila production in Guatemala appears bright. "This is a sewing country with the largest labor force in the Caribbean Basin. If overall stability remains, this country could easily grow and become the largest maquila production center in the region," predicted the U.S. Embassy trade attaché.[70]

The gross value of exported apparel figures is misleading because they report the value of the finished, ready-for-sale product when it enters a U.S. port. However, because generally assembly is the only operation that occurs in Guatemala, only a portion of this gross value is added in Guatemala. As will be seen below, Guatemalan inputs account for approximately one-fourth, or $87 million, of the gross value of exported apparel in 1991.

Of this Guatemalan value-added portion, however, there is significant evidence that the profits—constituting up to 40 percent of the revenue—rarely circulate as hard currency in the Guatemalan economy. In order to compete with other Caribbean countries for maquila investment, Guatemala permits unrestricted profit repatriation. Mainly due to insecure financial conditions and monetary policies in Guatemala and, specifically, an exchange rate set slightly below the market rate, foreign and domestic investors alike prefer to deposit all but their necessary expenses in U.S. or other foreign banks.

Many interviewed maquila owners confessed that they regularly divert profits to U.S. banks. Some arranged payments through a U.S. subsidiary to avoid converting dollars into quetzals. One Guatemalan entrepreneur boldly displayed his California identification card that he used "to open bank accounts in order to siphon off all but what is necessary to pay the bills in Guatemala."[71] So the actual gain of foreign exchange in many cases is limited to the expenses of the operation, while the profits pad North American bank accounts. On this profit drain, an industry consultant cynically commented, "More money goes to Miami banks than to Guatemalan ones."[72] Alvaro Colom and others estimate that at least 25 percent of the foreign exchange generated by the maquila industry never enters the country.

Korean bank accounts also receive substantial receipts from the sale of apparel assembled in Guatemala. In addition to depositing profits in Korean banks like their Guatemalan and U.S. counterparts, Korean investors universally contract Korean, instead of Guatemalan, supervisory and administrative personnel to manage their shops. This practice excludes hundreds of Guatemalans from the most skilled, and hence most lucrative, positions in Korean maquila factories. Since factories uniformly deposit these salaries, which range from $800 to $1,500 a month (well above the average Guatemalan supervisor's salary), directly into Korean bank accounts, Guatemala loses at least another $5 million a year in foreign exchange.

Maquila Factory Applications Registered under Decrees 24-84 and 29-89 [73]

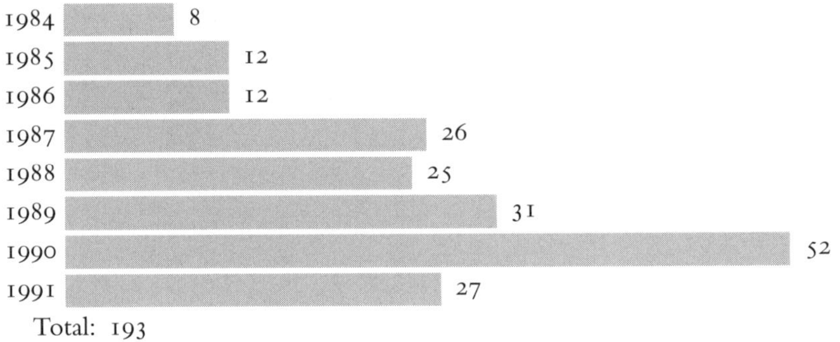

SOURCE: Economy Ministry/Office of Industrial Policy, March 23, 1992.

Along with injections of foreign currency, the creation of employment stands as the other immediate objective of the maquila strategy.[74] The maquila industry, thus far, has responded impressively to this end. At the close of 1984, the Economy Ministry reported about half a dozen qualified factories, employing less than two thousand workers who assembled garments for export. By the end of 1991, 193 maquila factories had registered for production with the ministry, and approximately eighty smaller sub-maquila factories were in operation.[75] These 270 or so factories employ an estimated fifty thousand workers.

Maquila workers presently comprise approximately 15 percent of all manufacturing workers in Guatemala. This figure may tell more about the limited size of the Guatemalan industrial sector than the growth of the maquila. According to the 1988 National Institute of Statistics census, out of nearly three million economically active employed workers older than ten, agriculture employed nearly 50 percent (1,423,439 workers) of the work force, whereas the industrial manufacturing sector accounted for about 14 percent (388,301) of all workers.[76] Hence, the maquila industry constitutes less than 2 percent of the total work force. Geographically, however, the maquila sector has had a more dramatic impact on employment, engaging approximately 5 percent of the total work force and 22 percent of the industrial manufacturing work force in the departments of Guatemala City, Sacatepequez, and Chimaltenango, the areas where the vast majority of maquila factories are located.[77]

The most important concrete indicator of long-term economic and industrial development is the magnitude of forward and backward linkages that the maquila industry forges with the rest of the economy. A conventional criticism of assembly-production exportation is that it functions in isolation from the rest of the country's economy, thereby adding little to the development of the economy as a whole. In the Dominican Republic, for example, the assembly-production operations are for the most part located in distinct geographic zones, physically separate from the rest of the country. Naturally, these industrial zones have developed into enclaves having minimal exchange with the rest of the economy, resulting in dead-end industrialization.

Since maquila exports, by law, must be reexported for sale in the United States, forward linkages to the domestic market do not exist. Even if there were major revisions in U.S. and Guatemalan trade laws authorizing the sale of finished products in Guatemala, the tiny market of potential purchasers would restrict any substantial forward linkages.

In contrast to forward linkages, Guatemalan law and maquila promoters encourage backward connections to the rest of the economy. The amount, or value, added by Guatemalan services and products, in addition to assembly labor, serves as the chief index of backward linkages. Traditionally, in assembly operations the value-added portion of the country where assembly takes place is very low. Commenting on this low figure, Eva Paus cautions: "When investment takes place in basic assembly-type production, one has to be careful not to exaggerate the positive effects. While such investments do create employment and generate foreign exchange, they normally create very few linkages with the rest of the economy."[78]

Consistent with Paus's warning, Caribbean and Central American assembly operations contribute less than 30 percent for all assembly operations, dropping as low as 10 percent for apparel assembly.[79] Unlike nontraditional agro-exports, where virtually the entire product is composed of domestic inputs—seed, land, and labor—the major value-added portion in export-processing industries is the labor. Additional internal costs include diverse expenses such as rentals, utility costs, and some materials; but, in most cases, these comprise a fraction of the added value.

Despite the traditionally low value-added component in regional industries, AID and other promoters insist that Guatemala has the potential to become a "full" maquila country; in other words, that the country, following the model of Korea and the other Asian Tigers, is capable of producing and manufacturing 100 percent of the product—from growing the cotton to manufacturing the textiles to cutting, sewing, and packing the garments. "It is my dream that 90 percent of the maquila factories in Guatemala will start selling full production—fabric, sewing, not only labor," said vice economy minister Alvaro Colom. "This is possible in our country because we have so many resources. Perhaps in two or three years we will start to export the entire package."[80]

However, based on current trends in Guatemala and the region, Guatemala's quest for full maquila production appears unreasonable and unrealistic. Although endowed with substantial natural resources, including the requisite climate and arable land for cotton cultivation, and an ample labor force, Guatemala, thus far, has maintained the regional practice of a low value-added component in apparel assembly and is likely to continue at this level. Labor constitutes the largest Guatemalan input, roughly $58 million a year, or 16 percent of the total value added.[81] Beyond labor, however, Guatemalan inputs for maquila production are extremely limited. In fact, the Economy Ministry reported that domestic contributions in 1990, excluding labor, accounted for a little more than 10 percent, which, if correct, raises Guatemala's value added to 26 percent, slightly above the regional average.[82] Confirming this estimate, for 1991 the Bank of Guatemala reported that apparel exports generated $86.8 million of foreign exchange, or about 25 percent of the gross value added. Relative to other exports, the foreign exchange generated by maquila exports, if correct, is still substantial, with only coffee and sugar exports creating more revenue.[83]

A handful of ambitious Guatemalan entrepreneurs are living up to AID's expectations of full maquila production, initiating companies and expanding established ones to meet the growing needs of the maquila industry. At least one laundering service, as well as button and zipper companies, has started in response to the demands of the maquila industry. When pressed to name significant links with the economy, one AID official proffered the hundreds of lunch stands that have sprouted up at the doors of maquila factories. Outside of labor and textiles, however, inputs such as these are relatively insignificant. The U.S. Department of Commerce estimated, for example, that in apparel assembly overseas freight costs and management support account for less than 2 percent of the total value of the item.[84]

Moreover, most of the textiles—by far the most substantial nonlabor input—used in Guatemalan maquila production are and will continue to be manufactured in foreign mills. In Guatemala, only one company, Liztex S.A., has responded in any appreciable way to the rising demand for textiles.[85] The largest producer of textiles and the only full service mill in Guatemala, Liztex, to be sure, has experienced phenomenal growth. Most of its fabric is manufactured from cotton grown on company plantations in Guatemala. In 1988, total sales for domestic and export production were $10 million; by 1990, they had surpassed $30 million. About half of this output is sold to Guatemalan maquila and domestic apparel factories, the rest is marketed to other factories in the region. For more than two years, the mills have been running at capacity.[86] In fact, Liztex is months behind on orders for maquila production, unable to expand fast enough to fill orders.

Despite Liztex's success, however, most owners use non-Guatemalan-made cloth and materials mainly because U.S. and Korean government trade policies and practices discourage use of native manufactured textiles. As a result, more than two-thirds of the textiles used in Guatemalan shops are manufactured in U.S. mills;[87] another one-fourth originate in Korean and other Southeast Asian factories;[88] and the remaining one-tenth or so are woven in Guatemalan and other Latin American shops, such as Liztex.

Although AID and U.S. Embassy officials proclaim the virtues of full maquila production throughout the region, the actual thrust of U.S. trade policy promotes offshore assembly but not self-sufficient manufacturing operations such as those found in Southeast Asia.[89] As mentioned above, the CBI excludes apparel from tariff reductions given to other nontraditional products. The only U.S. trade programs in which apparel assembled offshore is eligible for special duty treatment require that U.S. components compose no less than 65 percent of the total declared value of the imported product. Formerly referred to as 807 and Super 807, Harmonized Tariff Schedule (HTS) 9802.00.80 and 9802.00.60 programs subject only the foreign value-added portion to a duty.[90] Apparel imports qualify for this special treatment when the fabric is formed and cut in U.S. mills.

HTS programs exploit the Caribbean and Central American nations' natural comparative advantage of proximity to the United States, virtually prohibiting the development of meaningful textiles industries to supply maquila factories. By comparison, the distance between the Asian countries and the United States, to some extent, spurred the development of local textile production. The time and cost of sending cloth halfway around the world twice rendered the use of HTS 9802.00.80 impractical. With apparel exempt from preferred duty status under the CBI, HTS programs provide the sole option for U.S. corporations manufacturing and contracting abroad to limit high tariff costs. This policy makes it likely that the Guatemalan maquila industry will continue to rely on U.S. fabric.

The high proportion of non-U.S., foreign-manufactured cloth used in Guatemalan shops stems from Korean factories' widespread practice of assembling fabric manufactured in Korea. These factories prefer to use Korean-manufactured cloth in order to bolster the Korean textile industry which, like its apparel industry, has suffered the artificial ceilings of U.S. quotas since the mid-1980s. Korean factories in Guatemala provide a natural outlet for Korean textiles, an outlet also encouraged by its dominant government. So long as its domestic apparel and textile industries are throttled by the quota, Korean maquila factories in Guatemala will use as much Korean fabric as possible.

In sum, the maquila operations have produced close to fifty thousand jobs and approximately $87 million in annual foreign exchange. Alone, these figures—especially employment—appear miraculous; but the numbers are deceptive. These statistics do not reveal that the maquila industry has failed to develop lasting, substantial linkages within the Guatemalan economy and that much of the foreign exchange is repatriated. In particular, constrained by U.S. and Korean trade policy, the textile industry, the most promising backward linkage, remains newborn. As a result, labor costs and profits account for most of the value added in Guatemala. Perhaps more importantly, these figures fail to disclose the harsh nature of the recently created employment. "We read about the expansion of the maquila industry," commented a worker, "but this growth has not brought me or my coworkers much, except many headaches and pathetically small wages."[91]

3

The Market and the Players

Free Enterprise Personified

When asked to evaluate the investment climate of the Guatemalan maquila industry, an AID official called it "free enterprise personified."[1] Of this favorable environment, one maquila owner stated, "Any fool could make money in this business; it is just a matter of how much."[2] Even the entrepreneur who starts without managerial experience in the industry can operate an inefficient shop and still expect a high rate of return. Recent government policies to lure maquila investment, an "attractive" labor force, and low start-up and operational costs—including wages more than thirty times less than those paid in U.S. shops—ensure a healthy short-term profit for most maquila investors willing to accept the political risks.

In addition to promulgating an array of incentive legislation, the Guatemalan government devalued the local currency to attract foreign investors, particularly in the maquila industry. Before 1984 the quetzal was fixed at parity with the U.S. dollar. An even one-to-one exchange rate combined with protective tariffs had provided an edge to domestic manufacturers who supplied Guatemalan and regional markets. With the collapse of the Central American Common Market, this fixed rate hampered exports to markets outside the region. Under pressure from the World Bank and the United States, in 1986 and again in 1989, the Christian Democrat government devalued, or "floated," as the Central Bank called the move, the quetzal to encourage exports and foreign investment. Eventually, the government released the fixed rate altogether and adopted a freely floating exchange rate system. Applauding these efforts, an AID document hailed the devaluation as "a very significant positive step" that should "provide impetus to private sector capital repatriation, exports, and foreign investment."[3]

The government's currency devaluation has provided considerable benefit for maquila entrepreneurs. Since owner-investors are paid by U.S. buyers in U.S. dollars but pay workers and local vendors in quetzals, the "floating" rate guarantees owners a sizable profit on sales. Of course, these gains from devaluation would have been at least partially offset by parallel increases in wages. But wages in maquila factories have not kept pace, mainly because owners consider the government-instituted minimum wage a ceiling on compensation.[4] The last official increase in the minimum wage for garment and apparel workers occurred in 1987. Enacted during the "honeymoon" period of the Cerezo regime, the daily minimum wage for garment workers was set at Q5.50, or about US$2.75, at that time.

Even in 1987, however, the Q5.50 minimum did not keep pace with inflation. The real value of the 1987 minimum wage represented an almost 20 percent actual decline from 1980. To have maintained real wages at 1980 levels, an average minimum wage of Q7.64 would have been required.[5] Since then, the quetzal has continued to depreciate, presently sitting at about Q5.00:US$1.00, while wages have remained constant.

As an additional measure of structural reform demanded by international lenders, the government removed price controls on most goods. A consequence of these measures is runaway inflation; in 1990, the inflation rate was 75 percent.[6] Food and other essential items have tripled and quadrupled in price, placing maquila workers who earn minimum wage in a precarious predicament. Of particular concern for maquila workers has been the 300 percent rise in bus fares since 1989. In short, the government's decision to devalue the currency and withdraw price controls without increasing the minimum wage has created an exceedingly auspicious opportunity for exporters with eyes on the world market, at the expense of most Guatemalan workers.

The cost of starting and operating a maquila garment factory is extremely low. The garment-assembly industry is renowned as one of the least capital-intensive manufacturing industries. Little has changed in terms of garment production technology in the last hundred years.[7] The basic operation—assembling cut pieces of cloth on a hand-fed sewing machine—has yet to be replaced by sophisticated machinery or automation. Moreover, labor is still the lifeblood of the industry—and the cheaper, the better.

"Find a garage or a dance hall and some sewing machines and a factory is born," a union leader commented on the transient and inexpensive nature of the business.[8] In Guatemala, most maquila investors rent a warehouse and fill it with used machinery.

The next step is to post a "Help Wanted" sign and wait for the throngs of workers to arrive. Estimates of start-up costs range from $800 to $2,000 per worker. The higher estimate, provided by an "upscale" consultant, includes new machinery, salaries three times the minimum wage, and six months' training for each worker.[9] Perhaps two or three factories out of two hundred and seventy implement these more expensive practices; the rest of the shops import used machinery, pay no more than the minimum wage, and either hire only experienced workers or pay less than minimum wage during training periods. Hence, the more genuine estimate to start a maquila factory hovers near $1,000 per worker.

This economical start-up cost is complemented by inexpensive operating costs. Utilities, though burdensome on poor residents, are inexpensive compared to those in other countries in the region. The electricity supply in Guatemala, the most important local ingredient for production,[10] is more reliable than in many countries in the region and is cheaper than in any other country in the Caribbean and Central America.[11] Likewise, rental space is plentiful and reasonable; most factories pay between US$.47–.80 per square yard of space, again ranking it as one of the most inexpensive rates in the region.[12]

Guatemala's most attractive characteristic by far is its work force. Explaining his reasons for opening a maquila factory, an investor said: "It is really a very simple, straightforward situation. It is the labor. It is the cost of labor."[13] According to *Bobbin*, a textile and apparel manufacturers' trade journal, the cost of labor in Guatemala maquila factories in 1990 was the lowest in the Central American and Caribbean region. (In the magazine's 1991 survey, Guatemala maintained this position.[14]) This was the first time in the history of the magazine's survey that Haiti did not offer the lowest wages to investors. Including mandated benefits and minimum wage, according to *Bobbin*, an employer will spend Q1.80, or $.36, an hour per Guatemalan employee.[15] In fact, the actual wage is much lower than this estimate. According to this study as well as the reports of representatives of the Labor Ministry, most maquila employers do not comply with government wage and benefit requirements. The more realistic wage rate for maquila workers is between Q.70 and 1.30, or $.16 and .26 an hour, making Guatemalan maquila workers more than thirty times less expensive than comparable U.S. workers.[16]

Given this extraordinarily low payroll cost, profit in the maquila industry is a given; only the amount varies. Calculations of profit depend on variables such as volume of business; successful acquisition, quality, and duration of contracts; efficiency and reliability of the work force; and management proficiency. Nevertheless, the essential ingredients for a high rate of return—supportive government policies and low capital costs—await even the most careless, inexperienced investor. Foreign and local investors routinely begin operations without previous experience and with minimal capital. One North American owner began his business without any experience in the garment industry and, in less than a year, expected to make a nearly $25,000 a month profit from a small shop of 125 machines. Consultants and owners estimate profits at 25 to 40 percent of gross sales.[17] One estimated that each machine, on average, produces a minimum of $5,000 in sales per year. Of this amount, at least 25 percent, or $1,250, will return as profits. In less than a year, the investor can expect to pay back his initial outlay.

The Players: Workers, Suppliers, Entrepreneurs

A look at the "players" of the maquila industry in Guatemala—the workers, suppliers, and entrepreneurs—reveals some similarities and a major difference with other regional industries. On the one hand, the Guatemalan maquila worker shares the attributes of the "typical" maquila worker who assembles cloth or components in factories throughout the developing world. She is very young, often unwed, and is entering the job market for the first time. Further, as in the rest of the region, U.S. TNCs are the major suppliers of contracts and components and are the recipients of finished goods. On the other hand, the national origin of the entrepreneurs and capital differs radically from that in the other major maquila industries in the region. In those industries, direct U.S. investment in the form of subsidiaries or joint ventures dominates. Frequently, U.S. TNCs such as Hanes and Levis maintain large factories in free-trade zones throughout the region. In contrast, the major source of direct foreign investment in the Guatemalan maquila industry hails from the Republic of Korea. Local entrepreneurs account for the next largest presence, while U.S. garment maquila operations, the vanguard in the region, are inconspicuous in Guatemala.

The Maquila Worker: Nontraditional Worker for Nontraditional Manufacturing

In their seminal study of worldwide assembly operations, Joseph Grunwald and Kenneth Flamm conclude: "A feature that seems to characterize all assembly activities is a predominately female work force—an overwhelming proportion young and unmarried."[18] The workers in Guatemalan maquila factories confirm this classic image, as most of them are girls and young women between the ages of fourteen and twenty-four. The vast majority are single and living at home with their parents, where their income helps to offset household expenses. Some of these young women have children outside of marriage; others are recently married. At least four-fifths of the workers in maquila factories located in the city are women.[19] Factories outside the city limits, however, differ in composition, mainly because more acute poverty and fewer jobs force indigenous men into the labor pool. In rural maquila factories, nearly half the workers are men, most married with children. The predominance of female employees, particularly in urban factories, contrasts with the composition of the formal employment sector, in which more than three out of four workers are male.[20]

The maquila worker is particularly anomalous in the industrial work force. Male workers have historically dominated employment in industry, particularly in periods of industrial growth. In 1989, over three-fourths of Guatemalan factory workers were men. As a young, unmarried female, the maquila worker deviates from this norm. Traditionally, this class of worker has found employment in domestic work, and even in times of expansive industrial production their participation was limited to cleaning the homes of the managers and industrialists. During Guatemala's rapid manufacturing growth in the 1960s and 1970s, female workers actually experienced a decline in industrial employment.[21] By contrast, they are the work force of the thriving maquila industry. For the first time in Guatemalan history, then, female workers have taken the lead in industrial expansion.

In most factories jobs are nevertheless segregated by sex. Except in rural factories, sewing is almost exclusively the domain of female workers. "The work is more gentle, more appropriate for women. Men want to earn more, and the pay is very little in sewing," explained a manager from B y D Confecciones.[22] Advertisements for operators frequently request only female applicants. Women also account for most of the "finishers" who cut threads and check seams before shipping. Male employees fill the packing, cutting, and ironing sections of the factory, as these tasks are considered more "strenuous," and consequently more appropriate for men.

Too Few Workers?

Idleness is rare in Guatemala. Generally only the disabled who have the good fortune to receive disability pay from an employer or state social security can afford to be unemployed. Since unemployment insurance programs do not exist, most would starve without a source of income. As a result, though idleness is low, underemployment is enormous—almost two-thirds of the labor force work in jobs that either consist of less than forty hours a week or more than forty hours a week, with earnings below the minimum wage.[23] In urban centers the burgeoning informal sector of thousands of snack, hot dog, and shoe-shine stands vividly testifies to this underemployment.

Despite this abundance of available labor, a frequent, if not universal, complaint of maquila owners and managers is that there are not enough qualified workers.[24] Explaining this difficulty, one owner said: "We advertise [for workers] constantly, but there never seem to be enough. With so many factories, workers can choose where to work. We try to get workers to stay, but most of them leave, I guess, in search of better benefits."[25] Aggressive advertising demonstrates this intense competition for workers. One out of every five Help Wanted ads in newspapers is from a maquila factory.[26] Other Help Wanted circulars are posted on street lights, telephone poles, and walls throughout the city. Some owners even use radio announcements to solicit workers, which is reminiscent of the traditional means of recruiting migrant farm workers. One factory distributed flyers depicting a ten-quetzal bill to its employees, promising a real note to any worker who brought in a new employee.

How can there be a dearth of maquila workers in a country where over half the working-age population is underemployed? Although this study does not pretend to answer this question fully, some observations may be helpful in trying to understand the dynamics of the maquila industry and its work force. First, as mentioned, cultural stereotypes restrict the labor pool. Generally, both owners and potential employees consider sewing a female activity. Women, this view contends, possess the dexterity and patience necessary to perform the tedious operations. Subscribing to this stereotype, many men do not apply for openings in maquila shops, and when they do, they are often rejected because of their gender. "We only hire men to pack and ship. They don't have the patience or the skill to operate a machine," confirmed a personnel manager.[27]

Some personnel managers and owners assert that women are not only more dexterous but, just as important, are less inclined to be "troublemakers." These employers believe that women are more docile and respectful of authority than men, and hence less likely to rebel. "Men are more likely to form unions. Women do not have this mentality," candidly explained an employer. "They are more prone to do what you tell them without questioning. That they are better sewers is a bonus."[28]

In addition, preference for age and marital status further limits the available labor pool. Owners almost unanimously desire young, unmarried women in order to capitalize on their availability, youthfulness, and endurance. Millie Woc, a personnel manager at Este Oeste S.A., described this ideal worker:

> Eighteen to twenty-four is the ideal age. They should not be married because when they are married they tend to have added responsibilities. Before you know it they start to have children, which is a problem. We do not hire a woman if she has small children because it is likely they will become sick, and she will often need to go to the doctor. If a woman is large, she will likely get sick often and have to go to the

doctor as well. My ideal worker is young, unmarried, healthy, thin and delicate, single, lives close, and does not have previous experience. If they have experience they come with many vices. They do not like to follow orders. We like to teach them ourselves. Old people are also not good because they are sick often and do not look good anymore.[29]

The high turnover rate in the maquila industry also creates a continual need for employees. On average, factories experience between a 10 and 30 percent turnover of workers each month.[30] With few exceptions, owners admitted that workers rarely remain at their factory for more than a few months. Several owners called this transient behavior the "jumping bean syndrome." In some factories the entire work force changes every four months. Most managers, with the notable exception of Korean ones, attributed their employees' transience to lack of loyalty and irresponsible exploitation of the abundance of jobs. "So many take advantage of us," complained an owner. "They work long enough to master a new machine or a new technique and then they leave and go to work in another factory. We invest money in training but rarely see the results."[31]

Workers, on the other hand, confirmed frequent moves among factories but asserted that they were usually necessary for economic reasons. For example, one interviewed worker had worked at five different factories in less than two years. Dissatisfied with the conditions and salaries at each factory, he did not have difficulty obtaining work, but the pay and treatment never improved, leading him to quit and find another. "I have a family to feed," he explained. "So far I have yet to find a place that will pay enough to meet these needs."[32] A few factories reported higher retention rates, but these are usually the better-paying, more humane workplaces. This jumping bean behavior adds to the appearance of a surplus of jobs, but, more importantly, it demonstrates rampant discontent among workers with their salaries and working conditions.

Finally, and perhaps most significantly, the fact that maquila employment has outpaced the number of skilled operators and supervisors also contributes to the dearth of qualified workers. Workers learn how to operate machines in two locations. A small number, perhaps one or two thousand a year, attend training classes at the government's employment training project, Instituto Técnico de Capacitación (INTECAP), and at small nongovernment organizations (NGOs). The second and most popular place to learn how to sew is on the job. The onus of this training, however, falls almost exclusively on the twenty or so mostly Korean factories that are large enough to devote sufficient space and resources to training workers.

Funded by a 1 percent payroll tax, INTECAP attempts to train workers for new, emerging fields. At centers around the country, workers sign up for a free four-week sewing course and are provided with employment leads. Historically, INTECAP's impact on the development of a skilled work force has been modest. Threatened with meager, rarely enforced sanctions, many employers elect not to pay the payroll tax. Since these courses do not offer a stipend, few aspiring workers can afford to attend. Ironically, many maquila companies are reluctant to hire INTECAP-trained employees because these workers "learn other ideas as well," such as their legal rights.[33] As the largest NGO training program, Fundación Tecnológico (FUNTEC) trains less than thirty workers a month. Unlike INTECAP, this AID-financed organization charges tuition. "FUNTEC is a small NGO that struggles along, living hand to mouth," says an AID representative. "It is a drop in the bucket."[34]

Lacking significant training programs, most workers must learn how to operate machines inside the factory. Generally only the larger factories—those with more than three hundred machines—are financially capable of setting aside precious machinery, personnel, and time to train workers. In these larger shops entire lines are dedicated to training. Some factories, particularly Korean ones, prefer workers without experience because, managers contend, experienced workers are lazy and filled with "bad habits." In contrast, most shops, especially the smaller ones, only accept experienced workers. Upon application the worker is given a sewing test, which consists of sewing either a scrap of paper or cloth: if the applicant cannot sew or is not dexterous enough, she is not hired. Thus, the majority of the shops rely on the larger factories to provide training grounds for their future workers. "Thanks to the Koreans, we have huge schools of operators," said one Guatemalan maquila owner.[35]

Origins of the New Maquila Working Class: New Opportunity or Desperate Choice?

Precisely where this maquila work force emerged from is unknown. There are at least two explanations. But since detailed study on the background of the workers has not been done, both theories rely heavily on anecdotal evidence.

First, some observers contend that former and future domestic workers who traditionally have been young, single women from poor, low educational backgrounds compose the maquila work force. In pre-maquila days, these women, when necessary, could find work in the home of a middle- or upper-class family. In the last five years, the maquila industry has provided this class of worker with an unprecedented alternative to domestic work. As proof of the existence of this new option, some middle- and upper-class Guatemalan households report increasing difficulty in finding domestic workers.[36] One AID official stated, "You go to cocktail parties and at least one woman will complain how hard it is to get and keep maids, how her maid got up one day and said, 'I am going to work in a maquila.'"[37] Other elites lament that their maids are beginning to demand "better" conditions, such as weekends off, and employers feel compelled to grant these demands for fear of being unable to find a competent replacement. The maquila industry, they claim, has diminished the available pool of domestic workers.

The explanation that the maquila industry is competing with domestic work for the same class of workers could have substantial, long-term effects on the conditions and compensation for these workers. As the maquila industry continues to draw workers away from domestic employment, the competition between sectors will force improvements in domestic work, making it more attractive than maquila work. One high-ranking AID official claimed: "A common progression from field hand or domestic worker to maquila worker exists where young women may begin as maids but be drawn to the maquila factories because of the better pay, conditions, and enhanced freedom. The maquila, for the first time, provides these women and girls with a new and better opportunity."[38] However, there is little evidence beyond the above-mentioned anecdotes to indicate the rumblings of a substantial change in the demanding conditions and paltry wages within the domestic sector, and, as described below in Chapters 4 and 5, the working conditions and compensation in most maquila factories, by any objective standard, are deficient.

Second, some economists believe that the influx of young female workers into the maquila industry does not represent a major shift of workers from domestic employment; rather, they argue that increasingly desperate economic conditions, ironically caused in part by fiscal policies designed to lure investment in the maquila industry, have forced tens of thousands of girls and young women, who in previous times may have forgone paid work to assist in household chores and care of siblings, to enter the work force to supplement their families' income.[39] The recent explosion of the maquila industry has coincided with worsening economic conditions. Since the early 1980s, most Guatemalans have experienced particularly severe economic hardships, with the number of families living in poverty doubling between 1981 and 1986.[40] The United Nations reported in 1991 that 87 percent of Guatemalans live in extreme poverty, meaning 6.5 million of the nation's 9 million people go to bed hungry every night.[41] With prices rising daily and wages remaining constant, children are seeking work at younger and younger ages, and traditional distinctions between male and female household roles are deteriorating in the face of starvation. Thus, it is not surprising that in spite of the addition of more than fifty thousand jobs in the past four years, the unemployment and underemployment rates continue to increase rather than decrease.

While the maquila factory does provide young female workers with an option to domestic employment, these critics argue that most maquila workers are motivated to seek work because of a falling standard of living. One fifteen-year-old worker described this predicament: "I would not be working in this horrible factory for this demanding manager unless it was absolutely necessary. My father does not have a job and so we—the girls—had to find work. I went to the maquila because I knew they would hire me. I want to be in school but I am here. I do not like it but what is one to do?"[42] Under this economic strain, such workers would probably have entered the informal sector or found domestic work if the maquila revolution had not occurred. Moreover, the competition for young female workers that the maquila industry has generated does not appear to have improved the work conditions and wages for these workers. "In the past five years, we see more and more young girls leaving school earlier and earlier," commented an official in the Labor Ministry. "We also see this work force more and more abused and exploited."[43] Young girls and women work in maquila factories because the labor is highly gender segregated, because they are willing to work for lower wages, and because the management in these factories prefers to hire them.

The Suppliers: U.S. Transnational Corporations

U.S. TNCs contract nearly all of the garment production in Guatemalan maquila factories. As promotion officials readily attest, clothing for many well-known brand names, such as Liz Claiborne, Sears, Bugle Boy, OP, Levis, and Phillips-Van Heusen, is assembled in Guatemalan shops. Since few of these labels have elected to invest directly in the maquila industry, most business is conducted and monitored through company representatives or independent agents located in Guatemala. Representatives from about ten labels maintain offices in Guatemala City. They choose the factories to contract, facilitate communication between the factories and the parent company, and oversee the quality of production through regular visits to contracted shops. Other labels, such as Levis, send specialists to train managers and operators. Smaller labels often work through brokers, mostly Guatemalan, who at any one time may represent four to eight different brands. These brokers are independent middlemen—contracting, facilitating, monitoring in exchange for a commission on sales.

Many workers report frequent visits of North Americans to their factories. "They [the North Americans] come in and are rushed to the office where, I guess, they talk about business and drink coffee. When they come onto the floor, they usually only look at the finished products," explained a worker.[44] Timeliness and quality, not working conditions or wages, are the primary concerns of these representatives and agents. When asked about the conditions in the factories, one manufacturer's representative replied, "Our job is to make sure the garments are produced on time and have the highest quality. We can suggest ways to improve production, but how the factories choose to meet our demands is none of our business."[45]

The Entrepreneurs: Many Koreans and Guatemalans, Few North Americans

The most noticeable difference between the maquila industry in Guatemala and the rest of the Caribbean and Central America is the national origin of its investors and owners. Most other major maquila operations in the region—particularly, in Costa Rica, the Dominican Republic, and Jamaica—are dominated by U.S. investors and capital. In 1988, North American capital, for example, accounted for 87 of the 124 maquila plants in the Dominican Republic.[46] In addition, North American investors control the majority of production in Mexico's massive maquiladora operation.[47] Although large "brand name" companies tend to dominate, individual North American entrepreneurs and smaller labels have also found profitable niches in these countries. Local capital and entrepreneurs and, to a lesser extent, foreign investors from Southeast Asia account for the remaining factories.

In a radical departure from this model of North American investors as the leaders of the industry, South Korean capital and owners have emerged as the undisputed giants of Guatemala's maquila industry. Although the fifty Korean maquila operations are a minority of the two hundred and seventy or so total factories, these shops are generally larger, more modern, and more productive than their North American and Guatemalan counterparts.[48] Korean factories on average employ more than 350 workers, use more advanced production technology, and together account for nearly half of the maquila production.[49] Local capital has established over two hundred shops, but the great majority house far less than a hundred workers. Further, locally managed factories are much less productive than Korean shops because of less experienced management and inferior machinery; in all, Guatemalan-owned factories account for approximately 30–40 percent of the total production. Lastly, U.S. investors, occasionally in joint ventures with local industrialists, maintain assembly operations in about eight larger factories, which assemble less than 10 percent of the garments for export.[50]

As a whole, foreign investment has been slow to enter the maquila industry. From

1984 to 1989, foreign capital controlled perhaps eight out of sixty factories. Of these, South Korean investors operated six operations, while U.S. investors claimed the other two. Since 1989, North American investors have either invested or coinvested with Guatemalan entrepreneurs in about seven more plants. In comparison, South Korean (including Korean-American) investments have accounted for forty-four factories over the last three years.

As described in Chapter 2, a principal goal of AID's maquila strategy is to entice foreign investment to Guatemala. From the perspective of AID, "foreign" means the United States, not Korea. "Of course, when we develop policies designed to lure foreign investment, we hope that U.S. investors will respond. Historically, U.S. investors have responded to these policies. We expect that the same will be true with the maquila," confirmed the U.S. Embassy trade attaché.[51] In the region, a principle goal of the CBI is to encourage direct U.S. investment in production and distribution of nontraditional manufacturing and agricultural products.[52] In Guatemala, AID's primary objective is to create a healthy, secure climate for U.S. investment. GEXPRONT, for example, prints relevant incentive laws and promotional pamphlets in English and Spanish and distributes them to potential investors in the United States. Moreover, the combination of "free enterprise personified," an AID-constructed administrative structure, and cheap, abundant labor has resulted in prosperity for entrepreneurs with limited capital and a high spirit of adventure. In spite of this "sure thing," U.S. investors have bypassed direct investment in the industry.

Both individual U.S. entrepreneurs and TNCs have foregone the opportunity to invest in the Guatemalan maquila industry. Less than four individual U.S. citizens (non-Korean-American) have been willing to risk capital in a maquila factory. These investors, it seems, were not lured to the industry as a consequence of AID or GEXPRONT promotional efforts. Rather, they came upon the industry by chance; none appears to have "chosen" Guatemala as the result of a systematic search for an investment opportunity.

The experiences of two U.S. owners illustrate this haphazard, "fate-filled" investment strategy. One of the first maquilas, Internacional Exportaciones S.A., belongs to an American investor, Henry Robbins-Cohen.[53] Robbins-Cohen arrived in Guatemala during the mid-1970s with management experience and know-how from a spell in the New York garment district. In a short time, he built one of the largest garment factories in Guatemala, with over five hundred workers, producing clothing mainly for the regional and domestic markets. After the enactment of the 1984 maquila incentive legislation, Robbins-Cohen applied for the benefits and converted his factory to produce for the more lucrative U.S. market.

In an effort "to keep his wife busy," a second U.S. owner, Brent Holmes, purchased a small, thirty-machine shop, which at the time was producing clothes for the local boutique market.[54] Almost immediately Holmes was struck by the potential profits of export production. He sold his financial services business in California and joined his spouse full-time. Without any experience, he increased the number of machines and production fourfold and moved the factory to a larger building. In both examples, the reputation and promotional touting of the maquila industry were insignificant factors; only after discovering the lucrative earnings were these two men and a handful of others like them persuaded to dedicate their time and resources to the industry.

Phillips-Van Heusen: Lone U.S. Giant in Guatemala

Alongside these entrepreneurs, about four U.S. "brand name" TNCs, in several instances coinvesting with local investors, maintain assembly operations in Guatemala. By far the largest of these is Phillips-Van Heusen (PVH)—the world's largest manufacturer of men's shirts. Opened in June 1988, PVH's first plant, Camisas Modernas S.A.—a modern, well-equipped factory that is pictured in nearly every promotional brochure for the industry—contains 180 machines, employs over three hundred workers, and produces about 6,000 shirts a month. PVH has opened another factory for cutting and finishing fabric imported from Southeast Asia and regularly subcontracts to three middle-sized Guatemalan-owned and -managed factories. In all, PVH assembles more than 20,000 dozen shirts each month from over 1,000 machines in Guatemala, making it the company's largest "hub" in Central America and the Caribbean.

In collaboration with a prominent local maquila consulting firm, Megatex S.A., and the Guatemalan government, PVH has also begun a maquila development project in San Pedro, Sacatepequez, an indigenous village about 20 kilometers outside of the capital. For decades San Pedro was renowned for its manufacture of Western-style garments sold domestically. Scores of locally owned and managed microfactories of six to twenty machines—located in small, dimly lit, and unventilated shacks and houses—saturate the town. Combined, some 3,000 machines are worked by the 10,000 inhabitants. In 1989, PVH "adopted" the village, making a commitment to subcontract sufficient work to occupy the three hundred machines of a consortium of twenty local entrepreneurs. Other contributors followed PVH's promise to this entrepreneurial development project: Megatex S.A., Alvaro Colom's consulting firm, provided management and production assistance; the Guatemalan government installed new telephone and electrical lines; the army engineer corps built a new road from San Pedro to the capital; and then president Vinicio Cerezo donated several thousand dollars to further develop the town's infrastructure.

PVH and its collaborators view this project, known as "The Village," as a model of how the maquila industry can lead Guatemala into a new industrial age.[55] "Our best experience in Guatemala has been San Pedro," said Erick Sterkel, general manager of Camisas Modernas. "We are giving poor people an opportunity to grow and make money. If this were reproduced around the country, we could lead this country into prosperity and industrialization."[56] Others who are more critical point out the sweatshop conditions in these microfactories, which are some of the worst in Guatemala, and wonder why PVH provides employment, rather than classrooms, for boys and girls as young as seven years old.

While PVH's operation is one of the largest in Guatemala, the overall presence of direct investment from U.S. TNCs and entrepreneurs is modest. PVH's commitment dwarfs all other U.S. direct investment in Guatemala. The remaining TNC investments include such names as Gitano and Popsicle and are usually modern, larger facilities, employing between 250 and 500 workers. Including PVH, these firms, along with the few individual U.S. investors, account for less than one-tenth of the maquila production. Commenting on this lack of U.S. direct investment, one Guatemalan investor said, "You would hardly even know U.S. investors are here."[57]

Historic Anomaly

To be sure, U.S. labels and manufacturers' representatives have found Guatemala a prosperous venue in which to contract business. However, given the advantages of control that direct investment provides, the proximity to the U.S. market, and the generous profits of the industry, the dearth of direct investment by large U.S. corporations and smaller entrepreneurs is difficult to explain. This absence is more perplexing in light of the strong tradition of U.S. private investment in Guatemala beginning in the early 1900s when U.S. corporations transformed the country into a "banana republic." More recently, U.S. capital dominated the import substitution industrial growth in the 1960s and 1970s. In fact, by 1968, over 90 percent of all direct foreign investment flowed from U.S. corporate coffers.[58] Even today, U.S. investors claim 80 percent of all foreign investment in Guatemala but only about 16 percent of foreign investment in the maquila industry.[59] The absence of U.S. direct investment in the maquila industry thus contrasts with this rich history of U.S. participation in Guatemalan industrial growth.

The most common explanation for the low level of U.S. direct maquila investment is that the pervasive violence in the country diverts investors to more secure venues. To this claim, U.S. development and Guatemalan promotional and government officials respond that the reality of violence and political disruption is far less than the reports fabricated by the "liberal" Western press. They contend that melodramatic, biased news reports have unfairly prejudiced the mind-set of North Americans, especially investors, who have come to think of Guatemala as a land of terror, not free enterprise. Fanny Estrada, the executive director of GEXPRONT, articulated this view: "U.S. investors are scared by the reports of violence and instability. At this moment, they would rather set up shop in Costa Rica than Guatemala. Each day [U.S.] newspapers report on the atrocities which allegedly happen in our country. If I did not live here and know firsthand that investment in Guatemala is secure and profitable, I wouldn't invest either."[60]

Once this perception is corrected, Estrada and other promoters believe that U.S. TNCs will come to their senses and saturate the country with assembly operations. Hence, for promotion officials, the lack of U.S. investment is a public relations problem. "The problem [of few U.S. investors] is due to image. U.S. investors only hear negative things about Guatemala," explained an AID official. "We are working to change the image of Guatemala from that of a dangerous place to invest in to what it really is: an investment paradise."[61]

Promoters point to six years of civilian rule as the prime indication that lasting stability and peace have arrived. After a particularly brutal decade of civil war between the military and the guerrillas, in which tens of thousands were killed and nearly a million displaced, democratic elections were held. Vinicio Cerezo and his Christian Democrat party prevailed at the ballot boxes but barely survived their term, escaping three attempted coups d'état. Another civilian administration, though extremely conservative and well-connected with the military, was elected in 1991, offering some hope of a permanent breakthrough of democratic civilian rule. The Guatemalan people, however, have never witnessed the survival to term of two consecutive, democratically elected civilian governments.

Despite this apparent departure from the turbulent past, however, violence in Guatemala has not ebbed in the last several years. From 1986 to 1990, Guatemalans endured 4,000 murders, 1,300 disappearances, and 600 politically motivated assaults. In the first quarter of 1990, for the first time in modern history, more Guatemalans were shot, stabbed, or bludgeoned to death than died in motor vehicle accidents.[62] Further, persistent human rights abuses committed by the military have drawn scrutiny from the U.S. State Department leading to the U.S. Congress's withdrawal of official military AID in early 1991.

Thus, whether it is fiction or fact, the most common explanation for the scarcity of U.S. direct investment in maquila operations is that widespread political turmoil and violence in Guatemala scare off potential investors. One maquila consultant, for example, tells the story of a transnational undergarments manufacturer that expressed interest in opening a large factory in Guatemala. This interest, however, collapsed when the visit of high-ranking company officials coincided with an attempted coup d'état at the National Palace. These executives subsequently advised against investment, deciding that Costa Rica, though more costly, would provide a more secure and serene location for the production of undergarments. For this company and many others, the bottom line is clear: why invest, even in limited amounts, in a country with a tradition of violence and political turmoil? Are extraordinary profits worth the risks in a politically unstable climate, where the possibility of waking up one morning to a new government that no longer possesses the zeal for nontraditional exports is more than a remote likelihood?

This conventional explanation for the lack of U.S. direct investment, however, is not completely persuasive. If Guatemala were completely out of control, there would be few investors: Guatemalans would simply maintain their accounts in U.S. banks, and the Korean investors would have found another venue to set up shop. Yet the exact opposite has occurred: rather than stunted, unsure growth, the maquila industry based on substantial domestic and foreign investment has exploded.

In contrast to this period of abstention, U.S. investors, almost oblivious to the political climate, have traditionally financed industrial projects in Guatemala. From the Spanish conquest on, Guatemala has never experienced an extended period of political stability. Since the CIA-directed 1954 coup, the military has been engaged in a brutal war against guerrilla insurgents and any other group or person urging democratic or progressive reforms. In the face of this persistent political unrest, U.S. direct investment in Guatemalan industries, encouraged by Alliance for Progress policies, increased consistently in this period until the early 1970s when the Central American Common Market collapsed. Most often, these investments were long-term and highly capital-intensive. The operations required expensive, immovable machinery as well as a high level of technical know-how absent in garment-assembly operations.[63] The major investors were U.S. TNCs; in 1969, 70 percent of U.S. direct investment (and 60 percent of all foreign direct investment) was from Fortune 1000 companies.[64]

Little more than a decade later, political turmoil continues; Guatemala has embarked on a new industrial development path providing greater incentives for foreign investors than ever before; but U.S. investors have avoided participation. As a bonus, civilian democracy has arrived, presumably bringing with it increased stability. Other U.S. government organizations have joined AID in promoting Guatemala as a safe haven of investment. In 1987, the Overseas Private Investment Corporation rated Guatemala a promising site for U.S. investment and in 1989 increased from $500 thousand to $2 million the amount for which it was willing to insure for political risk. In the same year, the Export Import Bank also increased its financing to Guatemala. Most appealing to prospective investors, the maquila factory is a less costly, easier to relocate, and more profitable enterprise than previous capital-intensive investment opportunities in Guatemalan industry. In addition, Korean TNCs have given signs of resolute confidence in the industry, forgoing all risks and flooding the country with factories. The explanation, then, that reports of political violence are scaring away investors conflicts with the long-standing presence of U.S. investment in Guatemalan industry and the auspicious investment environment awaiting U.S. TNCs.

The Infamy of Transcontinentales S.A.

Rather than fear of widespread political violence, some observers, including several in the U.S. Embassy, believe that the underlying reluctance of U.S. investors to finance maquila operations stems from the untimely and widely publicized departure of a U.S. garment maquila factory, Transcontinentales S.A., in September 1987. Filled with the intrigue of a spy novel, the tale of this surprise exit lingers as a reminder that maquila operations are not exempt from political strife. According to the runaway company's version, a renegade manager and a persistent union "chased" the management out of Guatemala in 1987—the very time when U.S. investors were testing the waters of the industry. Thanks to the clamoring of the angry U.S. owners of Transcontinentales, the story of dual persecution by a vengeful manager and a rabid union rapidly spread from the garment district in New York City to the halls of the U.S. Congress. Although the precise effects of this incident are nearly impossible to document,[65] both anecdotal evidence and the fact that U.S. investment in the maquila industry halted after the exodus, and has still failed to materialize despite an "improving" political climate, suggest that this unexpected exit dramatically discouraged potential U.S. investors. "A result of this [Transcontinentales] unforeseen exit," claimed a U.S. Embassy official in 1990, "is that American investors have become extremely cautious. I do not think they have yet fully recovered."[66]

Established in the spring of 1987, Transcontinentales employed over five hundred, mostly female, workers, making it among the first and largest maquila factories in

Guatemala. Play Knits, Inc., a U.S. apparel company headquartered in New York City's garment district, provided the capital, contracts, and administration for the shop and, despite repeated denials, was responsible for its operation. (The link to Play Knits was initially established after workers found documents with the New York company's name and address under the heading of "Headquarters" in the factory.) Play Knits arrived in Guatemala with significant experience with foreign-assembly operations, having operated plants in the Philippines and South Africa. When the decision to invest in Guatemala was made, a local businessman, Michael Maldanado, was hired as a "political" liaison to ensure amicable relations between local authorities and the factory. Selected because of his political connections and clout, Maldanado, the son of a prominent general and former presidential candidate, was to "grease the wheels" so that the factory could operate without threat of government intervention. In return for his role as buffer, Maldanado was provided a sizable salary and significant benefits, including an apartment in an upscale neighborhood of Guatemala City.

In early 1988, the factory underwent a change in management when a North American administration was replaced by an Israeli squad. During this transition in management, Maldanado, without consent from upper management, began to involve himself in the day-to-day activities of the factory. In a matter of weeks, he gained a notable measure of control over the operations of the plant, especially in matters of personnel, for which he displayed considerable talent. Former employees recall that Maldanado regularly solicited potential workers on buses and went out of his way to sustain friendly relations with workers. When the new Israeli management arrived in the summer of 1988, they decided to remove this self-appointed interim manager. Maldanado resisted, viewing the Israelis as intruding on his newfound turf. The Israeli managers fired him. Maldanado vowed revenge. Almost immediately he initiated a union-organizing campaign with the workers, flooded the Guatemalan courts with breach of contract suits, and allegedly threatened some of the managers. These pressures and the threat of future acts of vengeance appear to have forced the company to withdraw its operations from Guatemala. Although the precise details of these events are cloudy, it is clear that the force the company had originally contracted to regulate their relations with the powers-that-be had suddenly turned against them. They could fight or leave. Play Knits chose to leave.

On Thursday, September 18, 1988, the eve of Yom Kippur, the company announced that, for their diligence and dedication to the factory, the workers deserved a four-day paid vacation in honor of the upcoming Jewish holiday. As a worker said later, "We thought it was a little strange since never before had they given us a free paid second, much less four days."[67] When the workers arrived at the plant early the following

Monday morning, they found an empty factory guarded by a private security force. Later the workers discovered that during the "paid vacation," the Filipino supervisors and North American and Israeli managers had worked for four consecutive days loading machinery onto trucks to be shipped out of the country.

There is no consensus on precisely why the factory fled. Any number of reasons could have played a part in this decision, including the presence of a union, fear of their former liaison-turned-traitor, or the rumored loss of their main client, Liz Claiborne. Whatever the exact cause or causes, after the clandestine departure Play Knits executives spread a tale of horror to peers in their industry and to their congressional representatives that Guatemala was not a safe haven for U.S. investment, that the country was chaotic and violent, and that the company had barely escaped firsthand experience of this.

The infamy was heightened when, in response to pleas for solidarity from the workers, North American labor unions became involved in a struggle to obtain the unpaid wages and severance pay of the workers. After a bombardment of letters, publicity, and threatened boycotts, a settlement was reached whereby Play Knits, though never formally acknowledging responsibility for Transcontinentales, paid several hundred workers $20,000 as "compensation" for their lost wages.[68] The notoriety of this factory closing severely dampened future investors from the intimate U.S. garment industry. Either story—the factory driven out by an enraged ex-employee or the greedy union chasing a parent company all the way to New York City for lost wages—has been sufficient to deter investors and steer them to more "civil" locations. The repercussions of this incident, combined with persistent reports of political violence, reverberate into the 1990s, as U.S. investors are still reluctant to deposit capital in the land of Transcontinentales.

South Koreans: Giants of the Industry[69]

Despite the absence of U.S. investors, foreign capital has gradually found its way to Guatemalan maquila factories. More specifically, since 1989 South Korean investors have seized leadership of the maquila industry. Korean TNCs have deposited more capital and constructed more factories in Guatemala than any other country in the region. Fifty Korean factories account for about 50 percent of the apparel production—five times as much as their U.S. counterparts. Nearly all these factories have parent corporations or factories in Korea, from which the Guatemalan siblings receive advice, contracts, and experienced personnel. For the most part, the investors are middle-sized Korean firms, but several large TNCs, including Samsung, which has five factories, have invested in the industry. The most distinctive feature of Korean factories is their fine-tuned system of repressive labor control. This system, though successful in terms of efficiency and production, is often condemned as inhumane and unjust.

While the Republic of Korea has singled out Guatemala as an investment target, the expansion of Korean assembly operations overseas results mainly from a rise in wages, labor unionism, and restrictive quotas within its domestic garment-assembly industry. As a result, the influx of Korean investment only really began in 1988, when these pressures overwhelmed Korean factories. The first Korean factory began operations in 1984, and by 1988 nine Korean factories were assembling garments. In 1989 eighteen factories opened (seven in October alone). By March 1992, while the pace of investment had slowed down, fifty factories were in operation, employing nearly 20,000 Guatemalans.

The Korean presence demonstrates that the threat of arbitrary violence and political instability is not an insuperable obstacle to foreign investment. Even though halfway around the world, Koreans seem to feel minimal anxiety over political instability. Putting it in perspective, the Korean ambassador, Key-Cho Sung, has said: "We have a border with a hostile nation twenty-four miles from Seoul. We do not have any conception of danger in terms of internal political problems."[70]

The disparity of enthusiasm between U.S. and Korean investors stems partially from the different functions their respective governments exercise toward private investors. In addition to combating either real or perceived communist aggression, U.S. foreign policy in Guatemala has followed the spirit of President Taft's statement: "Intervention is justified when it is made necessary to guarantee the capital and markets of the United States."[71] A primary goal of U.S. economic assistance has always been to preserve U.S. investments and create a secure enclave for future investments. In Guatemala, the arrival of the United Fruit Company in the beginning of the twentieth century meant that the U.S. government would and did resort to whatever means were necessary, including military force, to protect U.S. private investment. It is difficult to say which came first, the domineering corporations or the interventionistic government, but it is fair to say that the rise of U.S. influence was the result of an effective and ruthless collaboration of these two incestuous powers.

In comparison, Korean capital has only recently begun to seek foreign terrain for investment and production. Similar to the domestic economic growth over the last three decades, the export of Korean private capital is a planned endeavor, orchestrated by government technocrats along with the major Korean corporations, or *chaebols*. The Caribbean Basin, and Guatemala in particular, has been designated as a major recipient of this outflow of capital. As part of the plan, the Korean government, in the late 1980s, chose Guatemala as the primary node of Korean investment in the region. In less than three years, the country moved from the third largest to the largest presence of Korean capital in the region. The ultimate goal of this plan is to expand to nearby countries such as Honduras and Nicaragua. The nucleus and headquarters of this planned investment is the Korean Embassy in Guatemala City, which organizes and administers all regional Korean investments. Labor disputes, customs delays, and other problems arising from daily operations are immediately referred to the embassy for resolution. The Korean government is committed to supervising every detail of their capital to ensure a successful development.

This degree of micromanagement practiced by the Korean Embassy in the affairs of its investors far surpasses that of the U.S. State Department, which generally acts in the interests of its investors but mainly does so through macropolicies. One possible way to view this divergence in style is that, at least in some cases, the U.S. government follows U.S. capital, whereas Korean capital, at least in this case, followed the Korean government.

The "New" Breed of Entrepreneurs: The Progress of the Entrepreneur Is the Progress of Guatemala

Guatemalan maquila owners are for the most part the very young—mid-twenties to early thirties—sons of the wealthy landed elite. These entrepreneurs have strong ties and exposure to the United States. Most are recent graduates of U.S. universities or Guatemalan private universities, speak English fluently, and are extremely motivated and self-confident. These men are hailed triumphantly by GEXPRONT and paternalistically by AID as the "new breed of Guatemalan entrepreneurs," who have aggressively and altruistically assumed an active role in the economic development of their country while making money at the same time. Fanny Estrada, GEXPRONT's director, described the noblesse oblige credo of those her organization serves: "When that mystique disappears, when we are no longer doing something for the country as well as earning money, we will stop."[72]

GEXPRONT and AID officials frequently contrast the ethic of this new class of entrepreneurs with that of traditional business elites, members of the landed oligarchy, who inherit, as opposed to "earn," their wealth. The "work" of the landed oligarchy, as one GEXPRONT official sarcastically explained, "is showing up on weekends with their friends, showing off the coffee trees for an hour, and then lounging around the pool for the rest of the weekend."[73] As he suggests, few large landowners manage or worry much about their properties. They normally hire administrators to tend to these daily tasks. With sparse overhead, wages of a dollar a day, consistent production, and a competent administrator, so long as the guerrillas do not scorch the fields, they can depend on bountiful profits.

In contrast, the new class of Guatemalan businessmen are, from the viewpoint of GEXPRONT and AID, progressive revolutionaries and explorers of unclaimed territory. "While Guatemala's gun-bearing revolutionaries have made little progress in recent years," wrote a GEXPRONT official, "a growing band of private Guatemalan entrepreneurs are quietly changing many aspects of life for their countrymen."[74] In order to survive, these young men practice a vigorous work ethic based on dedication, determination, and discipline rather than indolent satisfaction with inheritance. "They look at coffee barons and other traditionals as Neanderthal types. . . . Very often the people in these nontraditional industries are the young members of the coffee families, not willing to wait for their father or uncle to die," explained a member of VESTEX.[75] The traditional elites have preset, centuries-old operations which, if left unmodified, will continue to produce. The new entrepreneurs do not have this luxury. Rather, they must be present each day at their factories, making crucial decisions and expending serious thought to achieve success. A GEXPRONT staff person commented: "If you own a maquila, you cannot go to Europe for a month during the summer or spend winters in Aspen skiing. You have to work at it day and night."[76]

This description of youthful, determined, and well-intentioned entrepreneurs devoted to the improvement of their country demands comment. The maquila industry, as explained above, is an almost infallible business. Most of these young men enter the business with minimal-to-no managerial experience. Despite this apparent drawback they flourish. This widespread success may be more indicative of the maquila industry's high profit margin than the zeal and talent of Guatemalan entrepreneurs, as the degree of factory efficiency and managerial expertise determines how much profit will be made, rather than if a profit will be made at all. In this sense, the traditional oligarchy and the new entrepreneurs both share relatively risk-free investments based on traditional capital pools. Nevertheless, there does appear to be a noticeable difference in the maquila manager's commitment of time and energy.

Just as the new class of entrepreneurs speak of the aging oligarchy as outmoded and reactionary, so the traditionally wealthy Guatemalans view these rising stars with skepticism. This industry, members of the landed oligarchy claim, is one for the "Turquos," literally meaning peoples from Turkey, but in the derogatory sense, an awkward combination of eastern Mediterranean nationalities, including Arabs and Jews.[77] One observer commented that the maquila industry is not yet "socially acceptable." It is not, he explained, "the sort of thing [where] you would go to the club and tell proudly that you owned a maquila factory."[78]

However, behind this rhetorical tension lies an inviolable bond of mutual interests. Both new and old capitalists agree on fundamental precepts of economic development and social change. Both reject state intervention and redistributive measures such as tax and agrarian reform.[79] Most noticeable when the Cerezo administration pushed for an income tax increase in 1987 was the fact that the aging coffee barons and budding maquila entrepreneurs joined forces to fight the increase.

The most significant advantage the new Guatemalan entrepreneurs hold over foreign investors is their understanding of how to do business in Guatemala. For example, they may know how to obtain an export license in a day instead of two weeks. Recognizing this benefit, many foreign-owned factories hire experienced Guatemalan businessmen to fill administrative positions that deal with government agencies. In particular, ex-customs officials, according to several owners, "are in high demand."[80]

The Guatemalan entrepreneurs, however, face their own set of problems. Most receive private financing from relatives or business associates, but the amounts are frequently much less than those of foreign TNCs. As a consequence, locally managed factories are undercapitalized and small—over three-fourths of Guatemalan-owned factories contain less than 150 machines, limiting the capacity, scope, and efficiency of production. These factories frequently lack specialty machines such as button sewers or double-needle machines, relying instead on standard, single-needle machines. A manufacturer's representative claimed that in some Guatemalan factories a double stitch has to be completed with two runs of a single-needle machine.[81] Further, since many of these shops contract from larger factories, the profits, and hence the wages of workers, tend to be lower than average.

Moreover, despite significant exposure to the United States, Guatemalan maquila owners often lack strong contacts with North American garment companies or their agents. Few attend American trade shows. Even fewer have consistent business contacts that provide year-round work.[82] In the first years of growth, the tremendous demand of U.S. suppliers has enabled Guatemalan factories to flourish by simply waiting for agents to contact them. And if they do search for contracts, it is usually done through manufacturer's representatives working in Guatemala rather than direct contact with U.S. TNCs. Many Guatemalan owners nevertheless expressed dismay over the lack of a year-round contract. The Guatemalan manager of Koram S.A., Philip Klose, claimed that his best business experience was obtaining a full-time contract with Levi Strauss. "With this contract we can produce forever," he announced.[83]

A consequence of the inability to obtain full-time contracts is irregular working hours for employees. It is commonplace for a Guatemalan factory to grant workers a "vacation" for several weeks due to a lack of contracts and two weeks later require them to work several nights in a row, nonstop, to complete an order on time. Inexperience, along with occasional overzealousness, prompts owners to accept more work than their workers are capable, under reasonable conditions and hours, of completing on time. Thus workers are forced to labor for intolerably long hours, the quality of the products diminishes, and shipments are often tardy. "Meeting deadlines," lamented one manufacturer's representative, "is the greatest problem of the maquila industry in Guatemala."[84]

Health and Safety Conditions

An unexpected aura of secrecy surrounds most Guatemalan maquila factories. The windowless, cinder block structures appear unoccupied. There is no distinct sound resonating from within, nor is residue spewing from smokestacks. Often, not even a sign announces the factory's presence. The sole indication that something of value is hidden inside the structure is the one or more machine-gun-toting security guards stationed at the entrance. The guards' charge is simple and direct: do not let anyone in until he or she has been cleared by the office. Commenting on the elaborate security, an Instituto Guatemalteco Seguridad Social (IGSS), the state social security institute, official quipped, with some truth, "It is easier to enter the National Police headquarters at midnight than a maquila factory in the middle of the day."[1]

From the outside, then, it is difficult to tell what these nondescript buildings could possibly contain to warrant such high levels of precaution and secrecy. Indeed, crime is rampant in Guatemala, but these factories only house scraps of cloth and sewing machines—not the most marketable items. Furthermore, internal employee theft is the crime that most worries managers, and hence every worker must endure a thorough body search at the end of each day. Nonetheless, guards are also instructed to treat visitors arriving in the middle of the afternoon, the most unlikely burglary suspects, with extraordinary scrutiny. Dismayed at his inability to gain access to most maquila factories, a Guatemalan university student conducting an investigation on the psychology of work commented: "What are they hiding in there? A secret society meeting?"[2]

The former director of statistics at VESTEX, Edgar Garzaro, claimed that most factories are inaccessible to outsiders because "the management is suspicious that visitors might steal trade secrets."[3] Considering that apparel-assembly industry experts readily acknowledge that the layout of most shops is dependent more on the size and shape of the building than on production philosophies or strategies, Garzaro's explanation is clearly inadequate. A labor inspector provided another, more plausible, one: "The secrecy is necessary to conceal the conditions in the factory, which are extremely poor and often inhumane. We always encounter difficulty trying to enter these factories, and for good reason: they don't want us to see the deplorable conditions."[4]

Even some who are official supporters of the industry are dumbfounded by maquila management's obsession with forbidding uninvited visitors. An analyst at the Executive Office of Quotas was astonished that two factories which received allocations of a garment quota refused entry to quota officials.[5] "We only came to count the number of machines in the factory, but they would not let us in," he explained. "They treated us as if we were from the Labor Ministry."[6] In a factory in Zone 13, a security guard was reportedly dismissed because he let in a labor inspector "without sufficiently delaying him."[7] The primary purpose of this heightened secrecy, suspicion, and security, it appears, is not to deter daytime thieves but to delay or deny access to those who have a right or a vested interest to examine the premises, most notably representatives of the Labor Ministry and the IGSS.

The Invisible Hand and Health and Safety

In July 1990, the IGSS held its "Fourth Annual Conference on Health and Safety in the Workplace" at its central offices in Guatemala City. For two days, over four hundred employees from dozens of industrial worksites gathered at the IGSS convention center to learn about and discuss techniques to prevent industrial accidents and diseases. Not a single worker from the maquila industry—the fastest-growing and perhaps largest sector of the industrial economy—attended the event. When several coordinators of the conference were asked about this absence, one responded: "Most of those owners will not even let our inspectors visit their factories. Do you expect these same owners to permit their workers to visit us?"[8]

Except on such rare occasions as this IGSS conference, the topic of health and safety conditions in Guatemalan workplaces is the lowest priority for employers, employees, and government agencies. In most workplaces, workers must be satisfied simply to be employed, earning something to secure their families' survival for another day. In fields and factories workers rarely, if ever, are equipped with adequate safety equipment. Unprotected use of dangerous machinery and toxic chemicals, as well as tremendous physical strain, are expected and accepted in return for employment. Preventive medicine, as a discipline and a practice, is virtually unknown in the private and public sectors. Even unions reportedly sacrifice health and safety concerns in pursuit of improved monetary benefits. "With starvation at the doorstep of so many, we put our efforts into increasing what the worker takes home to feed his children. Negotiations over health and safety are a luxury put off for another time," said a union official.[9]

Perhaps the best evidence of the government's disinclination and/or inability to monitor and enforce workplace health and safety standards is the fact that no official agency compiles data on work-related accidents and illnesses. The IGSS keeps reliable statistics on car accidents, but not work accidents. The Labor Ministry, the other major organ responsible for the regulation of workplace health and safety, likewise is devoid of this information. Lacking a concrete understanding of the nature of the problem, these agencies often are unable to articulate, much less enforce, minimal health and safety workplace standards.

The major consequence of this government unwillingness and/or incompetence to regulate workplace health and safety is that it is left up to employers' own means and discretion to determine the safety and health conditions in their individual workplaces. The lack of tangible government pressure, combined with a surplus of willing workers, creates vast opportunity for exploitation. In the garment-assembly industry, which by nature is extremely volatile, and in a country where the outstanding comparative advantage is cheap, abundant labor, most maquila employers are content to oversee crude, functional, and consequently hazardous plants. The nature of the business is low capital investment, high return. Since health and safety improvements—e.g., better ventilation, adjustable chairs—result, at least in the short term, in increased costs, most maquila owners consider them unnecessary. "Look, we made this investment for the labor, the very cheap labor," one owner admitted. "Like it or not, that's how we make money. The lower the overhead, the better. . . . This business has too many uncertainties. You make what you can when you can."[10] Encouraged by AID and the Guatemalan government, this entrepreneurial demand for unrestricted profit maximization means that workplace health and safety improvements, whether voluntary or coerced, rarely occur in Guatemala's austere maquila factories.

The Legal Structure of Regulation and Enforcement

What is written in law often differs radically from actual practice. In the case of the health and safety standards and their enforcement in Guatemala, the difference between the law and practice is usually modest and undetectable: both law and practice are generally ineffectual. Two sources, the Labor Code (Code)[11] and the IGSS promulgated "General Regulations on Hygiene and Safety in the Workplace" (Regulations),[12] furnish the legal guidelines and diagram the enforcement structures. In a parallel scheme, two government entities, the General Inspection of Labor (IGT) of the Labor Ministry and the Department of Preventive Medicine at IGSS,[13] are charged with setting, updating, and enforcing health and safety standards.

Neither the legal sources nor the administrative agencies are presently capable of articulating, monitoring, and administering health and safety standards. Written for an agricultural society, the two legal guidelines are antiquated, largely irrelevant, and—most significant—barren of effective sanctions. The agencies are underfinanced, justifiably intimidated by the powerful private business sector, and often corrupt. It is not surprising, then, that the level of health and safety conditions in maquila factories is severely deficient. In effect, the dominion of workplace health and safety has been passed on to individual employers. For maquila workers, this want of formal and effectual mechanisms of control has permitted the development of deleterious conditions.

The Labor Code, the "Bible" of the IGT, dedicates one brief and eclectic chapter, "Hygiene and Security in the Workplace," to defining and explaining health and safety standards and their enforcement. Since its inception in 1954, this section has never been modified or revised. Consisting of nine articles out of a total of 431 in the entire Code, the chapter contains a random collection of seven health and safety regulations ranging from mandating monthly medical checkups for food-preparation workers to calling for poundage limits for lifting, according to sex, age, and physical condition. This ad hoc mixture of mandates is largely irrelevant to contemporary Guatemalan industrial workers, particularly maquila workers.

In addition to these scattered articles, the section articulates several broad and vague mandates of employer and employee responsibility. Though well-intentioned, these articles lack direction and substance. The first defines the employers' responsibility: "All employers are obligated to adopt the necessary precautions for effective protection of the life, health, and morality of the workers."[14] Unfortunately, the Code fails to state what such "necessary precautions" might be. Instead, it hints that the content of these guidelines may be found in regulations promulgated by the IGSS.[15] Hence the Code fails to furnish any specific, relevant health and safety guidelines, appearing instead to defer to the IGSS for guidance.

In terms of enforcement, this chapter ends with a bold directive: "All authorities of work and sanitation must collaborate to the end of obtaining adequate performance, completion, and fulfillment of the dispositions of this chapter," as well as the regulations promulgated jointly and separately by the Labor Ministry and the IGSS.[16] Cooperation between the IGSS and the Labor Ministry, then, is the essence of enforcement. The Code, however, declines even to sketch the nature of this coordinated enforcement mechanism.

By default and statutory deference, the Code delegates to the IGSS the technical task of formulating health and safety guidelines and the practical job of enforcing them. The IGSS's formal acceptance of this responsibility is found in the Regulations, a tiny, twenty-five-page document published on December 28, 1957. Although the Regulations provides more specific health and safety guidelines, it, like the Code, has been neither updated nor modified since its promulgation.

Despite its size and age, the Regulations elaborates a more explicit and detailed method of coordinated enforcement than the Code. Article 11 states, "The Labor Ministry and the IGSS will have the responsibility in a coordinated manner over the application, control, and vigilance of the hygiene and safety in the workplace."[17] According to the Regulations, both agencies are to collaborate on developing technical assistance, investigating accidents, and promoting safety organizations within the workplace. As in the Code, however, the specific responsibilities of the two entities are not spelled out. The centerpiece of the Regulation's enforcement strategy is the formation of a "Safety Organization" in each workplace comprised of worker, management, and government representatives. By law, each Safety Organization should meet regularly and define individual workplace safety policies and practices. IGSS officials, however, were unaware of a functioning Safety Organization in any workplace, much less a maquila factory.

The Law in Practice

These obfuscated guidelines combine with inadequate resources, acute levels of corruption, employer noncompliance, and, most significantly, ineffective sanctions, to mute the efforts of even the most zealous IGSS and IGT inspectors. To begin with, both the IGSS and the IGT are dramatically underfunded and understaffed. The Department of Preventive Medicine at IGSS, under which safety inspectors work, functions with minimal resources. Thirty inspectors are responsible for monitoring health and safety conditions in all the workplaces in Guatemala City; another fourteen are accountable for those in the rest of the country.[18] Eight departments lack inspectors altogether, including the Peten, Quiché, and Solola. Luis Alfonso Hernandez Perez, an IGSS legal and technical consultant, candidly described the effects of this coverage, "Our budgetary restrictions have left us with so few inspectors that we cannot even begin to monitor and enforce standards adequately."[19]

The Department of Preventive Medicine's annual budget scramble demonstrates its paucity of resources. In 1990, for example, the department requested protective equipment for its inspectors. Because the inspectors investigate every type of workplace, from large plantations to chemical factories, the department requested, among other items, gloves, rubber boots, masks with filters, ear plugs, and sunglasses. Every item requested was denied except for one filterless mask and one pair of ear plugs for each inspector. "Each year we turn in the same budget requests because they [the IGSS administration] always fail to grant our request from the previous year," lamented Dr. Rodrigo de Leon Ovalle, the director of the department.[20]

A natural consequence of the lack of resources and personnel is that both IGT and IGSS inspectors take a reactive, rather than proactive, approach to the investigation of health and safety conditions. Such a method is universally recognized in the health and safety field as ineffective and insufficient. At the bare minimum, inspectors from each agency concur that each worksite should be inspected at least once or twice a year. However, practice diverges enormously. Describing his experience with IGSS inspectors, the manager of the main Phillips-Van Heusen factory, Erick Sterkel, said: "I have never seen one of them [IGSS inspectors] since we arrived two years ago. It is a shame, really, because they are supposed to evaluate the facilities. Unfortunately, we do not have that kind of concern here in Guatemala."[21] Whether it is "will" or "resources," or a combination of both, it is clear that Sterkel's experience is not anomalous. A subdirector of the IGT admitted: "We cannot work on a preventive level to deter abuses. Instead, because of our lack of human resources, we respond as best we can to denouncements made by individual workers."[22]

Usually, only when inspectors accidentally stumble upon serious violations, or when workers themselves initiate an investigation with formal or anonymous complaints, are these problems investigated. Incidental discovery of violations depends for success on fortune, rather than an aggressive, systematic search. With so much territory to cover, IGT inspectors concede as much. "We cannot focus on health and safety issues unless they are brought to our attention, because we lack the personnel to seek out problems, and even then our role is limited by a law without teeth," stated one inspector.[23]

The scarcity of unsolicited worker complaints to the IGT and the IGSS undermines the already limited effectiveness of their reactive approach. IGSS officials reported receiving one to three worker complaints concerning health and safety a month, while IGT offices reported receiving even fewer. There are multiple reasons why so few workers submit health and safety complaints, including widespread ignorance of legal standards and possible recourse for violations. The two most important causes, however, are a general lack of faith in the capacity of the IGT and IGSS to enforce the law and a paralyzing fear of retaliation by employers.

Workers, in general, place little confidence in the competence and effectiveness of government inspectors. For many workers, interaction with these agencies has been negative and discouraging. They repeatedly told of IGSS and IGT inspectors' visits to their factories, but most often these calls, from the worker's perspective, were informal, social, and ultimately futile. "Sure, they [the inspectors] visit once in a while, but it is a joke. All they do is talk with the boss over some coffee. They never want to talk with us, even though we are the ones who suffer," said a frustrated worker.[24] Whether these incidents reveal a pattern of systematic duplicity or not may be less important than the common perception among workers that their complaints to the IGSS and the IGT are hopeless, perhaps even prejudicial, to their employment.

The other major deterrent to worker complaints is fear of retaliation by employers. If an employer discovers the source of a denunciation, that worker knows her job is in jeopardy. "In Guatemala workers never search for help. They fear what will take place if they complain," explained Dr. de Leon. "They are fully aware that an army of unemployed workers is waiting to take their place, and the employer is often only too happy to open the front door to let one in."[25] Hence, in general, only in moments of extreme difficulty (or when there is a union) will workers resort to the IGT or the IGSS to denounce employment conditions. The response of a nineteen-year-old worker at a Korean factory, Daram S.A., to the question of why more workers do not complain to IGSS or the IGT illustrates this fear, particularly prevalent in the maquila industry. "It is very simple," the worker said. "You can't leave the factory for any reason or you may not have a place when you return. And because everyone is afraid of losing her job, we do not say anything."[26]

In Guatemala, bribes are an assumed cost of most transactions requiring government assistance, from riding a bus to exporting livestock. Anecdotes and rumors, most unconfirmed, abound in the area of employer-inspector corruption. Union officials and workers generally accept as a given that most inspectors have their price. Several maquila employers confirmed this perception. A North American owner, though he denied ever paying off an inspector himself, bluntly claimed, "The inspectors are bribable and everyone knows it."[27] IGT and IGSS officials deny that there is a significant problem in this area.[28] IGSS administrators did comment, however, that the job of inspector is one of the most sought-after, and that "[t]hese inspectors face immense financial pressure. Their salaries are unjustly low and some may feel they deserve a bonus once in a while."[29] Most officials agreed that the main cause of corruption was not greed but insufficient compensation. IGT inspectors earn Q600, or US$120, a month. Compared to those of maquila workers, this salary is well above average, but it is still less than what is considered necessary for subsistence.

As described above, a difficulty particularly prevalent in the maquila industry that IGSS and IGT inspectors have to face is aggressive employer resistance to inspection. Although inspectors have a legal right to enter the workplace and employers are obligated to permit entry,[30] inspectors are regularly delayed or denied entrance to maquila factories. Security guards posted at the gate routinely frustrate visiting inspectors, sometimes leaving them waiting outside the factory gate for over an hour.[31] "We [IGSS inspectors] go once, twice, three times, and they [the employers] have little interest in letting us enter," said an IGSS safety inspector.[32]

Employers' collective disregard for the right of the IGT and the IGSS to gain access to their factories points to probably the most trenchant problem with the entire health and safety system: ineffectual sanctions that have not been modified since 1958. As the subdirector of the IGT stated, "The most obsolete parts of the Code are the fines."[33] Quite simply, employers have no reason to fear representatives of the IGT or the IGSS. According to the Regulations, courts may only fine employers from Q25 to Q1,000, or US$5 to $200, for health and safety violations, depending on the gravity of the infraction and the economic capacity of the violator.[34] Except for extremely egregious "prohibited" violations such as negligent storage of dangerous chemicals, the maximum fine for less dangerous infractions is Q250, or US$50. When one labor inspector was asked about the consequences that delinquent employers faced, he argued that the most important sanction was the "secondary cost" of paying for legal advice and court fees.[35] Employers aware of this empty, toothless law have little respect for its mandates.

In addition to these low sums, the administration of sanctions is premised on a collaboration between the IGSS and the IGT, which, as demonstrated above, does not exist. "Cooperation would undoubtedly help the situation [of levying sanctions]," commented IGSS consultant Orlando Garcia, "but neither agency possesses the resources to contemplate an organized, formal relationship."[36] The more typical process is as follows. An IGSS inspector visits a factory, files a report, and gives the employer a deadline to remedy the violations. The inspector returns and finds the problem still persisting, so he submits the complaint to the IGSS legal department, which delivers a formal accusation to the labor court. The labor court judge then sends the denouncement to the IGT for further investigation. Only if the IGSS were to stay intensely involved in the case for months, if not years, a feat that requires remarkable diligence, might it convince the court to issue a fine. IGT inspectors are sent out, and they make another report to the court. If this report is uncontested (a rare occurrence) the court may fine the employer. Dr. de Leon described the outcome of most of these cases, "No one is able to enforce the sanction so it does not matter in the end."[37] According to IGSS officials, the last instance in which an IGSS-initiated health and safety complaint resulted in a court-assessed fine against an employer occurred in 1986. In that case, the employer was fined Q25, or $5, and the entire process took over ten months.[38]

In sum, the regulation and enforcement of health and safety standards rest on obsolete laws, trivial sanctions, and a confused, ineffective administration. Fully aware of this situation, employers are easily persuaded to streamline and cut corners in areas of health and safety in order to maximize profit. In particular, investors in the maquila industry, a business based on exploitation of cheap labor, have few incentives to improve working conditions. Even unions, aware of the lack of official support, appear to place the health and safety agenda on a lower tier of importance. "The issue of health and safety," said a labor organizer, "simply is not important to most people. Workers want wages, not masks. It is an ethos of desperation. Families are hungry, and only money cures this illness. The long-term effects of poor sanitary conditions are put aside for survival to the next day."[39]

WORKPLACE HEALTH

The Factory: A Warehouse in Disguise[40]

Over 90 percent of maquila factories are located in structures that were not originally erected to house labor-intensive assembly operations.[41] Most of these buildings were constructed as warehouses to store goods and machinery, not people. Megatex S.A., the premier maquila consulting firm, in their guide to prospective investors, states: "[A]s a rule, they [factories] are warehouses without adequate conditions; especially when it comes to access (usually they have only one in/out access), ventilation, and location."[42] Resembling airplane hangers more than factories, the buildings are cheaply and primitively constructed. The walls are composed of either cinder blocks and mortar or corrugated sheet metal; ceilings are formed from corrugated metal as well. Usually, the buildings have only two entrances—a small one for people, a garage door for shipments—and few, if any, windows. In Zone 12, known as "the Bermuda Triangle," dozens of these buildings are lined up block after block. Some of the structures do indeed store goods; others shelter machine and repair shops; and still others quarter garment-assembly factories. The choice made by most maquila owners to use these warehouses as factories exposes workers to serious short- and long-term health and safety hazards.

Cold Air, Hot Air, No Air

Two of the most harmful conditions inside these austere structures are dramatic fluctuations in temperature and poor ventilation. Although Guatemala is known as the land of eternal spring because of a mild climate, mornings are often cool in Guatemala City, dropping down to the 40s F, while afternoon temperatures can rise to the 80s. "I wear a sweater in the morning," said a worker. "In the afternoon a T-shirt, and by the evening I put the sweater back on."[43] Since none of the factories have insulation or a heating system on the shop floor, only porous concrete or thin steel walls shield workers from the outdoor elements. Hence, a chilly morning equals a chilly workplace. In a trade where manual dexterity and intricate movements are critical, frigid conditions make precise movements and concentration all the more taxing.

As the workday enters the afternoon, most factories transform into the stereotypical "sweatshop." When workers were questioned about the temperature inside the factory, almost 90 percent responded that they endured daily periods of extreme heat and perspiration. "Our work is constantly interrupted because we have to wipe sweat from our faces," explained a nineteen-year-old maquila worker. "Some operators wear excess pieces of cloth as headbands to absorb the moisture."[44] In many instances, the sheet-metal roofs act as ovens, conducting the heat from the sun. Further, without adequate ventilation the air becomes stale, stuffy, and at times unbearable. One group of workers reported that in their factory a particularly humane manager would let them go outside for fifteen or twenty minutes when he felt it was too hot to work. "It probably got too hot in his office," cynically added a worker.[45]

In "strict" factories, where workers are denied morning and afternoon rest breaks and are restricted in movement and access to potable water, accounts of operators fainting and collapsing due to exhaustion and dehydration are commonplace. In most factories, workers reported at least one incident of a fellow operator slumping to the floor from fatigue or heat exhaustion. "Because many people live so far away and often do not have time for breakfast and because they need to be there on time and they do not let them eat anything, not even a cracker, and because they work without a break, these workers sometimes faint," one worker recounted. "If you try to eat, they yell and take it out of your hand and throw it out. So many people pass out from this hunger. . . . The boss then drags them outside for air, but does not give them any food."[46]

Ventilation is extremely limited in these "warehouse-factories." Some buildings lack windows altogether; others have them but they stay permanently closed; and still others have windows that open, but these are generally small and too few.[47] A general manager of a factory in Zone 12 bluntly described his factory: "This building is so old that most of the windows do not open anyway."[48] Ventilation, then, is usually either limited to an internal system of fans, or, more commonly, the factory lacks any flow of air to cool workers and remove dust, chemicals, and odors.

While almost all offices in the factories are equipped with air-conditioning systems, less than one out of every ten factories contains any fans on the shop floor. Even fewer have sufficient fans to provide adequate levels of circulation. And in factories with fans, workers are quick to point out the absurdity of a self-enclosed ventilation system. Fans may cool people off, but they fail to expel dust and chemicals—the more dangerous nuisances—because they simply move these irritants from one part of the factory to another.

Bathrooms and Cafeterias

In general, maquila factories lack physical amenities for workers. In particular, the quantity and condition of bathrooms and cafeterias are inadequate. The IGSS Regulations mandate that each factory must have sufficient eating space and bathrooms for its work force. Maquila factories fail, in most cases, to meet these requirements. The main reason for this delinquency is that these factories were designed to store goods; hence, the buildings would require physical modifications to meet the needs of workers. Few, if any, shops have made these changes; and it seems unlikely that the law will persuade them to. A labor inspector explained, "They [management] tell us that the space is being rented, and the owner of the property will not allow the maquila factory to make these types of improvements, like more bathrooms, because the lease forbids it. A fine is unlikely to change their minds, so we don't even bother."[49]

According to the "logic" of the Regulations, every workplace must have at least one clean bathroom for every twenty-five men and one for every fifteen women.[50] Although the original rationale for these precise ratios is not known, the purpose of the rule is clear: workers deserve the dignity of having sufficient and sanitary bathrooms. Maquila employers, however, rarely comply with this regulation. The average ratio in this survey was forty workers per bathroom. In at least a dozen factories, less than five bathrooms serve more than three hundred employees: workers either have to leave the factory to relieve themselves or forego it altogether during working hours.

Workers tend to complain more about the unsanitary conditions in the bathrooms than their numbers. Too frequently the facilities are unclean, unsupplied, and broken. "We only have two boys who clean the factory and the last thing they clean each day are the bathrooms. Sometimes they do not have time to do much of a job," explained a maquila worker in a large factory.[51] Rolls of toilet paper dangle from individual work stations, as workers, instead of their factories, regularly supply their own paper. Most factories do not maintain their toilet facilities. As a result, broken seats and plumbing problems are commonplace. Yet, in the same factories, separate bathrooms—clean, operational, and fully supplied—serve the white-collar administration.

Unsanitary and substandard rest rooms are an assault upon the self-esteem and dignity of maquila workers. Workers face more dramatic hardships, such as weary bodies and woeful wages, yet most presented their criticisms about the condition and number of bathrooms with exceptional vigor and indignation. A nineteen-year-old operator, for example, commented: "The conditions in the bathrooms are horrible. They are filthy, they have no toilet paper, and they often do not work correctly. What kind of animals do they think we are?"[52] The complaints of workers, much like the preceding one, focused on feelings of exasperation and indignation that the management considers their most elemental human needs unworthy of dignified treatment. Further, if management routinely ignores employee requests for clean bathrooms and toilet paper, acquiescence to an increase in wages seems even less likely. "When the owner will not even supply toilet paper in a bathroom, how can workers expect to receive just wages or more humane hours?" queried a labor inspector.[53]

The IGSS Regulations also mandate that employers must provide adequate space and equipment for workers to prepare and eat meals. Each factory, according to the Regulations, should maintain a cafeteria, large enough to accommodate all employees either at one time or in shifts, and a place to store and reheat food.[54] Of the 270 or so factories, less than half have a designated space for workers to eat. In those shops with a cordoned-off space, a small area, next to the floor, adorned with a few tables or counters, is known as the "cafeteria." These areas are almost always too small to hold all the workers, and few contain facilities to cook and reheat food. Perhaps fifteen factories actually maintain adequate cafeteria space for their workers.

At factories without a cafeteria or with too small an eating space, workers eat outside—exposed to the elements—either at food stands[55] or literally in the streets. In Zone 12, noon signals a massive exodus of workers onto the unpaved, dusty roads. At Este Oeste S.A., a factory located adjacent to an busy four-lane avenue, workers eat their lunches on the "island" situated between the lanes of traffic, as cars and trucks speed past on both sides. Several factories are located on a road to the municipal dump. The garbage trucks that pass daily on this road spill their contents on the bumpy, unpaved street. At lunchtime workers sit on the curb alongside scavenger birds feeding off the spilt garbage. During the rainy season, lunch hours for employees without a cafeteria are furious hunts for shelter, as workers are forced either to find cover under a tree, awning, or in a small restaurant or become drenched. Of course, they also have the option to remain inside the factory and work, an option usually not discouraged by management.

WORKPLACE SAFETY

No Way Out: A Few Locked Exits

The means for workers to flee a burning building quickly and safely is a universally recognized fire precaution. This need to escape is increased when a region, like Guatemala, also has frequent earthquakes that transform primitive and inexpensive structures into instant rubble. Recognizing this need, Article 18 of the Regulations reads, "All workplaces must possess a sufficient number of doors. . . . The number and width of doors . . . must be calculated in such a way that all personnel can evacuate in the minimum amount of time and a secure manner."[56] This rule obviously allows for wide discretion, but nevertheless the consensus among IGT and IGSS inspectors is that the vast majority of factories lack sufficient exits for their workers. Again, the problem is one of design. Since the buildings were not constructed to house workers, most have one large garage door for loading and unloading and a smaller door for people to enter and exit.

The layout found in many factories, in which the administrative offices are located in the front of the building, both forces visitors to pass through the office section before reaching the shop floor and poses a significant obstacle for workers who need to exit the factory during an emergency.[57] A factory where employees must file through a narrow hallway and a series of doors in order to leave would have calamitous consequences during a fire or earthquake. "I pray that God will protect us because not all of us are going to get out," answered a maquila worker when asked what would happen during a fire.[58]

In nearly all shops, management keeps the few doors of the factory locked during working hours to discourage unwanted intruders and unpermitted exits. Often only a few management employees and sometimes the security personnel have a key. In case of a fire or earthquake, workers would pile up against the inside of a locked door while the person with the key struggled through this hysteric group to unlock the door. In one factory, Internacionales de Exportaciones S.A., workers reported a frantic, potentially tragic scene when hundreds of workers dashed for the door as the floor shook with tremors. The key to the door was in the office, and the manager was unable to fight through the crowd to open the door. A worker commented on the incident, "When the tremors started, everyone got up and started running for the door, bumping into each other, and in the end no one could get out."[59] Fortunately, no one was hurt in the incident, as the tremors quickly subsided.

Except for perhaps the dozen or so buildings that were constructed as garment-assembly factories, maquila factories fail to meet the threshold requirements for adequate exits found in the Regulations. Prison-like conditions compound this confinement. Some workers have reported small electrical fires, and considering the shoddy electrical systems and the flammable materials in the factories, the potential for a major blaze is high. "A tragic accident is sure to happen soon," predicted Dr. de Leon. "Whether it be a fire or an earthquake, these workers will be trapped."[60]

Primitive Shop Floors

The primitive shop floors in maquila factories are ergonomically unsound workplaces, ripe for the proliferation of long-term muscle-skeletal illnesses endemic to garment-assembly production. In the last hundred years, little has changed in this industry. Sewing machines have grown faster and more sophisticated, but they still perform the same task—assembling pieces of cloth. Guatemalan factories resemble the earliest North American sweatshops. As Jimmy Eager, a manufacturers' representative in Guatemala with management experience in factories in Mexico and the United States, confirmed, "Guatemala is in 'Pampers' compared to the large factories in the United States and Mexico."[61]

The quality and age of sewing, cutting, and pressing machines generally vary according to the size of the factory. The larger factories, especially the foreign-owned ones, tend to use more modern and varied machines and equipment, while the smaller shops normally purchase used models. The submaquila shops with less than thirty machines—more than a hundred in all—may only contain one or two types of machines.[62] The older machines are more prone to break down—a much dreaded occurrence for operators, who are regularly held financially and morally responsible for the damage.

Workers labor on crudely designed and constructed shop floors. During their ten- or twelve-hour shifts, rows of operators sit in wooden chairs or on backless wooden benches and dozens of others stand while cutting excess threads without an opportunity to sit down.[63] The chairs are unadjustable and hard; the benches additionally subject the worker to hours without any support for her spine. Operators often sit on pillows brought from home to ease the strain of a long workday. The flat tables on which the sewing machines rest are also made of wood and are unadjustable. Hence, except for the few operators who happen to be the appropriate size, workers either are forced to slouch awkwardly over the machine or extend themselves onto the table in order to operate the machine. Shorter operators must stretch their feet to reach the pedal of the machine. Sitting for ten or more hours a day on hard, wooden, unpadded seats without back supports in awkward postures is an invitation to long-term back trauma.

Another serious problem found on these primitive shop floors is improperly rigged electrical and lighting systems. Since most of the warehouses were built with modest electrical systems, significant rewiring has been necessary. This wiring has often been done unprofessionally or in haste, resulting in dangling and exposed wires and plugs. More than half of the workers mentioned incidents of electrical shock when an operator touched a machine after prolonged use. Others noted high rates of overheated machines and short circuiting. In at least ten accounts, small electrical fires were reported. One worker said, "I fear the locked-up factory and what could happen if one of these short circuits becomes serious. Already we have had two small fires, and we have had to wait for the owners to come from their offices and open the doors."[64]

Unlike garment shops in urban areas of the United States or Southeast Asia where crowded conditions are a given of the industry, cramped quarters are not prevalent in Guatemalan apparel-assembly plants. To be sure, dozens of smaller shops are located in crowded zones of the city, stuffed into former stores, restaurants, residences, and apartments. In these plants, crowding of machines and people poses significant safety risks. Machines and tables are virtually on top of one another, restricting movement and blocking access to exits. One factory in the downtown zone of Guatemala City is situated on the second and third floors of an apartment building. There, the tables are so close together that workers must turn sideways to pass between them.

For the medium to large factories in the industrial and exterior sections of the city, lack of space and overcrowding are not noticeable problems. The abundance of cheap, available warehouse space, thus far, has exceeded the demand. In many factories, floor space is left unused with the hope that in the near future it can be filled with machines and workers. An example is the North American company Fantastica S.A., which moved to an ex-car dealership warehouse. With its 125 machines, the working area presently covers less than one-half of the available space; the rest of the floor is empty. The owner hopes that his business will occupy this space in the future but is unworried about the present "waste" of space because the rent is so inexpensive.

Accidents, Illnesses, and Treatment

Workers and owners concurred that few serious accidents occur in maquila factories. The simplicity of the shop floor—chairs, tables, and machines in straight rows—and the relatively safe machinery minimize most immediate, life-threatening industrial accidents. Workers, managers, and inspectors agree that the most common injuries by far are pierced and cut fingers and hands from sewing machine needles and sharp cutting edges. Fainting because of prolonged sitting and heat exhaustion also frequently occur. The prevalence of electrical shocks and burns from improperly rigged or overburdened electrical systems and burned-out machines varies according to factory but accounts for the third most common accident. More serious accidents happen less frequently. In only one in twelve factories did workers report accidents, such as broken bones, which required extensive medical attention.

In contrast to the limited number of sudden and dramatic industrial accidents, the potential for a plethora of cumulative health and safety problems is extremely high. The intensity and length of work periods pose serious risks to worker health. The Code states that workers are entitled to morning, lunch, and afternoon breaks. No factories provide regular afternoon breaks, and management in almost half of the factories forces workers to skip morning rest-breaks. Many other workers choose not to take their breaks because they want to increase output and income. As a consequence, tens of thousands of workers labor four or five hours consecutively, break for a half-hour lunch, and then return for six to fifteen more hours of continuous sewing. During this time, they sit on uncomfortable and back-straining benches, lean over inappropriately sized tables, concentrate on tediously pushing cloth through the machine, breathe in noxious chemicals and dust, and sweat profusely because of the heat and poor ventilation.

The lack of adequate ventilation and protective masks means that workers daily inhale and are exposed to chemical fumes and dust from the cloth. Since there are no specific regulations limiting the chemicals used in garment and textile production, workers also risk inhaling large doses of carcinogenic and other harmful substances, such as formaldehyde. Dust from the cloth, particularly around the cutting machines, is a constant irritant. Workers mentioned that the dust and chemicals frequently clog and irritate their nasal passages, eyes, and skin. One sixteen-year-old worker commented, "The dust comes out of the clothes and makes it very difficult to breathe and your eyes start to water."[65] Further, over half the workers said they experienced skin irritations and rashes from the constant, unprotected contact with the cloth.

Every interviewed worker complained of headaches. "There is so much tension.

The noise and the movement of the machines affect the nerves. Concentrating and constantly looking strain the mind," explained a worker. "All these add up to a constant headache."[66] Few workers can afford glasses, so many are forced to squint to compensate for impaired eyesight. Lights hanging five feet from the floor and the chemical smell intensify these headaches.

Workers also told of varying degrees of wrist, back, and neck pain caused by the padless wooden seats and awkward postures. For many, the prolonged sitting also caused cramps and pains in the stomach area and lower back. "Sometimes when they will not let us go to the bathroom, I want to scream from the pain," commented a worker.[67] A majority of workers spoke of wrist or hand pain due to the repetitive motions of the work. Others described total fatigue. "When I leave at the end of the day, I can barely stand up," said a fifteen-year-old worker with eight months' experience in the factories. "Every part of my body hurts, but especially my arms and back. I thought I would get used to it but so far the pain seems to be getting worse each day."[68]

Because the industry has grown substantially only since 1988, the long-term effects of the maquila revolution on workers' bodies is unknown. Some workers are already complaining of respiratory and eyesight problems. On a larger scale, conditions are ripe for an epidemic of cumulative trauma disorders (CTDs), illnesses that plague workers in the garment industry in the United States.[69] Caused by repetitive motions, forced exertions, awkward postures, and vibrations, CTDs are illnesses of the musculoskeletal and nervous system that involve damage to tendons, muscles, and nerves in the hands, wrists, elbows, arms, backs, or legs. The primitive factory conditions, the pressure to produce, and the lack of rest periods in Guatemalan factories create ideal conditions for this illness. One health and safety official in Guatemala believes that unless dramatic restructuring of the workplace occurs immediately, "an entire generation of workers will be physically disabled by these illnesses."[70]

Factory Medical Services: Aspirin, Alcohol, and Cotton

"Since I am a volunteer fireman, I am called to treat all the injuries. Whenever a worker cuts herself, I go and help her clean and dress the wound. At first my manager didn't like me moving around, but now he lets me do it. If I didn't, no one would be helped," said a worker of his factory's accident treatment policy.[71] Like this worker's factory, few maquila plants provide adequate medical supplies and services beyond cotton and alcohol for cuts and aspirin for headaches. "People get stuck with needles all the time. If there is alcohol, which there is only some of the time, you clean the puncture. If not, there is no cleaning and you return to work," explained an operator.[72]

About 10 percent of the factories provide medical care beyond aspirin, alcohol, and cotton, ranging from a complete medicine cabinet to a part-time doctor. In approximately ten factories, medical personnel, either a doctor or a nurse, visit periodically. These factories, however, do not dispense or reimburse for medication. Thus, workers frequently remarked that the doctors are unable to treat ailments because they have no access to medicine—except for aspirin.

Most maquila employers perceive little need to provide services for injured workers. They argue that injuries are few and usually minor; thus the need for medical services is very limited. And, if more services are needed, they assert, workers can visit IGSS hospitals and clinics. The personnel manager of Sam Lucas S.A., for example, claimed that his factory of over nine hundred employees, located some fifteen miles from the nearest medical facility, had not yet acquired the services of a doctor because the "operation is so new."[73] At the time of the interview, the factory was more than a year old; the implication was clear: the health and safety of the workers did not merit attention.

The IGSS: Employee Medicine

All employers with more than three employees are required to register each employee with the IGSS and pay a tax of 10 percent of the monthly payroll to the IGSS. This requirement, however, is "really optional," admitted several IGSS officials, because enforcement is "rather ineffective."[74] Nevertheless, more than 22,000 employers and 700,000 employees are registered with the IGSS, representing approximately one-fourth of the economically active population. There is widespread sentiment among IGSS officials that maquila factories, in particular, underreport their number of employees. The number of maquila workers without IGSS cards supports this contention.

"It is painful to use the medical services of the IGSS," reported a worker.[75] She was not referring to inept treatment by IGSS doctors but to her manager's vigorous resistance to permitting visits to IGSS hospitals for treatments or checkups. Workers have a legally protected right to use IGSS services without fear of reprisal—even wages are not to be deducted for lost time. Despite this law, even in factories that contribute to the IGSS, workers consistently said it takes great courage to request permission to visit IGSS clinics or hospitals because of the anticipated negative employer response. Almost all factories discourage use of IGSS facilities; the degree of resistance, however, varies. The policy in a few factories is to interrogate the worker about the purpose of the visit but allow her to go if the excuse appears valid. Most factories are not as lenient, either prohibiting visits altogether or penalizing workers with wage discounts, and sometimes dismissal. Workers routinely reported reductions in salary for visits to IGSS services, and in some instances workers are presented with an ultimatum: "Go to the IGSS clinic but don't come back to work here."

Even when the injury requires immediate medical attention, the worker often must transport herself to an IGSS hospital or is required to wait until after work. A Guatemalan line supervisor, for instance, suffered a broken arm and finger (both were in a cast during the interview) when an iron he was operating fell on him. The accident occurred at 10:30 P.M., after fifteen hours of uninterrupted work. Since buses had stopped running for the evening, the manager agreed to transport the injured worker to the IGSS hospital—but only after his work was completed. Management told the supervisor to continue his task. Following this command, he worked for another two hours until the order was finally completed and packaged. The injured worker arrived at the IGSS hospital after 1 A.M., three hours after his accident. "I continued to work with my one good hand until they took me to the hospital," he said of the incident. "I was told there was work to be completed and my injury, which they said was my fault anyway, would simply have to wait."[76] When the worker returned to the factory after a month-long recuperation, he was told he no longer had a job.

Rosa: The Future Maquila Worker?

The story of "Rosa," a disabled, former maquila worker, illuminates the long-term prospects of this work. For more than three years, Rosa worked as an operator in a half-dozen maquila factories. "They were pretty much all the same," she said. "We worked without breaks, sometimes into the night, and earned very little."[77]

Today, Rosa suffers from extremely weak kidneys, which confine her for several days at a time to her bed. She and her doctor attribute this illness to three factors prevalent in her experience as a maquila worker: uninterrupted sitting, limited access to potable water, and restricted use of the bathroom. When she asked for water or to use the bathroom, the supervisors would say: "Just bear it a little longer!" "Don't be weak!" "Keep up the production, my little girl!"

After a year and a half as an operator, Rosa's kidney became infected for the first time. She visited an IGSS clinic, where a doctor told her to rest for a week. Her employer, however, informed her that he could not hold her place open for a week. Since she needed the income, she continued to sit and sew. The kidney grew more painful. Finally, she was forced to retire from the maquila industry well before the age of thirty because she was unable to sit for the necessary time. "What I fear is that thousands of women will suffer the same fate," she lamented. "And all for the sake of stupid clothing that Guatemalans never even wear."[78]

Three Deaths and More to Come?

The most dramatic series of industrial accidents in the short history of the Guatemalan maquila industry were the deaths of three workers who were hit by cars as they exited from their factory, Sam Lucas S.A. Located on a winding, two-lane, unlit highway between Guatemala City and Chimaltenango, the plant is the largest maquila in Guatemala, with nearly a thousand machines. The fence surrounding the premises lies about ten feet from the edge of this highway. Frequently workers are not allowed to leave until well after nightfall.

On three separate occasions, a weary worker walked out of the factory onto the unlit highway and was struck and killed by a passing car or a bus. Despite these tragedies, the factory has not installed lighting, posted signs, or constructed an overpass. Of the accidents, a worker said: "The factory is right on the edge [of the highway] and they do not do anything! They didn't help pay for the burials. They refuse to take responsibility for the accidents, saying 'Once we leave the premises, we need to be careful.'"[79] When asked about injuries or accidents in the factory, the personnel manager of the factory, Salvador Fijardo, enthusiastically responded: "We are very proud of our accident record. Workers rarely are injured on the job. Maybe a needle stuck in a finger once in a while, but nothing more."[80]

These deaths poignantly demonstrate the desperately inadequate state of health and safety conditions in Guatemalan maquila factories. By default, the onus of setting and enforcing standards has been placed on the owners of the factories. The result is an industry that exploits at will the health, safety, and welfare of fifty thousand, mostly young and female, workers, leading one veteran labor inspector to say, "I have seen only one decent, humane [maquila] factory."[81]

5

Working Hours, Compensation, and Labor Relations

The General Inspectorate of Work

The IGT is the sole government agency responsible for the administration and enforcement of legal standards for working hours, compensation, and labor relations. Although most inspectors feel more comfortable in this role of labor rather than health and safety inspector, the result is the same: an overburdened, underfinanced IGT is unable to execute an antiquated Labor Code.

Thirteen labor inspectors are responsible for more than twelve thousand businesses in Guatemala City. This responsibility is complicated by the multiple roles that the Code calls each inspector to perform. In addition to the regulation of health and safety standards, labor inspectors are expected to monitor and facilitate union formation and collective bargaining; intervene and conciliate labor disputes and strikes; resolve individual complaints brought by workers and employers; issue work permits; audit company books; and enforce basic employment standards such as minimum-wage and maximum-hour laws. In comparable U.S. law, Guatemalan labor inspectors are responsible for the Fair Labor Standards Act, the Occupational Safety and Health Act, the tax code, and the National Labor Relations Act. As the U.S. Embassy Labor Attaché explained, "Their role is so ambiguous that they do not know themselves what to do."[1]

In practice, limited resources restrict the labor inspector's expansive charge to that of a passive recipient of worker complaints. Instead of aggressive enforcement of varied duties, labor inspectors spend most of their efforts settling disputes over severance pay.[2] Since the IGT conducts business during the hours when most employees are working—8 A.M. to 4 P.M.—and since few workers are able to request time off to file a complaint, the IGT receives complaints primarily from those who are unemployed. If an ex-employee believes she is due more severance pay than her employer offered, she risks little except time to lodge a complaint with the IGT. Inspectors explain that their extensive experience with fired workers is a result of a law that is ineffective in protecting worker rights. "The law fails the worker," said a labor inspector. "The law offers no job security so all we can do is get them their indemnification."[3]

Yet even in disputes over severance pay, employers can, if they choose, defeat their former employees' petition. In a typical situation, the employer will either refuse to compensate a discharged worker or offer her a fraction of the correct amount. The worker spends a day at the IGT, files a complaint, and an inspector is sent to resolve the dispute. If the inspector is unable to settle the complaint and he believes the employee's claim has merit, he can submit it to the labor courts, which are notoriously slow and ineffective. "At this point," lamented an inspector, "we give up hope of a victory for the worker. We are incredibly frustrated. Whatever we try to do, the courts and lawyers minimize."[4]

Moreover, if he chooses to avoid the above procedure, the employer has ways of wearing down his ex-employee. He can reschedule appointments, negotiate in bad faith, bribe the labor inspector, or file frivolous, time-consuming motions in court. Workers normally do not possess the time and resources to consistently pressure the IGT to pursue the case in the labor courts. For example, a nineteen-year-old maquila worker, "Clara," who, on the advice of a doctor and after informing management, took a week off to recover from a respiratory ailment, was refused reentry to the factory. When Clara was finally able to speak to the manager, he informed her that she was due Q300 in severance pay. She believed the amount to be more than Q700 and declined the offer. Hence, Clara lodged a complaint with the IGT and awaited the outcome. Weeks passed without word despite several visits to the IGT. The inspectors only told her what she already knew: the manager was extremely obstinate. In the meantime, Clara's mother became ill and, because of mounting medical costs, she broke down and accepted the employer's original offer. Clara said of the situation, "He knew that my stamina was less than his, and he simply exploited it. The IGT tried, but they are too weak."[5]

Perhaps most debilitating to the work of the IGT is the workers' lack of confidence in the law and in the IGT's willingness to assist. If workers really believed that the law and the IGT would protect and redeem their rights, they would file complaints in more situations than merely when they have been unjustly denied severance pay.

Moreover, though much of this worker hesitancy derives from a belief that the IGT is impotent, many workers go so far as to contend that the IGT is too often an ally of the employer. Bribes are rumored to be commonplace. The manager of Modas del Este S.A. alleged that many inspectors are "very direct in their approach. They ask for money before they tell you why they are there."[6]

Some inspection reports support this claim of an alliance between inspectors and employers. For instance, after investigating anonymous worker reports of "inhumane, degrading, and abusive" treatment by managers at Sam Lucas S.A., a factory renowned for repressive labor practices, an inspector wrote in his report: "I met and spoke with the personnel manager of the factory. He showed me that the company was not treating workers poorly and that in fact a great deal of harmony and understanding existed between workers and management. In virtue of this finding, I have found these complaints without merit."[7] These workers, no doubt, were relieved that they made their complaints anonymously.

The Flood of Complaints from Maquila Workers: A Six-Month Survey

Within the last three years, the IGT has witnessed an unprecedented deluge of complaints from maquila workers. The recent explosion of maquila exports has brought an even greater increase in denouncements from maquila workers at the IGT. Labor inspectors and I quickly acquired the skill of picking out maquila workers in the IGT waiting room. Of this increase, one inspector commented: "In the last two years we have been overwhelmed with complaints from the maquila. They take up more space in our waiting room than any other class of worker."[8]

In order to determine the frequency of maquila complaints and to gain a sense of the type of complaints, I undertook a survey of the IGT archives in their Guatemala City office. Of the first 770 worker complaints mediated by inspectors from January to August 1990, more than seventy, or 9 percent, were filed by maquila workers. Of these complaints, more than forty different factories were represented. At the time, approximately forty to forty-five thousand workers were employed in the maquila industry, which constituted about 5 percent of the total work force within the jurisdiction of the IGT office in Guatemala City.[9] Thus, during this period, complaints from maquila workers accounted for almost twice their representation in the work force. Moreover, the frequency of these complaints is rising. The first two weeks of the year, maquila complaints comprised less than 5 percent, while in July these complaints represented more than 16 percent.

Consistent with the predominance of severance pay complaints, more than 85 percent of maquila worker petitions concerned postemployment issues. Of these, almost half alleged that the employer had fired a woman because of pregnancy without the legally entitled severance pay or pregnancy leave. The other half mainly consisted of denouncements filed by minors who alleged dismissal without compensation. The remaining 15 percent dealt with a variety of complaints from "unfair and inhumane treatment" to dismissals for having used the IGSS services during working hours.[10]

The Minimum Wage and the Maquila

One significant accomplishment of the decade of democracy from 1944 to 1954 was the implementation of a government minimum wage. For the first time, Guatemalan workers were guaranteed a minimum amount of compensation for their labor. The Code declares, "Every worker has the right to enjoy a minimum salary that covers the normal necessities of material, moral, and cultural order and that permits him to satisfy his duties as leader of the family."[11] The 1986 Constitution reaffirmed this right, guaranteeing "fair compensation" for work and "equal wages for equal work performed under equal conditions."[12]

The Code sets out an elaborate scheme of minimum-wage commissions to ensure that each individual occupation receives a just wage in accordance with the cost of living and relative value of the job to society. A National Salary Commission is authorized to create regional and industry-specific minimum-wage commissions comprised of employer, union, and government representatives. These commissions are to meet periodically to analyze economic data and adjust minimum wages accordingly.

In practice, the commissions rarely meet and, according to some observers, the members seem more driven to increase their stipends than the minimum wages. The U.S. Embassy labor attaché called the commissions "scandalously ineffective."[13] Out of this system, thirty-eight separate minimum wages have been set, ranging from bank employees to agricultural workers.

The minimum wage is calculated on a daily basis and is usually paid biweekly. The Code requires that all work performed beyond forty-four hours a week be compensated at a rate of one and a half times the regular wage. If an employee works forty-four hours, or six days a week, she is compensated for an extra day's wage, known as the "Seventh Day."[14] Since 1987, the minimum wage for garment-assembly workers has been set at Q5.50, or about US$1.10, a day.[15] If she works full time and receives the Seventh Day pay, she earns Q165, or about US$33 a month. At this rate, workers earn less than US$.20 an hour.

In addition to a guaranteed minimum wage, workers also benefit from two mandatory bonuses. First, a 1965 decree requires employers to pay all workers who have at least one year's experience an "aguinaldo" bonus at the end of each year.[16] Each employee who qualifies for the bonus effectively receives an extra month's salary at the start of the new year. Second, in December 1989, the Guatemalan Congress, in response to the rising cost of living and runaway inflation resulting from a devalued currency, instituted a mandatory raise for every worker. Agricultural workers were given a 20-centavos-an-hour raise, or Q48 (US$9.60) a month, and industrial workers received 30 centavos an hour, or Q72 (US$14.40) a month. This *bonificación*, as it is called, increases the government-mandated minimum wage in maquila factories to Q237, about $47, a month.

Most maquila employers in Guatemala understand the minimum wage to signify the maximum wage. Employer after employer assured, "We pay what the law says." A union official explained, "Of course they [maquila employers] pay the minimum. It is so pitifully small, it would be hard to pay workers less."[17] Yet despite these assurances, maquila worker denunciations of minimum wage violations are frequent at the IGT. A labor inspector described the depth of the problem in the maquila industry: "In some factories, they pay minimum wage. In others, they do not even pay the minimum. . . . Some of the businesses use incentives to make the salaries adequate, but you can count these on your fingers."[18] In addition, according to a 1990 Labor Ministry study of 1,200 businesses, only 16 percent of all employers are paying their workers the government 1989 *bonificación* of thirty cents an hour.[19] IGT officials suspect, and worker interviews indicate, that even fewer maquila factories are paying this bonus.

In conflict with this testimony, promoters of the maquila industry at GEXPRONT and AID assert that most factories pay workers substantially more than the government-set minimum. A senior AID official in the Private Sector Development section claimed that wages in the maquila sector have doubled in real value over the past three years.[20] Yet the GEXPRONT official most knowledgeable about individual factories, Gary Garzaro, was unable to identify ten factories that paid above Q12 a day, or Q360 a month.[21]

In this survey, over 80 percent of the workers reported receiving exactly the minimum wage. Another 10 percent said they received less than the minimum. Some factories pay minors and workers in training less than the minimum. In two such factories, these workers earned less than Q4, or US$.80, a day. The other 10 percent of the interviewees said they earned more than the minimum wage. In addition, the survey of IGT complaints revealed that of the fifty-five maquila worker complaints on severance pay which were settled, workers received the minimum wage 75 percent of the time. The average of all these settlements was Q175 a month, approximately 6 percent more than the minimum wage. Even the Phillips-Van Heusen factory, Camisas Modernas S.A.—considered by promoters as the most benevolent factory—compensated a fired pregnant worker at the minimum wage in a settlement. Since severance pay is based on the most recent paycheck, these findings illustrate that most maquila workers earn the minimum wage—but no more.

The Misplaced Incentives of Piece-Rate Compensation

Management in apparel-assembly factories uses two compensation systems: by day and by piece. Nearly every factory, with the notable exception of Korean shops, pays operators according to their production. Employers set the price of each operation, such as sewing a seam or a button, based on the time it takes to complete. When a worker finishes a dozen of any operation, she attaches a coupon onto a sheet, which is collected at the end of each day, and the coupons are added up to determine the day's wage. This wage system effectively makes each operator an independent contractor. The faster and more productively the operator sews, the greater her earnings. Since income depends on output, the incentive to work as rapidly as possible is the driving force for most workers.

In theory, this system encourages workers to improve efficiency and increase wages. The practices of most factories, however, discourage and impede this progression. Often, piece rates are kept so low that no matter how fast operators sew, their wages will not exceed the government minimum. At a factory in Zone 1, for example, workers are paid piece rates which are continuously revised and updated. At this same factory, however, the employee wages are identical—everyone earned exactly the minimum wage. No one is able to sew rapidly enough to exceed the minimum. Boasted the factory's owner, "I still pay them the minimum wage whether they earned it or not."[22]

Another management practice workers reported was the deliberate reduction of piece-rate pay as a worker becomes more proficient, so that her wage never exceeds the minimum. The continual turnover in apparel styles further limits earnings, because workers never practice a particular style enough to become proficient. Pressured by the need to exceed the minimum wage, workers often labor through breaks and lunch, or work overtime "voluntarily" without increased compensation. "Sometimes I won't get up from the machine because I want to make more," said a worker. "Some people eat in secret at their machines because they do not want to break. Of course, they know that this is not allowed, but they want to make money."[23]

Most employers also manipulate the piece-rate system by not increasing rates by 50 percent, as required by law, when workers begin overtime. In other words, the rates remain the same whether the worker is beginning the day or her fourteenth hour. Only one interviewed operator mentioned a rise in piece rates for overtime work; the rest were unaware that this law applied to piecework. Employers enjoy the benefit of these extra hours but apparently do not feel compelled to compensate for this time.

The other compensation system—day rates—is almost exclusively found in Korean-managed factories.[24] This scheme is less complicated, with employees receiving a daily wage usually based on seniority. The incentive to produce rapidly is diminished, as workers lack real or perceived control over the amount of compensation offered by the piecework system. Most employers provide raises of Q.50, US$.10, a day every six months. Despite this stated policy, more than a dozen workers reported working more than a year at a factory without receiving this promised raise.

Discounts and Reductions: Ambiguous Law, Clear Practice

The Code lacks adequate guidelines to protect wages from unscrupulous employer deductions. It permits employers to deduct from wages as a form of punishment and for employer-provided services, except for tools necessary for work.[25] Because of this ambiguous standard, some of the most blatant instances of employee exploitation are arbitrary reductions in and deductions from workers' salaries. Inspectors at the IGT explained that workers in all industries are subject to random and inexplicable salary discounts, but, as an inspector noted: "What is a worker to do? He can only argue with his employer so much before he loses his job. Then he arrives here without work, and usually without proof of the employer's theft of his earnings."[26]

Tardiness is probably the most common reason for payroll deductions. Nearly every maquila factory has rules designed to deter lateness that punish workers through their paycheck. In close to half the factories, the doors shut at a specified time, and thereafter workers—no matter what their excuse—are refused entry. It is not uncommon to see workers dashing to the entrance of the factory before the doors are shut for the day. The reasoning behind this rule, as an employer explained, is simple: "If I let one in late the next thing you know everyone will show up late. We cannot tolerate this. We make money only while we are producing. Lateness takes time away from production."[27] The consequences of arriving late vary between loss of the day's wage and the "Seventh Day" pay to a Q1 penalty for every minute late. In one large Guatemalan-owned factory, every worker who arrives late is required to work an hour overtime without compensation.

Workers denounce these policies as unfair, arguing that a sick child, family troubles, or, more commonly, transportation problems sometimes cannot be avoided. Transportation, for many workers, presents the biggest difficulty. Most workers rely on buses and minivans to carry them from home to work. Bus schedules, however, are unreliable and breakdowns are frequent, leaving passengers at the mercy of the efficiency of the various bus companies. A twenty-one-year-old mother of two describes the daily difficulties:

> They [the employers] do not understand what it is like to wake up at 5 A.M., straighten up the house, feed and get the children off to school, run to catch two buses, and then run again to make it inside the door before it closes for the day. If one thing goes wrong, if the bus is late, if a child is sick, I will be late. But they do not want to hear about this excuse. They just want us on time, to be punctual, to be responsible, to be efficient, to be, as they say, like workers in the United States. But when it comes to treating and paying us like workers in the United States, they don't even come close. Maybe when we're paid like American workers, we'll start to respond like them.[28]

Many workers contended that employers continually search for excuses to discount salaries. "[The management] is always finding reasons for taking away our wages. If it's not tardiness, it's too much time in the bathroom," said a worker. "There are more incentives designed to reduce income you already have earned than to increase income."[29]

As noted above, the Code forbids salary discounts for tools, equipment, and supplies that are "indispensable" for work.[30] Despite this prohibition, management in more than four out of five factories charges workers for the replacement and repair of tools and machinery. Scissors, for example, are obviously indispensable to an operator, yet most operators either must supply their own pair or purchase them from the factory. The cost of replacing scissors equals at least one day's wage for most workers. Operators, in many cases, are also held responsible for other essential work items such as bobbins and needles and when lost or damaged, the paycheck is reduced accordingly. These internal regulations seem to be implemented more to curb theft than carelessness. An employer explained this rationale: "These workers would steal the scissors if we did not make them pay for them."[31]

In the majority of factories, workers who accidentally damage cloth are held responsible. If the cloth is reparable the worker is generally required to fix the mistake during unpaid overtime. If, however, the damage is irreparable, the worker will most likely be forced to pay for the cost of the cloth. In reported cases in which the worker was obliged to pay for the damaged cloth, the expense exceeded weekly wages. Like damage to clothing, the cost of sewing machine repairs are often discounted, regardless of fault, from the wages of the operator. One worker reported that his wages were garnished for several months to compensate for a sewing machine that broke while he was using it.

Slow production speed and "wasted" time provide another excuse for wage deductions. Many supervisors have high, frequently unrealistic, expectations for the workers in their charge. If a worker does not meet these levels of production, salaries are sometimes adjusted accordingly. Slow workers, so the theory goes, deserve less pay. A union official responded: "Workers will work for the amount they get paid. If they are paid the minimum wage, they will work the minimal amount."[32] Several factories discount wages for "wasted" time, that is, time spent not sewing. If a worker rises without permission or spends too much time in the washroom, for example, her pay is docked.

Forced Overtime: The Enslavement of Workers

Forced overtime is probably the most flagrant labor rights violation in the maquila industry: overtime is almost always obligatory and rarely compensated for at the legally mandated rate. According to workers, almost nine out of ten factories regularly practice forced overtime. (Over six out of ten employers also reported the practice of mandatory overtime in their factories.) Most workers are required upon pain of dismissal to labor at least two, and up to ten, hours of overtime each day. Thus, the average workweek of a maquila worker ranges between fifty-five and seventy hours, with some workers reporting normal workweeks of more than eighty or more hours. In more than three-fourths of the factories, management forces workers when it deems "necessary"—ranging from four times a week to once a month—to work overnight for one or more days straight. Few, if any, factories compensate workers for these extra hours.

Workers literally labor until the doors are unlocked at the end of the day. Requests to leave the premises early are routinely met with threats of dismissal; leaving early usually merits dismissal. One worker explained the common practice in her factory: "The manager locks the door, stands in front of it, and says, 'One more hour, please.' He walks away and we wait for him to come back later and open it. Then we know it is time to punch out and leave."[33]

The 1986 Constitution—as a sign of "humanizing" the workplace and complying with the International Labor Organization's standard—reduced the maximum workweek from forty-eight to forty-four hours. Subsequent hours are considered overtime and must be voluntary, and the maximum workday may not exceed twelve hours. Despite this clear guideline, IGT inspectors have found violations of hourly limits to be the gravest and most common infringements on the rights of maquila workers.[34] "They work them like slaves. Breaks are surrendered. Sleep is denied. Just work, work, work. Nothing else matters," commented a labor inspector.[35]

According to labor inspectors, forced overtime is one of the easiest abuses to assess, but the most difficult to monitor. The enormity of this problem, combined with inadequate government resources, has caused pessimism about inspectors' ability to combat this abuse. "There is no way we can regulate that [overtime] because we do not have the personnel, and the instances of violation are too numerous to count," explained an inspector.[36] Moreover, most workers are reluctant to complain. For many, extra hours of piecework mean more income, a "bonus" few workers can afford to turn down, much less report an employer for.

Employers defend their policy of forced labor by saying it is a consequence of the volatile nature of the garment-assembly industry. The needs of the apparel industry, they argue, vary according to seasonal and market demand, and hence factories need a flexible work force to meet these fluctuating production deadlines. The manager of Maldanado Higueros S.A. explained: "I cannot have problems with [people not wanting to work overtime] because that is one of my rules. You know, in this business you cannot be stopped by self-seeking operators. . . . They have to collaborate. If they refuse, they get fired. If one worker does not work overtime, the entire line may crumble. I find that in most cases they are very cooperative."[37]

Almost two-thirds of the interviewed managers unabashedly said that they frequently force their employees to work overtime in order to complete an order. One manager from Sae Han S.A. admitted to the unheard-of in Guatemala—work on Sunday. "Every day we work from 7:30 A.M. until at least 8:30, and then sometimes until 12:30 or all night, depending on what is needed." He continued, "We even work on Sunday if there is a lot of work."[38]

Other employers, realizing the illegality of requiring obligatory overtime, attempt to introduce the propriety of voluntariness. For instance, workers in at least five factories reported being forced to sign a card stating that they agreed to work overtime when requested. Another employer explained that his policy was voluntary, because "[w]hen we hire them we make it clear that they need to be free until midnight every evening. They can choose at that moment whether they want to work overtime."[39] Finally, a few employers have convinced workers that "regular" work hours include overtime. When asked what hours they worked, employees at Sam Lucas S.A. reported that their regular working hours began at 8 A.M. and ended at 6 P.M., with a half-hour lunch break. On Saturday, the workers arrived at the same time but regularly quit at 12:30 and spent Sunday away from the factory. The workers explained that all work beyond these hours was overtime; in other words, the workers had been led to believe that the first fifty-two hours were regular, expected hours, compensated at minimum wage.

More than three-fourths of maquila factories force their employees occasionally or regularly to work through the night. When obligated to work overnight, workers typically arrive in the morning and are then told, normally without warning, that the regular shift has been extended until midnight or later. Few workers object, as all know the consequence of dissent is dismissal. A short dinner break is provided, with a catered meal of rice and tortillas. When management decides to end production, the machines stop, the lights are extinguished, and the workers scramble for a clean, warm place to rest.

In addition to the hourly limits, the Code prohibits owners of commercial and industrial businesses to permit workers to sleep or eat in the workplace. They are required, if necessary, to provide other facilities for these activities.[40] In the maquila sector, no one seems to bother. Cloth scraps and remnants become makeshift blankets, protecting employers against frigid nights. Covered by these scraps, the workers huddle together on the floor, or on a bench or table, in an attempt to sleep until early the following morning, when they are awakened an hour before work for breakfast and a brief wash. Then the operation begins anew.

It is not uncommon for factories, under pressure to complete an order, to force employees to work several nights in a row without interruption. In one factory, two seventeen-year-old operators casually reported that during especially busy periods they worked straight through an entire week, never leaving the factory from 7 A.M. on Monday until 5 P.M. the following Saturday. A manager would announce on the preceding Saturday that workers were to bring a change of clothes for the coming week. They brought the clothes and worked from 7 A.M. to 12 A.M. every day—over ninety hours for the week.

These excessive hours naturally create other problems besides severe infringement of the worker's freedom. Most buses, the major source of transportation, stop running shortly after nightfall, leaving workers stranded at factories. Child care is another serious problem. Children are often left with friends, relatives, or older siblings for the day, but in the case of two or three hours of overtime, these resources may become less reliable and understanding. Moreover, when a mother returns home after 10 P.M., her children are already asleep. Weeks can slip by without there being significant contact between the parent and the child.

Children and Women: The Most Vulnerable Employees

"By far the two largest pools of complaints from all workplaces we receive here are child labor and illegal dismissals of pregnant women," reported the subdirector of the IGT.[41] Fittingly, women and minors share a chapter of the Code. As minors and females comprise the overwhelming percentage of employees in the maquila sector, these problems are intensified in the garment-assembly factories.

"When a maquila factory lets out for the day," commented a union organizer, "it looks more like a high school than it does a factory."[42] Maquila factories have become notorious for their exploitation of child labor. Indeed, between 30 to 45 percent of the maquila work force is under the age of eighteen.[43] Close to one-fifth of the workers are under the age of sixteen; and in factories outside the capital as many as half the workers are minors, some as young as six years old. For example, in the village of San Pedro Sacatepequez, where Phillips-Van Heusen contracts large volumes of cheap flannel shirts to dozens of small household shops, children as young as six work alongside their siblings and mothers, usually snipping excess thread from finished garments.

The Code prohibits employment of minors under fourteen years of age, except when it can be shown that the child will work in the capacity of an apprentice or that "extreme poverty" warrants the child's contribution to the family economy.[44] In such cases, workers are required to demonstrate this proof to the IGT, and, if successful, will be issued a special, limited work permit. Economic reality dictates a less formal regime. According to census data, nearly 20 percent of children between twelve and fourteen are working to supplement their family's income.[45] Few of these children have work permits. In the Phillips-Van Heusen San Pedro sweatshops, none of the children had obtained work permits.

Pregnancy as Impediment to Production

The Code provides relatively generous benefits and rights for pregnant women. In addition to a prohibition against discrimination in discharge, a paid maternity leave of thirty days pre- and forty-five days postdelivery is a statutory right. After giving birth, mothers are entitled to return to their jobs. Upon return to work, moreover, mothers possess a special "right to lactation": two thirty-minute breaks set aside for mothers to nurse their newborns.[46] Further, if a business has more than thirty employees, the law stipulates that the employer must supply day care for children of the employees.

Most of these protections and benefits, however, are rarely, if ever, provided to maquila workers. To begin with, not even the Labor Ministry provides day care for children of employees. In its guide for prospective investors, Megatex S.A., a maquila consultant, states, "By law, enterprises employing more than ten [*sic*] women must have Daycare Center [*sic*]; nevertheless, in practice 'nobody' does it, not having been practical to date."[47] Lactation breaks are also unknown in worksites and pre- and postnatal paid leave can be obtained only after lodging a complaint with the IGT. Finally, in the maquila industry, dismissal based on pregnancy is routine.

Maquila employers consider pregnancy to be the greatest single enemy to production. "Nothing disturbs our production more than women getting pregnant," stated one employer.[48] "These women are irresponsible. They do not seem to be able to control themselves. I have workers leaving weekly because of pregnancy," complained another manager at a large factory.[49] More than one-fourth of management representatives contended that women take advantage of their ability to get pregnant, entering the job market early in their pregnancy with the intention of obtaining the paid maternity leave. Philip Klose, manager of Koram S.A., explained: "Some workers are trying to pull our leg when they come to the factory. We hire them and they start acting strangely. Then you fire them and she comes back and says she is pregnant. . . . A lot of women when they become pregnant apply to work at a maquila so they can receive the benefits when they are fired."[50]

From the day of application, most managers scrutinize and discriminate against female workers on the basis of their capacity to give birth. Upon application for employment it is a common practice to require medical proof from female workers that they are not pregnant. Other employers use cruder techniques to weed out these undesired employees. Millie Woc, a Guatemalan personnel manager at a five-hundred-machine Korean-owned shop, Este Oeste S.A., explained her method of "weeding out" pregnant women: "I have the luxury of many years of working in this industry. When an applicant comes through the door for the first time, the first thing I look at is her stomach. If there is the slightest lump, or mound, she will not work here. Children take time away from production. We cannot have that in this factory. We try to discourage pregnancy on the job. We may soon bring in a family planning organization to teach these girls about birth control."[51] Workers have no actual recourse when denied a job on this basis because the Code, though proscribing discrimination between married and unmarried women, does not forbid hiring discrimination based on pregnancy.

The IGT does process numerous complaints of female maquila workers fired because of pregnancy. Although the law requires employers voluntarily to provide paid maternity leave, only in exceptional cases do maquila employers supply this benefit uncoerced. In the majority of cases, maquila employers dismiss the worker when they learn of the pregnancy. Typically, the worker will be given another reason for the dismissal, such as a drop in production, and maternity benefits will be denied outright. Then the employee presents her complaint to the IGT, where it is processed. In most cases, an accord is reached in which a worker accepts partial compensation for the maternity leave but relinquishes her right to return to work after delivery of her child.

Several workers reported management attempts to force pregnant workers to resign, thereby avoiding paid maternity leave altogether, because resignations void this entitlement. In such cases, management either tries to frustrate workers into resignation—for example, by assigning these women new jobs or machines which they do not know how to operate. In a piecework system in which wages depend on production, the inability to operate a machine efficiently guarantees low wages. Placed in these situations, the worker quickly loses confidence and self-esteem, and, most often, resigns. Sometimes the employer will not give the worker material to assemble, again creating frustration and isolation. Whatever the means, the common practice of management in maquila factories, with few exceptions, is to act as if the right to paid maternity leave did not exist. The result for many workers is the insecurity of giving birth to a child without having any source of income.

Sexual Abuse

Labor inspectors report that sexual abuse of women employees by fellow workers and management is rampant in Guatemala. "From the plantations to the factories, this [sexual abuse] occurs all too frequently," lamented the IGT subdirector.[52] Despite this regularity, the IGT receives less than ten complaints of sexual abuse a year. In the summer of 1990, the only case in a maquila factory of which inspectors were aware was that of an employer justifying the discharge of a security guard because he had impregnated a worker in his factory. A combination of embarrassment, mistrust, cultural factors, fear of losing employment, and nearly impossible chances of successful prosecution keeps most complaints outside the formal system.

Another explanation for the lack of complaints is a common definition of sexual abuse that excludes all behavior except for rape and violent molestation. Most workers seem to consider touching and fondling to be an annoyance, but not abuse. For example, ex-workers in a factory on the Caribbean coast regarded a Guatemalan manager who routinely grabbed the bodies of women workers and requested that certain women come to work in bathing suits more of a playful nuisance than an abusive supervisor. Of this conduct, a sixteen-year-old worker said: "He was just a pain and most thought of it as a stupid joke. Once he grabbed the breasts of a worker, but she smacked him, so you can see we never let him get too far."[53]

For obvious reasons of privacy, workers were very reluctant to discuss sexual abuse in their factories. Nevertheless, evidence of widespread abuse surfaced in interviews. One woman claimed that she was raped by a supervisor and was then subsequently fired for pregnancy. Another reported constant advances from male supervisors and threats of reprisal if sexual acts were not performed. Several labor inspectors claimed that a few Korean factories had come to resemble brothels more than factories. Allegedly, Korean supervisors at these factories forced women workers, under penalty of dismissal, to engage in sexual intercourse. A former worker at Jobtex S.A. reported, "The Korean supervisors like to touch and touch the legs, the rear, and the breasts."[54]

Job Security: At Will Dismissal

"There is no job security in my factory. They [the management] hire and fire you at will. You never know what might get you fired," said a seventeen-year-old maquila worker.[55] Most workers in maquila factories share this sentiment that job insecurity is a condition of work. A production decrease, an intemperate supervisor, or a late bus might be enough to provoke the loss of a job. Only at the factory Pindu S.A. were workers who belonged to the factory's union confident that their jobs were permanent. Yet, even there, workers arrived one Monday morning and found an empty factory. Most other workers are at the mercy of fluctuations in the market and the arbitrary decision making of employers.

A high turnover rate, including both resignations and dismissals, indicates the inherent instability of employment in the maquila sector. Most managers and owners claim a turnover rate of 10 to 30 percent of the workers per month. They blame their low efficiency and production levels on the constant need to hire replacements, placing fault on workers for their irresponsible "jumping bean" behavior. While this theory is credible, it cannot entirely explain the extraordinarily high rates of attrition. The fact that most workers who restlessly move among several factories in the hope of finding better wages, conditions, and benefits infers that this "jumping bean" effect is largely the result of dissatisfaction inside the workplace. It is the poor earnings, long hours, monotonous, exhausting work, and no chance of advancement or promotion that motivate workers to try new shops.

The voluntary transferral of employees among businesses only accounts for a portion of this high turnover rate, however. Most factories dismiss workers for a host of reasons at very high rates as well. Encouraging these "flexible" discharge policies, the Code is based on the "employment at will" doctrine, which, under the assumption of equal bargaining power and the absence of a contract, allows either party in an employment relationship to sever the arrangement for any reason. The first article in the section entitled "Termination of Work Contracts" articulates this doctrine: "The work contract is terminated when one or both parties who formed a labor relation chooses to end it."[56] Hence, in the absence of a stipulated contract between employer and employee, either party is free to conclude the labor relationship at any time.

The major benefit available to discharged workers is a provision for severance pay of one month's salary for every year of work. Under this scheme, if the worker was dismissed for an unjust cause or resigned for a just cause, she is entitled to one month's salary for every year employed.[57] The Code defines a just cause dismissal to include industrial sabotage, fighting another worker or member of management personnel, sharing trade secrets, or missing two consecutive days of work without justification. If an employee resigns, with a few exceptions, she forfeits the severance pay. Only if a worker can prove she resigned because of malicious treatment by the employer or was being forced to work in a dangerous environment is she entitled to severance pay.

For most maquila employers, severance pay, like paid maternity leave, is another cost to be avoided. Almost always novices to the formal employment sector, maquila workers are unaware of most of their rights, including severance pay. In addition, as mentioned above, employees have little faith in the IGT to protect and ensure these rights. Most maquila employers take advantage of this ignorance and lack of confidence, rarely dispensing the legally mandated severance pay without the intervention of the IGT. Labor inspectors admitted to expending most of their time and effort on dealing with dismissed workers who demand proper compensation.[58] One inspector commented on the practice of employers: "Their general rule is: Don't pay unless you are forced to do so. This means that workers will only receive their correct benefits if we are brought into the incident. This places a great burden on our time and leaves us little time to protect workers who are having problems while still employed."[59]

Employers use more active means as well to avert compliance over severance pay requirements. Maquila workers and labor inspectors reported a common practice of employers forcing workers to resign, thus negating this right. Other factories sacrifice a stable work force, practicing a policy of never retaining an employee for an entire year. In several shops, when management desires to terminate a worker with more than a year's experience, they will, as in the case of pregnant workers, attempt to force the employee to resign "voluntarily."

Finally, it is common for workers, when they accept a job, to sign a piece of blank paper in the expectation that the sheet will later be dated and drafted into a statement of resignation. This practice is prevalent in all industries and trades. In the maquila industry, at least two attempts to unionize have been thwarted by this tactic. An experienced employer tells the story of a worker entering his office on the first day and handing him a blank sheet of paper with his signature on it. In every past employment experience the worker had followed this procedure and assumed it was the lawful practice.

Fall in Production, Illness, Education, and Other Reasons for Discharge

Beyond the pressure to resign, workers are subject to other work conditions and internal regulations that threaten their job security at any moment. First, workers are vulnerable to the rise and fall in production of the factory. If, for whatever reason, production should decline, it is not uncommon for workers to be given a "vacation" until work picks up again. "In this type of industry you have to anticipate vacations. When production is down, you give them their vacations," explained a Guatemalan manager.[60] Hence, workers are placed at the mercy of inexperienced owners and managers in the garment-assembly industry who often accept orders without realistic consideration of the factory's production capacity. This strategy has earned Guatemala the reputation for slow and unprofessional service among some U.S. brand names. It also forces workers to depend on overambitious, inexperienced employers for their livelihood. An organizer with the Confederación General de Trabajadores de Guatemala explained: "We have told them [owners of Pindu, where the federation had a union] over and over that the problem is that the owners make the contracts without the assent or advice of the workers. They accept more work than they have capacity to deliver. They do not make realistic assessments. The owners then say that the workers are lazy, that they do not respond, but the fact is that they are overwhelmed."[61]

"Excessive" absenteeism and tardiness are also not tolerated in maquila factories. Although the Code stipulates that absenteeism for two consecutive days, or six days tardy in a month without justification, are just cause for discharge, maquila employers generally exercise their own rules. Most factories tend to have, depending on the point of view, flexible or arbitrary means of treating workers who are absent. Employers complain that absenteeism, next to pregnancy and inefficiency, is the largest problem with workers, who counter that if the factory provided transportation or day care, they would rarely arrive late or miss work. Management decisions to terminate because of absenteeism generally vary from case to case. If an employee is especially valued, she will receive more leniency than an employee who is less experienced. Another common management policy is to force workers to sign admissions of fault for every tardiness or absence. In this way employers can, if necessary, justify the fact that they fired a worker because of her failure to show up on time.

Maquila workers who become ill for even a few days frequently return to the factory to find that they have been fired. "If you get sick, you know that you had better find new work when you get well. The boss is unlikely to hold your position open, and I would not count on getting a job there later, either," explained a maquila worker.[62] Some maquila employers consider illness a sign of poor performance and just grounds for dismissal. "We simply cannot afford to employ people who cannot stay healthy," said a personnel manager. "We run a factory, not a hospital. If a girl cannot stay healthy, we will hire another."[63]

Along with pregnancy and use of medical services, many maquila employers view education as an impediment to production. Tens of thousands of Guatemalans work full-time during the day and take classes, either high-school or college, in the evening. For most maquila workers, the long and unpredictable hours that production demands have usurped this traditional opportunity to further educational objectives. "It is impossible to do both [work at a maquila and attend evening classes]," explained one worker. "My manager will not give anyone permission to leave early for any reason. He claims if he gives one person permission, everyone will want to leave. Night school is out of the question."[64] Another worker, explaining his reason for leaving a factory, said, "When I took the job I was told I could go to school, but every time I asked permission, they begged me to stay the extra time. Then, one time I just left so I could get to class. The manager yelled at me not to bother coming back the next day."[65]

In response to such complaints, some employers contend that their workers' education is in the factory, not the classroom. "This is the first time many of these workers have been inside a factory. Everything they learn will be useful for the rest of their lives, from discipline to learning how to use a sewing machine. Most do not need to go to school, since it will not give them the practical experience of the factory life."[66]

Another major category of offenses that result in dismissal are broadly categorized as "disobedience." Nearly every employer described instances in which he discharged a worker because she was causing trouble, disobeyed a supervisor, or simply refused to work with the rest of the group. Management considers such workers nonconformists. From their actions and attitudes, employers identify them and let them go. An experienced Guatemalan owner explained this theory of management: "The most common reason for letting workers go is because they are not part of the group. We treat everyone as part of the group; those who lag behind, those who do not work overtime, those who do not pull together with the group, we replace with someone who is really interested in producing. You produce or you leave."[67]

Workers, for the most part, understand that conformity helps to ensure job security. Most simply accept their fate, follow the dictates of their superiors, and find solace in the common plight of their coworkers. "If you disagree with anything they say, you are fired," lamented a sixteen-year-old worker. "We sit, listen, and obey. Otherwise they point to the door and tell you to leave."[68] An eighteen-year-old worker, "Irma," was fired from a factory because management ordered her to resew a piece of garment she allegedly had stitched incorrectly. She was told to do this without pay. When Irma denied that she had made the original mistake, the supervisor grew flustered. Because Irma refused to back down, she was fired. "I had endured so much grief in that factory. I just couldn't allow them to blame me for something I hadn't done," she explained.[69]

Management Paternalism

More than once, labor inspectors and other observers compared the control the maquila management wields over its employees to involuntary servitude. Workers more often likened the relationship to that of a teacher or parent with a child. "They [the management] treat us like little children. We cannot do anything without their permission. You have to raise your hand, just like in grade school. I feel like I'm in school most of the time," complained a maquila worker.[70] The combination of excessive, rigid rules and practices and overbearing, abusive supervision subverts individual expression and behavior. Workers are expected to act like machines. Although it is more flagrant in Korean-managed shops,[71] nearly every worker articulated feelings of inferiority and humiliation arising from the treatment by managers and supervisors. One worker explained, "They treat us like small animals, not letting us do anything for ourselves and never trusting us."[72]

In fact, maquila employers often do consider their role comparable to that of a parent. One Guatemalan personnel manager at a factory outside Guatemala City said: "I have to educate people to use the toilet and teach them how to use it. When you see the result of your work you feel very comforted that you have done something for your people, and that is the feeling I have now, working in the maquila, doing something for my people. . . . In this job, I feel like a father, like a doctor, like a psychologist. My people are very simple; some of them went to school for only two or three years. And if they have a problem, they believe it is the end of the world. I have to let them know that their problem is not that big."[73] Another employer stated: "I am very tough with my people. When I started to work in the maquila, my character was so different from now. I used to work with people in an office; but when you start to work with these people, you need to change because they need to look at your face and see a very tough, strict person. They need to almost fear your face. This change in my demeanor comes from experience in this industry."[74]

At least one Guatemalan-managed factory practices a crude form of group punishment, in which everyone is penalized for the actions of a minority. In this shop, someone wrote graffiti on a bathroom wall. When no one took responsibility for the act, the manager forced all the workers to share the cost of cleaning the wall. In another incident, the cleaning boys allegedly left the water on in the bathroom overnight. Again, no one admitted guilt, so all the cleaning boys were made to pay for the repair of the water damage. "We try to teach them [the employees] to take responsibility for their actions," said the manager of this factory. "Some of them never went to school and have had poor parenting, so we try to instill these values that were never instilled."[75]

Owners and managers consistently expressed a view of workers as incapable of controlling their actions and even their lives. "The workers have many problems in their homes. Many do not have water or electricity and have a very low salary," said a manager. "Usually they have too many children. . . . Our aim is to make the workplace a better environment than the home. There is order here, something many are not accustomed to. It is not beautiful, but it is better than most of their homes."[76] The most prevalent example of this attitude was the view that young women workers "lack control over their reproductive capacity." One manager, mentioned above, was seriously considering holding birth control sessions to enhance production. Employers were puzzled over how to stop the rampant single motherhood and attributed it to lack of responsibility.

Employer views of unions provides another example of this paternalism. Besides dreading unionization, most employers believed that maquila workers are too uneducated and illiterate to manage a labor union competently and responsibly. "You have to understand that we are, unfortunately, an underdeveloped country," explained a Guatemalan manager. "And a lot of people do not know how to read or write. . . . My workers do not understand the philosophy of a union. It is not like the States. If they cannot read or write, how are they supposed to comprehend how a union works?"[77]

6

Unions and the Maquila: The Battle Against Impunity

Depending on the source, between 2 and 8 percent of the economically active population in Guatemala belong to functioning unions;[1] in the maquila industry, as of May 1992, there were no active unions. Since the first maquila factory opened in 1984, the government has issued more than two hundred export licenses for maquila operations; but it has granted legal status to only two unions in the industry: workers at Internacional Exportaciones S.A. (Inexport) and Pindu S.A. Today, these two unions exist only on paper. After management illegally discharged scores of union members at Inexport in the summer of 1989, the union collapsed when the government refused to reinstate the workers; and the workers at Pindu are without a factory, as the owners, in the summer of 1991, relocated overnight to an unknown location outside the country.

Despite the absence of official union membership, dozens of groups and hundreds of individual workers have tried to organize unions in maquila factories. None of these efforts, however, has succeeded. These failures do not imply a lack of will on the part of maquila workers to organize collectively, or widespread complacency with working conditions, or a docile work force. Rather, the fact that the maquila industry is not unionized demonstrates the government's inability or unwillingness to protect the workers' constitutionally guaranteed right to organize unions and to bargain collectively. Through both negligence and complicity, the government allows maquila employers to destroy worker attempts at self-determination with impunity.

Labor History, Guatemalan Style

Trade unionism has had an erratic and precarious existence in Guatemala. Until the 1940s, the most effective labor laws were forced labor laws. Then, with the "October Revolution" of 1944 and the ensuing decade of democracy, the government initiated seminal changes in working conditions and labor rights. The 1945 Constitution set the ideological foundations, recognizing the right to associate and organize. Two years later, the Labor Code (Code) was passed, which significantly enhanced these new rights. The Code set a minimum wage and maximum hours of work, restricted female and child labor, and established procedures for the formation and function of private- and public-sector unions. These laws, and a supportive administration, ignited the rapid growth of a formidable labor movement. By 1953, more than 100,000 workers, some 10 percent of the economically active population, belonged to 536 unions.[2]

But, like most other reforms of this period, the rights of workers were abolished immediately following the 1954 CIA-instigated coup. The post-coup government, propped up by the U.S. State Department, immediately issued Decree 21, dissolving all unions organized under the previous "Communist" regime. Brutal repression accompanied this legal annulment. Numerous unionists were jailed and executed; hundreds more fled into exile. In 1961, fifty unions representing slightly more than 23,000 workers, 2 percent of the economically active population, remained. Subsequent regimes, some more reform-minded than others, have refused, or been unable, to lift the cloud of repression. Several times during the 1960s what appeared to be political openings led to flurries of union activity, but the result each time was a violent narrowing of the political space. By 1973, the union movement counted only 1.6 percent of the economically active population.[3]

Membership and activity in unions rose significantly in the 1970s. Guatemala's emergence as the major industrial power of the region and the Catholic church's call to serve the poor were two key factors in this growth. Perpetuating this cycle of opening followed by violent closure, a wave of repression in the late 1970s and early 1980s squelched this surging union activity. In systematic fashion, hundreds of trade unionists and popular activists disappeared, were tortured, and killed. Dozens more fled into exile. This wave of repression devastated the movement, particularly in the industrial sector. In the aftermath, most unions existed on paper only.

One remarkable bright light that emerged from this swirl of destruction was the union at the Coca Cola bottling plant in Guatemala City. Beginning on February 17, 1984, union members occupied the plant for more than a year in protest against the company's announcement of its intention to close the factory in order to destroy the union.[4] After intense negotiating and substantial international pressure, the factory, with new owners and a union contract, reopened a year later. The militant union is considered the mainstay of the labor movement of the 1990s.

Guatemala's economic and political composition presents trade unionism with extremely difficult obstacles. Agriculture is the society's economic and political foundation, and the number of industrial workers are few: for more than two decades, only 15 percent of the economically active population have been employed in the industrial sector. Moreover, the two dominant political groups—the military and the landed oligarchy—have ruthlessly resisted trade unionism, generally regarding unions as subversive, "Communist" fronts for the guerrilla insurgency. Applying these labels, the army and the oligarchy, often in tandem, have relentlessly employed repressive measures against trade unionists. Faced with this deadly atmosphere, trade unionism somehow perseveres. In the words of one union leader, unions must "constantly overcome the psychological crisis terrorism continually generates."[5]

A New Era or Bitter Rerun?

The rebirth of democratic, civilian rule in 1986 seems, at least on paper, to have expanded the space for union activity. From the beginning of the Christian Democrat administration, officials pledged to protect and encourage the interests of workers and, in particular, trade unions. On her first day in office, the new labor minister, Catalina Sobernis, promised that trade union persecution had ended.[6] The 1986 Constitution abolished the thirty-year ban against union formation for public-sector workers. As concrete proof of this new era, the Christian Democrat Labor Ministry constantly pointed to the unprecedented spurt of union applications and recognition. In 1985, the year before the Christian Democrat victory, seven unions were legally recognized; in 1988, the third year of the regime, sixty-five unions had achieved legal status. The Labor Ministry published meticulous charts and graphs, boasting of this new freedom of association, which by government estimates reaches over 8 percent of the economically active population.

Despite this political opening and the ensuing resurgence of union strength, repression of unionists has continued. The persecution has been more selective but has served as an effective reminder of the past to workers and activists. A new tactic of terror has been to murder rank-and-file members of unions. Instead of threatening and assassinating high-profile union leaders, ordinary members are being selected for random execution, sending a warning to fellow members that no unionist is safe.[7] At least twenty unionists in 1991 were forced to leave as a consequence of death threats.[8] A prominent labor unionist remarked at the end of the Christian Democrat tenure: "Unions are indeed reactivating and new ones are forming but always keeping an eye over their shoulder and their passports in their pockets. No one knows for sure when this 'freedom' will expire.[9]

The Formation of Labor Unions under "Reasonable Labor Laws"

GEXPRONT's 1992 maquila promotion brochure for U.S. investors, "Guatemala: A Manufacturing Country by Tradition," lists on the first page Guatemala's most attractive qualities. Among characteristics such as proximity to the United States and an idyllic climate, "reasonable labor laws" are mentioned prominently.[10] When GEXPRONT officials were asked what this phrase meant, they called attention to the "clarity" and "completeness" of the Labor Code, which placed employers and workers on "equal footing."[11] The Labor Code, however, is anything but clear and complete.[12] Moreover, the phrase "reasonable labor laws" has obvious implications to potential investors. In the words of a labor federation official, "The Code is ridiculously biased in favor of employers."[13] A U.S. Department of Commerce document intended to inform potential investors modestly confirmed the official's analysis, "On the whole, labor laws favor employers over their employees."[14]

Both the Labor Code and the 1986 Constitution protect the right to associate, bargain collectively, and strike so long as all legal requirements are fulfilled.[15] It is the opinion of most union officials that these "requirements" more resemble burdensome obstacles than legal safeguards. As James Goldston points out: "Perhaps the greatest obstacle to union formation is the complexity of the law itself. In general, Guatemalan unions must contend with an excessive degree of government supervision in the stages of formation, recognition, and operation."[16] After a union fulfills the legal obligations, both the labor minister and the president must formally recognize the union's legal right to represent and collectively bargain for its workers. Before obtaining these signatures, the group of workers, however, are bereft of meaningful legal protections.

The process to achieve legal recognition is theoretically straightforward. Workers can initiate a union with the formation of an ad hoc committee of three to six persons. This committee acts as the organizing base and is protected from reprisals through an injunction, called an *emplazamiento*, which prohibits the employer from altering labor relations without acquiring approval from the judge. In particular, the injunction requires the employer to refrain from retaliatory measures, including dismissal for any reason, unless authorized by the court. The committee outgrows its function once the next stage, formation and election of officials, is reached. The Code mandates that at least twenty workers are necessary to form a union and that this body must elect an executive committee as its first step.[17] At that point, the union submits to the government an application and list of members for legal recognition. Then begins the obstacle course.

Although legally limited to sixty days,[18] the actual process to obtain legal recognition often drags on for years. The primary cause of the excessive delays, from all accounts, is the Labor Ministry's obsession with detail, including grammar and the number of lines on a page. Ministry officials are infamous for returning union submissions for legal recognition for revision and resubmission because of minute mistakes in one of the 214 required steps.[19] Union members awaiting this critical imprimatur expressed skepticism about the government's motivation: "What does a misspelled word have to do with granting legal recognition? It is clear with which side the Labor Ministry sympathizes."[20]

For the two unions in the maquila sector, Inexport and Pindu, legal recognition was granted twenty-seven and twenty-six months, respectively, after the process was initiated. Moreover, with only a handful of labor-side lawyers left in practice (most have been either murdered, or exiled, or intimidated into leaving the practice), many prospective and functioning unions are unable to seek and gain access to the advice they need to comply with the Code.

In contrast to the Labor Ministry's overbearing supervision of the process of union formation and recognition, their vigilance in regulating and sanctioning employer practices during union organizing drives is severely deficient. Guatemalan labor laws and their selective enforcement offer a paradise to the potential investor seeking to avoid intrusive government supervision of the operation of his business. "The Labor Ministry is like a little mosquito," confided a Guatemalan owner. "Sometimes a pest, but easy to swat away. We rarely worry about serious opposition from them. It is the workers themselves who create the problems."[21]

For workers and unions, hope in the present Code and its enforcement is slight. In 1990, the Labor Ministry expressed optimism about a newly composed Labor Code, but, like a dozen before it, it stalled in Congress.[22] Although not the sole cause, the lack of legal guarantees and protection has virtually ensured that unions do not exist in maquila shops. Thus, the combination of too few inspectors responsible for applying a toothless, complex, and largely irrelevant Code would only appear "reasonable" to those more interested in maximizing short-term profits than protecting labor rights.

Labor's Paralyzing Fear of Unionism

Most interviewed workers indicated a substantial interest in forming and belonging to a union at their factory. "Sure we want a union. We will take anything that will improve our situation," said a desperate maquila worker.[23] Workers equated the presence of a union with job security, increased wages, benefits, and more dignified treatment. However, these same workers believed that forming a union at their factory was an impossible feat. In fact, workers almost unanimously feared that serious attempts to organize would result, at the very least, in dismissal, if not physical violence. A pervasive belief that the employer would surely suspend or terminate production if a union should take root further overshadows hopes of collective victory. "For me it is a difficult choice," lamented a worker. "If we could organize together we might win some real benefits, but the consequences are so grave. Even if all that happens is that we are fired, the present economic situation makes this an especially terrible event."[24]

Fear of job loss and physical injury paralyzes the transformation of any thoughts of organizing into concrete action. Workers in every sector of the economy fear reprisals for even minimal participation in a union campaign. In the maquila sector, this fear is compounded by the transient nature of the industry. With only machines to transport, factories can and will relocate if deemed necessary. Maquila workers well understand the consequences of this possibility. An official at the IGT described the situation: "In the maquila industry, when workers have tried to organize, they have faced such huge problems, they have gone through so much and often lost their place of work. A lot of workers choose not to form unions because they see a history of failed attempts and fear losing their source of income."[25] "The companies will often say if you want to form a union, we will leave," a union federation official added. "This is a direct threat to the worker who has economic needs. Out of fear, she opts to live with the problems of work because she wants to bring food to her home. Bare subsistence is better than nothing."[26] This fear expands beyond simply the loss of a job to the possible loss of life. As employers are eager to demonstrate, many unionists suffer grave persecution, even death. "We are so filled with fear of what terrible fate may happen that we cannot even think about organizing," explained an operator.[27]

Management's Ruthless Fear of Unionism

Employers fear unions in their factories more than any other man-made calamity, including coups d'état. Better than half of all managers answered that the "worst event or experience" they could imagine would be the presence of a union in their factory. When asked about whether his factory had a union, one manager in a large factory exclaimed: "No, thank God! At the moment our people are not educated enough to have labor unions. I have heard of some companies that have suffered the fate of labor unions, and they immediately go broke. It is not like other countries, when they have labor unions, they show that they want to work. They ask for a raise but they will work for it. Here, they ask for a salary increase and they want to work less. . . . I could work with a labor union because I understand what they are about, but not one from this country."[28] Harboring similar sentiments, most owners are willing to take extreme measures to prevent surges in union activism in their shops.

Owners argue that their fear of unions is rational. Unions, they assert, especially Guatemalan ones, disrupt production and shift control to the workers. "This industry is very delicate and intolerant of disruptions," said Carlos Arias of Cardiz S.A. and a U.S. university graduate. "Unions by their nature disrupt and, hence, must be avoided."[29] The garment-assembly industry, as Arias notes, is a fragile, time-sensitive business; a contract not completed on time can jeopardize future business. Factories with a reputation for missing shipping deadlines generally have difficulty surviving. For management, all disruptions are therefore insupportable. Since unions have the propensity to upset industry through strikes and work stoppages, their presence is a genuine threat to production and long-term stability. "They [unions] strike. They stop work. They refuse to work overtime," explained an exasperated young Guatemalan owner on the prospects of a union in his shop. "We ask, 'Do you want to work tonight?' 'No, we decided we do not want to work tonight,' they say. This attitude can kill production, and production is your income. If a union showed up in the factory, it would be our worst nightmare."[30]

In several highly publicized instances, employers have reacted to the rise of union activity with closure and relocation. Most famous of all, the "soap opera" departure of Transcontinentales S.A. erected a wall of fear between U.S. investors and the Guatemalan maquila industry. Likewise, stories of the "labor troubles" at Inexport have circulated among owners and managers and helped convince many that a union inevitably leads to a factory shutdown. A union means trouble and, if not eradicated immediately, financial ruin. One owner of a sizable factory elaborated: "The sad fact is that unions destroy factories. Look around, how many maquila factories have unions? When unions arrive, they bring industrial cancer."[31]

Driven by this dread, companies have adopted and practice two basic union-prevention strategies. A handful of maquila companies implement a "pacification" approach. The philosophy of this strategy is that a union-free shop is indicative of a contented work force, and that only unhappy workers start unions. "The key is to keep them happy, so that they do not have anything to complain about," explained a proponent of this approach.[32] The vast majority of employers, in contrast, use an overtly hostile approach to squelch unionism. These owners have few pretensions to being benevolent employers. They acknowledge their goal of profit and seek to maximize it by whatever means necessary.

These two managerial styles, however, are not mutually exclusive. In fact, most of the pacification camp likely will—and at least one has—if pushed far enough, resort to cruder methods of labor control. Likewise, the managers who practice the second approach are unlikely to conceive of themselves as performing heinous acts, believing that their practices are in the best interests of the factory, and ultimately the workers. Together, these models have helped to impede unionization in Guatemala's maquila industry.

The Pacification Approach: Keep Them Happy

The more sophisticated approach to union prevention is the pacification, or as one manager described it, the "as long as they're happy, they won't revolt" theory of management. The idea is as follows. Workers only feel the need to form a union when they are dissatisfied with the conditions of their employment. Unions thus develop exclusively in workplaces where management fails to provide the minimal benefits for employees. The solution lies not in hostile actions and attitudes but in placating ones. In practice, pacification involves slightly better than average material benefits, positive employer-worker relations, and strong identification with the company. Alvaro Colom, known as the "Godfather of the Maquila Industry" for his experience and knowledge, is a vigorous proponent of this view: "A union is the first effect of very, very poor personnel management. If a company has a union, it is because it does not have the proper attitude toward its workers. There is absolutely no reason for a union to form if the factory is run correctly. . . . If you do not pay on time or pay too little, you will provoke a union. I do not have bad feelings toward unions, but I feel one is not necessary if you have good relations."[33]

The factories in which this management strategy is implemented are generally larger, more capital-intensive, and strongly linked to the U.S. business community. Their managers are well-educated and enjoy extensive contact with U.S. TNCs. Pictures of these well-lit, modern plants fill trade journals and promotional brochures; the pride of AID and GEXPRONT, they are also the factories to which these promotional agencies direct inquisitive journalists for interviews and tours. Workers are often paid more than average and enjoy other benefits unknown to most workers, such as voluntary overtime and liberty of movement. For example, a seventeen-year-old male worker at such a factory reported that his manager gave him and other young workers permission to attend evening university classes, though this meant missing overtime. His girlfriend, employed at a more "typical" shop, jealously responded, "My boss says 'If you leave early, you leave for good.'"[34] Erick Sterkel, the general manager of Phillips-Van Heusen's (PVH) main factory, Camisas Modernas S.A., boasted that his factory treated its "associates" (it is PVH's policy to call its employees "associates") so well that the plant had not lost a single operator in three consecutive months.[35] Considering that the average operator turnover rate is between 10 and 30 percent a month in most factories, this statistic—if true—is extraordinary.

The Perfect Balance

These more sophisticated employers realize that it is not necessary to squeeze every dime out of their employees in order to make a substantial profit. They are willing to expend extra money for worker amenities in exchange for a union-free environment. Owners and managers openly admit that unions are defeated through money and bonuses. "Our workers are happy. They are paid well. This is the one and only way to keep a union out of the factory," asserted a Guatemalan owner.[36] Union prevention, then, need not mean overt intimidation and suppression of the work force. "Unfortunately, one way to prevent unions is to have benign personnel practices," admitted the U.S. Embassy labor attaché. "Providing benefits to prevent unions from forming is common in Guatemala industries."[37]

This style of management is most effective because it is so much more sophisticated than the crude, abusive strategy employed at most worksites. A maquila worker explained, "Workers who expect to be treated as animals are relieved to receive more humane treatment."[38] Slightly better than average treatment tends to work to the employer's advantage since workers' allegiance to the company grows, so they stay longer and become more efficient and productive.

This management theory, of course, assumes that "the happier the worker, the less likely she is to rebel." These managers never assent to the possibility that workers may want more than mere material benefits, that they might desire more control over their destiny, especially a part in the decision making in the plant. Commenting on this sophistication, a union official said: "These factories, usually transnationals, have a different path, not as brutal but just as effective. They partially subvert the most fundamental cry of Guatemalan workers for more bread. But they are unlikely to give any real control."[39]

Extreme paternalism frequently results from this approach, as managers assume they know what is best for their less educated employees. The distinction between meeting the needs of workers with dignity and treating them as helpless, ignorant children is fine and often breached. In one illustrative instance, an owner-manager of Confecciones Iberoamericanas S.A., Ilsa Husmann, considered herself the mother/caretaker of her workers: "I've been married for over nineteen years without children, and I identify with these people. They are the children I never had."[40] Of this University of California graduate, a former worker said, "She yelled and screamed a lot and called us 'girls,' but at least she didn't hit us."[41] In addition, these factories are renowned for dispensing patronizing bonuses for the completion of mundane tasks. Workers, for example, who remember to punch in their cards each morning for two consecutive weeks might receive Q10 (US$2). The goal of these rewards is allegedly to increase reliability and responsibility. However, the real effect is to control every movement of the employees.

These managers also portray Guatemalan workers as incapable of forming a "U.S.-style union." By "U.S.-style" they mean "a professional, nonviolent union willing to compromise and negotiate while truly representing the interests of the workers." The most important qualification for forming and running a union, according to these owners, is education. And since most maquila workers are of school age, they are de facto incompetent. Owners point to the lack of education and literacy of the workers as a clear sign that the country is not yet ready for trade unionism. "How can a worker with a sixth-grade education lead a group of workers?" asked a personnel manager.[42]

Phillips-Van Heusen: Pacification Gone Awry

Since this pacification approach has, thus far, successfully prevented the formation of unions, the question of what these "benevolent" employers would do if an organizing campaign started has yet to be adequately addressed. Would they respond with increased benevolence, placating employee concerns and thereby making the union appear unnecessary? Would they respond with the traditional ruthless, union-busting tactics? Or would these firms accept the wishes of their employees and accede to their demands? Skeptical, a labor-side lawyer asked pointedly: "They know that a few cents extra will not sink the factory. Who could complain of this generosity? But ask them what they will do if workers begin talking about a union. What will they do then?"[43]

The case of Camisas Modernas S.A. I and II, PVH's factories and the jewels of the Guatemalan maquila industry, strongly suggests an answer to these questions. Officials at the U.S. Embassy have praised PVH's management as "a true leader in labor relations."[44] And PVH considers itself "a model company, if not the model company, in Guatemala in terms of pay, benefits, and working conditions."[45] Lawrence Phillips, the CEO of PVH, has visited the factory and met with every one of the company's "associates." On the basis of this intimate knowledge, Phillips stated, "Our contributions toward the uplifting of the standard of living of our associates in Guatemala are significant."[46]

Despite this benevolence, on at least two separate occasions, in late 1989 and early 1991, workers at Camisas Modernas solicited assistance from a labor federation, the AFL–CIO-affiliated Confederation of Guatemalan Trade-Union Unity (CUSG), to stage an organizing campaign. Three factors seem to have contributed to the eruption of dissent and unionism in the factory. First, both union campaigns reacted to unannounced drops in piece-rate prices. Workers, accustomed to earning a set amount, were outraged at the unilateral decrease in prices. A worker stated, "One day we were making good money, and the next day they tell us there has been a cut in pay. We simply will not put up with it!"[47] Second, the above-average conditions at Camisas Modernas, while virtually eliminating turnover, allowed workers to form strong and lasting bonds. Workers became friends, not simply persons who coincidentally sat beside one another for eight hours a day. In most maquila factories, workers come and go so quickly that worker solidarity never forms. In fact, in Korean factories, the policy of high turnover appears to be a designed effort to deter organizing. In contrast, PVH unwittingly appears to have created an atmosphere where workers form stronger loyalty to one another than to the factory.

Finally, the workers expressed a growing resentment of the paternalistic and often dehumanizing practices of management. "They do not treat us like persons, and we simply are tired of this," said a union leader in the factory.[48] Management systematically maintained total control over workers. The factory sought to regulate their movements, their arrival and departure, even their access to bathrooms. While clean and functioning, the bathrooms were accessible only if a worker could persuade a supervisor to open them. One worker summed up the growing frustration: "We are adults, not children. We can decide when we want to use the bathroom. We have worked there long enough to know the system. But they continue to tell it to us over and over."[49]

In 1989, when workers first showed signs of unionizing, management responded with increased benevolence, providing them with a "company store" and liberalizing its loan policy. This reaction, combined with the discharge of union supporters, defeated the union drive. In March 1991, the workers touched off the second union campaign. This time management's tone and reaction were different. CEO Phillips asserted that his associates, who in conversations told him they were satisfied with their treatment and compensation, did not instigate the union campaign; rather, without substantiation, he accused U.S. unions, vengeful for their failed attempts to unionize U.S. factories, of initiating the campaign.[50] PVH officials, proud of their union-free shops in the United States, declared that they would do everything legally possible to prevent the union.

Management personnel at the Guatemalan factory either did not hear this message from above, ignored it, or received alternate instructions, because their reaction has been consistently illegal and violent. The very day the factory was served with an *emplazamiento*, Erick Sterkel—the same manager who bragged of the strong loyalty of his associates—allegedly offered the leaders of the organizing drive severance pay and an additional $2,000 bribe to resign from the factory.[51] Although the leaders rejected this offer, dozens of colleagues later accepted similar sums to resign from the organizing drive.[52] In violation of the *emplazamiento*, management shifted union members to new and more difficult tasks in an effort to reduce productivity and pay and immediately suspended several services, including the cafeteria and the loan program. The company formed its own union and a *Solidarismo* association (see below). Supervisors began to intimidate the workers with threats that the factory would shut down if the union were victorious. At least one of PVH's personnel managers issued death threats, claiming that "everyone who is involved in the unions is going to die" and calling the union a guerrilla front.[53] In Guatemala, accusations of guerrilla activity are extremely perilous and often mark the accused for assassination.

On September 8, 1991, a death threat was almost realized when unknown assailants shot Aura Marina Rodriquez, one of the three top union leaders, in the head on her way home from work. Rodriquez survived the attack, as the bullet grazed her temple and severed part of her ear. A day or two later, unknown men, pretending to be from the factory, came to her house and asked where she was. Fearing further violence, Rodriquez then fled to a hidden location. Although Larry Phillips sent the workers a letter deploring the incident and disclaiming any responsibility for it, Rodriquez and her frightened coworkers are certain the incident was meant to deter formation of the union.

Unfazed by this violent and illegal onslaught, workers have persevered. Another union organizing drive began in the second PVH factory. By September, CUSG claimed more than 150 members in both PVH plants and submitted the documentation for legal recognition to the Labor Ministry in late March 1991. Despite the sixty-day limit for certification and the union's and international human rights groups' vigilant pressure to comply with the legal limit, as of May 1992 the president and labor minister had not accepted the application. CEO Larry Phillips, meanwhile, continues to insist that his associates do not want a union.

The Violent Rejection Approach

"In Guatemala, there is a violent rejection of unions in most workplaces and especially the maquila industry," claimed a union organizer at UNSITRAGUA.[54] Like PVH, most employers are openly hostile toward real and suspected union agitators. "The day a union arrives at this factory, I will leave, because I want to survive," announced a Guatemalan personnel manager in a large Korean factory.[55] Armed with this uncompromising determination, many managers are willing to implement a wide range of tactics, including dismissal, threats and violence, flagrant disobedience and manipulation of the law and its instrumentalities, and, if necessary, relocation of the factory.

"Right or wrong, you get rid of those you think might start a union. This is one thing an employer watches for here. This is probably not officially permitted but, let's face it, it is done all the time," candidly admitted Brent Holmes, a North American maquila owner.[56] The dismissal of workers thought to be organizing is easily the most common and effective managerial tactic. In fact, workers who are merely suspected of union propensities are routinely discharged with no legal recourse. Employers are more apt to throw a wide net for possible conspirators, which results in the discharge of numerous "innocent" workers. Hundreds, if not thousands, of workers are dismissed each year from maquila factories because of suspected or real intentions to organize.

The subinspector of the IGT confirmed the practice of dismissing suspected unionists: "What happens is that as soon as the employer suspects they [workers] are attempting to organize a union, it is certain management will find a reason to fire them."[57] Moreover, the law does not offer protection from these retaliatory discharges for union activity. Limited official protection for union organizers begins only at the stage when workers form an ad hoc committee and at the same time obtain an *emplazamiento* from the Labor Court. Before this stage, employers are free to dismiss workers at will.

The pervasiveness of discharging suspected union activists is attested to in sample interviews with owners and managers. Of the fifty-four interviewed management representatives, twenty-five admitted to at least once dismissing workers whom they had reason to believe were staging a union campaign. Many were candid. A Guatemalan manager of a factory in Zone 12, for example, told of a recent incident in which "three 'troublemakers' began to spread union rhetoric." These workers were immediately "conciliated," explained the manager, as he made a scissors-like motion with two fingers.[58] Another manager described how his cousins, who worked in the factory as administrators, had overheard some workers plotting a union campaign. "They were gone the next day, and I would do it again in a second," he concluded.[59] "I fire all the troublemakers," referring to those "rebellious, nonconformist people you think might start a union," said another owner.[60]

Potential agitators are frequently screened at the outset. Most job applications ask about prior union affiliation. An affirmative response elicits automatic rejection. Moreover, more experienced personnel managers claim to possess the special gift of filtering out potential activists. "If a worker consistently voices complaints about conditions and wages, and if she draws a crowd at lunchtime, her time is limited in this factory," explained one such manager.[61] In addition, blacklisting of union members is commonplace. Workers who belonged to the union at Inexport reported numerous instances of dismissal at other factories once management learned of their previous union activities.

Beyond the ability of individual managers to uncover subversive employees, many attempts at unionization are thwarted because of employer "spies" on the shop floor. Workers seeking the favor of a manager find it easy to denounce fellow employees for a special perk, most often a few quetzals. An employer describes one such experience:

> I do not have to worry about organizing in this factory because my workers don't want it. Last year, a girl who was only sixteen had the mentality of creating problems and she started here. She would go to the bathroom and start telling the people that "they are not paying us well. I think we should stop working and complain." A lot of people know about unions and they do not like it because of what has happened in other factories. So right away they told me, and I confronted her. . . . "I am sorry but this factory has been very clean and you will have to go." She said, "Well, I will take it to the Labor Ministry.". . . I told her to go. I paid the severance pay. I did not want any problems, and you know the people themselves did not want it. They were the ones who came and told me.[62]

This network of informants makes even the mention of the word *union* anywhere in the factory potential cause for dismissal. A discussion of working conditions with a particularly ambitious, ruthless, or desperate fellow employee may lead to termination.

Post-*Emplazamiento* Tactics

A different scenario normally exists once workers have submitted their intention to organize a union to the labor court, which then immediately issues an *emplazamiento*. Workers normally take a day off from work without notifying their employer to present their petition to the court. The IGT then sends an inspector to serve the *emplazamiento* on the employer, forbidding him from altering the employment relationship. From that moment forward, the employer risks legal consequences for reprisals against employees. In many cases this order is ignored, if not flagrantly violated with impunity.

In the maquila industry, between the time the first factory opened in 1984 and May 1992, at least seventeen groups of workers from thirteen different factories have managed to solicit and successfully obtain an *emplazamiento* from the courts.[63] Of these seventeen, only two groups, those at the Pindu and Inexport factories, have been allowed to mature into legally recognized, functioning collective agents. For a host of reasons, the other fifteen ad hoc committees failed to develop into official unions with juridical personality. In most of the cases, the attempts were stifled within a few weeks after procurement of the *emplazamiento*.

Surprisingly, most maquila employers have taken the *emplazamiento* seriously enough not to violate it egregiously with outright dismissal of the leaders. Instead, they have illegally responded to *emplazamientos* with a combination of three basic tactics. First, on the shop floor management applies relentless pressure both on leaders to abandon their task and on other workers to refrain from joining. To achieve this end, bribes, threats, isolation, and intimidation are the most commonly used tools. Second, employers wage a war in the courts, manipulating the law and delaying the proceedings. As a last resort, if management believes a union is indefatigable, relocation of the factory may be the only viable alternative to a union shop. A number of factories, when confronted with a strong union campaign, have fled, leaving workers without means and hope.

At the outset of most organizing drives, workers who want to unionize seek the advice of one of the major federations on legal and other practical matters. During this period, experienced union officials brief workers extensively about the potential risks of union-organizing drives. They are told that the decision to seek an injunction against the factory is a dangerous path, that the employer will oppose their intentions with all his might, and that psychological and physical warfare will likely follow. Despite these strong forewarnings, workers who become leaders of the drive are understandably often unable to withstand the threats and enticements of employers. As a result, the majority of organizing campaigns falter in the early stages.

In what has become an automatic response to an *emplazamiento*, employers, as in the case of PVH, immediately offer significant amounts of money in return for a resignation. This makes sense. Employers know that sewing-machine operators who attempt to organize have wage increases as a main objective. Thus, a well-placed bribe may fulfill the worker's need, thereby temporarily removing part of the motivation for unionization. Commenting on the troubles at PVH's factories, a North American manufacturer's representative correctly predicted: "They will do as everyone else does. They will bribe and be rid of the sympathizers in short fashion. It always works. 'How much?' is the only unknown."[64] The sums and perks that management has offered union leaders to resign are astounding. At Inexport, workers report that management offered each member of the executive committee $10,000 to renounce her position and affiliation with the union.[65] In that case, the leaders rejected the offer, but in other situations workers have succumbed to the temptation.

A Bribe in Action: Mi Kwang S.A.

Bribes often wear down a group of workers. If one leader accepts, the others feel pressured and even more isolated. If another capitulates, the core is shattered, unless other workers step forward and seize the leadership. The case of the workers in Mi Kwang S.A., a Korean firm located in Villa Nueva, a modern industrial center outside of the capital, displays the capacity of monetary inducements to debilitate a union campaign.

Several workers sought the counsel of a labor federation to organize a union and soon after obtained an *emplazamiento* against the factory.[66] When notified of this legal order, the Korean management of Mi Kwang was startled and alarmed, taking immediate reprisals against the workers named in the injunction. A federation lawyer described their antics afterward as almost "childish." "It was as if someone had just stolen their favorite toy," he continued.[67] Their complete unfamiliarity with the law (the factory had been operating less than six months) and lack of contacts in the country seemed to cause a frenzied response to the insurgency. The managers singled out members of the ad hoc committee and interrogated them about the prudence of their chosen path. These workers contacted the IGT and the labor federation for assistance. Representatives from both arrived the next day and found a confused manager, pleading for relief from the uprising.

Then the management discovered the potency of the bribe, and a sudden tranquility overcame them. A leader of the campaign reported to federation officials that a fellow organizer had accepted payment and resigned from the factory. Two days later, a second call told of another bribe and the subsequent resignation of another leader. The federation contacted the factory, and this time a composed manager asked what amount the federation officials desired to withdraw their support. Two weeks later, unable to reach the remaining union leader, federation lawyers contacted the manager again. He explained that all those listed on the *emplazamiento* had resigned and that there was no need to speak further. A member of the federation's legal department involved in the situation said of the whirlwind change of allegiance:

> The workers arrived in our offices with an earnest desire to reform their factory. They wanted justice in the workplace. But they fell like dominoes, one after the other. . . . What can we do in such a situation? The economic power lies with the owner. We can advise workers not to accept bribes, that they will betray their cause and companions. However, when thousands of quetzals are placed in front of them and the only obstacle to putting them in their pockets is a signature, what good is our advice? People have to eat.[68]

The personnel manager of Mi Kwang presented a different account of the event. "It is true we had a problem with a union," he explained. "A few workers wanted to put a union in the factory. We explained to them that a union means no production, and no production means no salary. We would have to close the factory. These workers resigned and left."[69]

Threats and Intimidation

If bribes fail to induce resignation, management usually subjects workers to a variety of threats and intimidation. In every case of a union drive in a maquila factory, management, on company time, has recounted to its employees the tragic history of factories damaged irreparably by unions—for instance, Transcontinentales. The same fate, they assert, will befall their factory if a union is allowed to develop. Workers recognize an element of truth in this argument, aware that the lightweight contents of the factory could be moved overnight to a new location and that the management, if pushed, may react in just this manner. The threatened loss of income, for many employees, is a sufficient deterrent.

Employers also inundate workers with propaganda describing the tragic plight of unionists while subtly (or not so subtly, as in the case of PVH) informing them of the ultimate reprisal which management, or right-wing death squads, may be ready to take. The aim, of course, is to intimidate both leaders and other workers into resisting union formation. One employer posted a photo of mutilated torture victims with the caption, "Look what happens to unionists."[70] Most employers are less blunt in their approach, but just as effective.

In one poignant example of the effect of this intimidation, four workers at Booco

S.A., a Korean-owned factory in Zone 12, obtained an *emplazamiento* in May 1990. Management immediately began a campaign to persuade workers to oppose the union drive.[71] In an unprecedented event, according to workers, the manager invited groups of employees to lunch and explained: "Look at the unions in this country. See what problems they have. If you continue to build the union, you will end up on the side of the road, dead, like the rest of the unionists. For your own good, for the good of your families, for the good of your children, please reject this union!"[72] The committee gradually weakened as they saw their support dwindle. By the end of two months all the committee members had resigned.

The force of Booco management's campaign can be fully appreciated when the inhumane conditions of the factory are examined. Not only were wages often less than the government minimum and paid irregularly, but, according to a former secretary at the factory who was not involved in the union campaign, the workers were subjected to humiliating treatment. Verbal and physical rebukes were common, and incidents of sexual abuse committed by Korean supervisors had reached an especially troubling level.[73] Even though workers endured these horrid conditions for six days a week, the management was still able to persuade them that a union was not the solution and might in the end compound their suffering.

A step beyond mere descriptions are threats of physical harm. These tactics seem necessary only when a union already has a stronghold in the factory. Workers at Inexport, Pindu, PVH, and other factories gave detailed accounts of death threats.[74] The union leader at PVH so far has been the only victim of an assassination attempt, but the potential of death is real enough to impede the goals of all but the most courageous activists.

As another technique of intimidation, managers also stigmatize and isolate the leaders of the organizing campaign. The goal again is to force these workers to resign, thereby crippling hopes for a union. At Inexport, during the first day of the campaign the leaders were made to stand in the middle of a circle while the North American owner screamed: "These people are killing our factory! We will not tolerate this, will we?"[75] These workers were also placed at machines in the corner of the factory and not given any work. They sat idly in a sequestered area for weeks, struggling to combat isolation and boredom. In another factory, the leaders were daily switched among different machines in order to frustrate them into capitulating.

Relocation: A Threat Realized

Motivated at least in part by a union-organizing drive, at least five maquila owners have either transferred their installations from Guatemala completely or relocated within the country.[76] Certainly the relatively low capital investment necessary to start a garment-assembly shop eases the burden of relocation, but, nevertheless, a decision to suspend business and transfer several hundred machines and pieces of furniture is rarely taken lightly.

As described in Chapter 3, the most infamous case of relocation caused by unionization is the runaway factory called Transcontinentales that fled overnight in 1987.[77] Play Knits, a U.S. firm, opened this factory of six hundred workers as one of the first Guatemalan maquilas in 1984. It was also the first to shut down. In 1987 workers, at the urging of a vengeful ex-manager, initiated a union drive. Wielding his political influence, this ex-employee retaliated against the factory with a flurry of legal claims and the instigation of a union.

Fearful of the union and this ex-employee, the company chose to flee. Filipino supervisors and Israeli and U.S. managers worked round the clock during a "paid vacation" given to the workers in honor of Yom Kippur. When workers arrived on Monday morning after the four-day holiday, they found a nearly empty factory guarded by a private security force. A year later in New York City, the union, assisted by U.S. labor activists, negotiated a settlement for $20,000 with the parent company, Play Knits, to compensate for unpaid wages and separation pay. The agreement was reached on the condition that this payment was not to be interpreted as an acknowledgment of responsibility, but rather as simply a gesture of "goodwill" on the part of Play Knits. The effect on U.S. direct investment in the maquila industry was paralyzing, as U.S. investors subsequently avoided the industry, considering it too risky.

In Guatemala, this unexpected exodus reverberated in two significant ways. First, the government was left embarrassed and determined not to let the event be repeated. Second, the case became the paradigmatic example of the effects of unionization on employment in the maquila sector. Owners could always recite the Transcontinentales tale to employees as a likely consequence of their organizing efforts.

Since the Transcontinentales incident, four more factories have elected to close their doors rather than permit a union to enter. Lockouts and relocations, as mentioned above, are illegal so long as an *emplazamiento* is in force. However, employers do as they wish in terms of location and duration of operation. Sometimes shutdowns do not result in relocation but in temporary stoppage of production, essentially equivalent to a lockout. The employer claims there is no more work because prime materials have not and will not arrive for an unknown period of time. Although the enjoined factory is legally prohibited from changing the labor relationship without authority from the courts, there is little that workers can do once the shop closes other than wait for it to reopen. And by that time it is likely these workers will have found new employment, and hence be ineligible to be rehired.

Come Back in a Few Weeks: Diseños Panamericanos S.A.

At Diseños Panamericanos S.A. several workers formed an ad hoc committee and obtained an *emplazamiento* in August 1988, largely in protest of the management's proposed merger of the shop with another located eight miles away. The workers were also seeking to remedy the unsafe conditions and illegal practices of the factory, which included inadequate bathroom facilities, faulty electrical wiring, and nonpayment of social security and health insurance. It was soon discovered that the factory with which the enjoined shop was to merge was full to capacity, that "there was not one space open for new workers."[78] Employees realized that the transfer of the factory would effectively eliminate their jobs. The IGT visited management and reassured workers that a relocation would be illegal so long as the *emplazamiento* was in force. Nonetheless, on September 4, when the workers arrived, they were shocked to find the installations locked. A sign posted on the door stated:

> To workers and management. . . . From September 4, 1989, to September 16, 1989, the company will be giving a paid vacation to all employees. . . . During this time, the company will repair electrical and plumbing problems and clean the factory, especially the bathrooms. The company has decided to do this in order to reward workers for their dedicated service and to provide them with better working conditions in the future.
>
> —The Secretary.

Faced with the sealed factory, the workers immediately contacted the IGT, which documented the incident. Despite the promises of the posted note, no repairs were made, and the factory never reopened. The workers were suddenly without employment. Moreover, the employer never compensated workers for the promised vacation period or gave them severance pay. The workers filed a motion with the Labor Court to enjoin management from transferring the machinery, in the ultimate hope of selling it and using the proceeds as separation pay. As of March 1991, the Labor Court had not ruled on this motion. Union officials were not optimistic that requisition or sale of the equipment would occur in the near future. The factory meanwhile continues to operate, but in the new location.

Three Strikes and You're Out: Dong San S.A.

Two months after Diseños Panamericanos, another factory, Dong San S.A., a large, four-hundred-machine plant, transferred its operation in Guatemala to avert imminent unionization. Located in ZOLIC, the state-administered free-trade zone on the Pacific Coast, and owned by the Korean multinational Sam Phoong, Dong San employed Korean personnel in most of the managerial and supervisory positions. The factory began operations in January of 1987 and soon earned a reputation for insufferable working conditions, particularly the brutality of the administration; even the general manager of the free-trade zone compared the owners to "slave drivers."[79]

Workers reported numerous incidents of beatings for minor errors resulting in bruises and contusions. "The management treated us horribly," said a former operator. "If you made a piece wrong, they would throw it in your face, screaming 'bad, bad.' The workers cried a lot."[80] For more serious acts, such as marring a garment, workers were placed outdoors in the hot sun for several hours without cover or water. The ex-employee described another common punishment: "At times the personnel manager would lift boxes and throw them at us or dump the cloth over workers who were talking." Employees worked until nine or ten at night and were rarely paid for this time. "It was a miracle if we left at 5 P.M.," she said.[81] The factory, constructed of corrugated sheet metal, relied on two large doors for ventilation. In the tropical climate the result was an extraordinarily hot factory. In short, the conditions in the factory were abominable.

Confronted with these conditions, workers began to organize. On two occasions, workers formed an ad hoc committee and began the process of unionization. The company easily defeated the first attempt, which occurred in November 1988. The pressure and intimidation exerted by the factory, including a prohibition on talking even during breaks, pathetically inadequate support from the local IGT office, and incompetent legal advice caused the drive to crumble within two months. The injunction was lifted and the organizers summarily fired. In January 1989, another group of workers formed an ad hoc committee, enjoined the factory, and demanded the same changes in conditions and practices. This action broke the back of the factory.

Management elected to shut down the factory and relocate to Guatemala City rather than combat another union drive. One afternoon the owner announced to the workers that, starting the following day, "there would be no more work." Because of "questions of climate," the Korean ambassador would later claim, the factory packed up and moved to Zone 13 in the capital, where it reopened under the same name and management a week after the second injunction. Meanwhile, most of the workers received only partial severance pay. A sixteen-year-old member of the first ad hoc committee told of her dismay: "Always during the campaign, our goal was never to close down or harm the factory. We simply wanted them to treat us better. The only thing we were struggling for was our rights as workers, to be treated better, to work only eight hours a day without the obligation of overtime. Instead, we lost our jobs."[82]

Failure of the Legal System

In every case where a union drive fails, deficiencies in the legal system are abundant. Whether it be a corrupt labor inspector or judge, or a toothless or excessively detailed legal process, inadequate protection and enforcement of the freedom to associate constantly stifle workers' efforts. "Numerous attempts to organize [in the maquila industry] have been frustrated by things the law should have been able to prevent but did not. It is easy for the entire process to reach the lowest common denominator," confirmed the labor attaché at the U.S. embassy.[83] Former workers at Dong San, for example, alleged collusion between the management and labor inspectors. "We tried to get them [the inspectors] to understand that we were, like them, Guatemalans," said a union organizer. "But they accepted the rationale of the owners and said we were irresponsible. They told us that the company is paying a sizable sum of money to the government to start a factory here. Essentially, they had them bought off."[84] Management in Dong San was also critical of the IGT, but for a different reason. The personnel manager of Dong San applauded the efforts of the IGT but lamented that the inspectors were powerless in the face of the blind intransigence of some workers who were determined to destroy the plant.[85]

Foiled by a Sign: The Levi's "Dockers" Factory

Perhaps the most shocking example of the government's failure to protect the right to association occurred in the fall of 1988 at a Guatemalan factory, Koram S.A. (Koramsa), which assembles Levi's "Dockers" for children. On August 21, 1988, five workers formed an ad hoc committee; they submitted their petition to the labor court, which immediately enjoined the factory. The committee's main requests were for more dignified treatment and a regular forty-four-hour week with *optional* overtime. The management often required workers to work entire nights, and the supervisors were notoriously brutal with words and fists, regularly striking workers in the head with their knuckles.

On the petition for an *emplazamiento*, the workers used the name written on the sign outside the entrance to the factory, "Koreanos Americanos S.A." Since the workers were always paid in cash, they had never seen a receipt with the name of the firm on it. Thus, they had no way of knowing that the actual name of the company registered in the Mercantile Registry was "Koram S.A." A week after the *emplaza-*

miento was issued, on August 29, the committee members were fired, along with several other "sympathizers." A few days later, a representative of the company filed a motion stating that the injunction did not apply to Koram S.A. because the order referred to a different firm, "Koreanos Americanos S.A." The committee responded by presenting a motion correcting the company's name, arguing that the original *emplazamiento* was obviously binding upon the factory in which the named employees worked.

On October 5, 1988, the court announced that the workers' second motion contained a genuinely new issue, that of the name change. Thus, the court granted a new injunction for the factory named "Koram S.A.," which was effective "from this moment forward." In essence, the court ruled that the original injunction had never applied to the very factory in which the petitioners worked. Since the workers were fired before this second injunction commenced, they were not eligible for reinstatement, as—technically—the factory was not enjoined. Because the workers had innocently used the incorrect name of the company—found on the wall of the factory—their original plea for protection against reprisals never took effect. An official from the labor federation that provided advice and assistance to the workers speculated that in the "Koram S.A." case the judge almost certainly was bribed, because the company was "making a lot of offers to everyone involved."[86] The unionization attempt, however, did initiate some improvements. Soon after the dismissals, the company provided free coffee to those forced to work all night, and a *Solidarismo* association was introduced.

Solidarismo: An Assault of Ideas, Not Bullets

The most recent addition to the arsenal of antiunion tactics is the arrival of the *Solidarismo* movement from Costa Rica. *Solidarismo* refers to a theory of cooperative industrial relations which is effectuated in the form of worker-employer organizations, or "associations." As a philosophy, *solidarismo* argues that "employee dignity arises from economic empowerment and labor-management harmony" rather than class struggle and communism.[87] The theory envisions an unlimited pie of which both workers and owners can partake, but only if they pool their resources and work together. The movement seeks, in the words of one advocate, "to make capitalists out of workers as well as employers. Unions want workers to be workers all their lives. We give alternatives to change their destiny."[88]

Begun in 1947, the *Solidarismo* movement has achieved remarkable success in Costa Rica; by the late 1980s it encompassed more than 25 percent of the work force in more than three thousand companies. Over 90 percent of the U.S. TNCs in Costa Rica have associations. After failed attempts to penetrate Guatemala's extremely conservative business sector in the 1960s and 1970s, which at that time viewed all forms of employee organizations as baneful, a group of Guatemalan businessmen founded the Guatemala Solidarista Union (USG) in September of 1983. A rapid and extensive development of *solidarismo* associations followed. By 1990, USG officials were claiming more than eighty thousand members in more than 350 associations, far outpacing the growth of the union movement.

The *Solidarismo* movement is extremely controversial in Central America. On the one hand, proponents such as Curtin Winsor, Jr., ex-ambassador to Costa Rica, extol the movement as an unprecedented tool of democracy. Winsor wrote, "The *solidarista* association is . . . perhaps the most original and significant ideological Latin American contribution to the West."[89] On the other hand, unionists view it as a vehicle of destruction. The former Christian Democrat labor minister, Maldanado Ruiz, stated, "*Solidarismo* deceives and violates the irrefutable rights of the workers."[90]

In the workplace, *Solidarismo* takes the form of employee-employer investment associations that use funds most Latin American countries require to be set aside for retirement or severance pay. Every month, employees contribute at least 5 percent of their salaries to the association, and employers match the contribution in the form of a non-interest-bearing loan as a contingency reserve for severance pay obligations. When workers quit or resign, they receive their original contributions and a portion of the profits or interest. The employer's matching contribution is either given to the ex-employee as the legally required severance pay or remains in the association accounts if the employee was discharged for good cause. The board of each association, composed of employer and employee representatives, is responsible for investing the fund.

According to *solidarismo* theorists, associations pass through three increasing stages of investment. First, in the "capitalization" stage, the association, using the monthly contributions and accumulating interest, builds a base of capital to issue consumer and housing loans to "associates." At the second stage, the "services" level, the association invests capital in services, such as discount food stores, cafeterias, and libraries, for its associates. In its most mature stage, "production," the association finances entrepreneurial ventures, including the creation of peripheral businesses and purchase of stock in their company.[91]

Proponents are quick to point out instances in Costa Rica where the associations are minority stockholders of their workplace or have ownership of subsidiary operations.

More often, associations, hampered by small contributions, high turnover, and lack of interest, remain less grandiose endeavors, creating—at most—company stores.

Solidarismo and Unions: Inevitable Conflict or Potential Harmony?

In theory, unions and *Solidarismo* associations share the same general end of improving the lot of the worker, but they propose entirely different means for achieving this seemingly honorable goal. Unions use collective representation and bargaining to improve working conditions and material benefits. Associations, on the other hand, look outside of the employee-employer relationship to better only the employees' financial situation. Employees gain only if the investments of their association succeed. As such, associations provide workers with a voice in investment decisions but not workplace decisions. The association, in contrast to a union, does not provide a venue for workers to even discuss, much less negotiate, better salaries and improved job security.

It is therefore theoretically possible for a trade union and a *Solidarismo* association to coexist peacefully, just as credit unions and trade unions do in U.S. workplaces. In this hypothetical situation, the union would work to improve working conditions and wages while the association would independently invest employee earnings. This complementary scheme, however, has never been realized in practice, since associations are almost always used to counter and defeat an existing union or fledgling union drive. Even the historically cautious U.S. Department of Labor, in its annual report on Guatemala, commented that associations "normally replace them [unions], particularly in enterprises with a conflictive labor history."[92] Indeed, for employers the *Solidarismo* movement presents the perfect alternative to a union: employees are promised financial rewards without the employer having to surrender profits or bargaining power.

Time and time again employers have instituted *Solidarismo* associations with the explicit intent of destroying a union. One study found that, through May 1990, associations had replaced unions in at least seventeen workplaces. In eighteen more businesses where unions exist, employers have introduced associations, but the unions have thus far managed to survive.[93] Dozens more employers have founded associations either to crush a swelling union drive or to preempt a potential one. A founder and active supporter of the USG, Joseph Recinos, admitted: "We know that some employers see us as a vehicle to destroy a union, but these are the ones we try to avoid."[94] Critics are more straightforward, charging that the *Solidarismo* movement is nothing but a more sophisticated, modern way of eliminating unions. One study concluded about the movement: "Most important of all, it [*Solidarismo*] seeks to displace trade unions as a form of worker organization. . . . They [associations] aim to neutralize and coopt workers through persuasive rather than coercive means."[95]

The *Solidarismo* movement, though touted by proponents as a joint labor/employer movement, is actually an employer institution. According to the USG officials, "because the cooperation of both parties is required" only employers can request the formation of an association.[96] After the employer's initial inquiry, USG representatives make their well-polished pitch, which includes everything from glossy brochures to color comic books, to workers on company time. Workers are thus forced, on pain of lost wages, to listen to this professional appeal. Once formed, employees routinely elect management officials to key positions on the association board, mainly because they fear reprisals and believe that employers are better versed in "financial" matters. Explained one maquila owner with an active association in her factory: "They know I have experience with accounting and money so they chose me as their treasurer. I am pleased to serve them. We even took a survey, and they were very happy with the directors."[97]

Because they are totally dependent on management's initiation and support, the level of managerial commitment determines the fate of individual *Solidarismo* associations. The most successful associations are ones where management is involved in day-to-day promotion and decision making. At Cardiz S.A., an association sputtered out within weeks of its initiation. "We tried and people did not want it," Manager Carlos Arias explained. "They did not like it. *Solidarismo* only works if management constantly works in it and sells it to the employees."[98] Typically, after the association has expelled a union or debilitated a union-organizing campaign, management's enthusiasm for the association, drawn to other tasks, dwindles. As a result, up to half of the associations the USG claims to be operational are no longer functioning.[99]

Solidarismo in the Maquila Industry

The maquila industry shows in microcosm the effects of the *Solidarismo* movement on unionization. Through May 1992, at least twelve maquila employers introduced associations into their factories.[100] Of these, at least seven were in factories where unions either already existed or workers had started the legal process toward unionization.[101] In another factory, Manufacturas Best S.A., which assembles and exports work gloves, the owner installed an association within weeks of opening to deter union activity. At three of his rubber plantations on the southern coast, unions have a foothold, and he has found that the best way to avert this "monster" is to form a competing association.[102]

Some maquila employers freely admit that the intent and effect of *Solidarismo* is to avoid and destroy unions. Philip Klose, manager of Koram S.A., a factory in which an association was introduced with this end in mind, stated: "Maybe *Solidarismo* was intended to be, or it was believed in the beginning that it could be, beneficial like a union, but a good one, and to make workers believe they are part of a union, but a productive union. But not anymore, everyone knows what it is and why employers use it."[103] The life span of the typical association in the maquila industry is this: an association is introduced, the employer supports it just long enough to destroy the union movement, then, without much fanfare, the association dissolves. Of the twelve associations in the maquila industry, less than half are still functioning. Of the seven cases in which associations waged direct combat with unions or organizing drives, only one association remains.

When management keeps a *Solidarismo* association in a maquila factory after its primary purpose of halting union activity is complete, the organization faces serious practical difficulties. Since most factories and businesses in Guatemala employ less than a hundred people, few associations would have the financial capacity to launch significant entrepreneurial initiatives. In the maquila industry, the size of all but a handful of factories with five hundred or more employees (none of the larger firms have associations) limits the role of associations to that of a girl scout troop rather than a venture-capital firm. For example, in one maquila factory with a very active association of 150 workers, monthly activities to raise funds for the association included a car wash, a bake sale, and a raffle. Another limitation on the association specific to the maquila industry is the high employee turnover, which makes for an impossible accounting mess. "We have *Solidarismo*, but it is very, very difficult to carry an association in this type of industry because there is such a great rotation of personnel," an owner confirmed. "In fact, ours is not working very well at all."[104]

Despite these shortcomings, proponents of *Solidarismo* argue that an association benefits workers more than a union does. Rina Sanchinelli, the director of the USG, explained: "Unions are political and offer the people political solutions. *Solidarismo* is economic and offers economic solutions. People are tired of the political promises and now want economic improvement. We do not want to fight the unions, but if they want to fight, we will; but this time we choose to attack ideas with ideas, not bullets."[105]

Inexport and Pindu Unions and New Levels of Union Destruction

Only two organizing campaigns have ended in legally recognized unions. In 1986, early in the development of the maquila industry, the Labor Ministry certified the first, and only, unions in the maquila industry for workers at Pindu and Inexport factories. For union members at these factories, however, legal recognition did not reduce employer repression; on the contrary, formal recognition has led to new levels of union destruction. By 1991, neither the Pindu nor the Inexport union functioned in the factories. Management hostility toward unionization, facilitated by government complicity and incompetence, has resulted in the total absence of a functioning union in the maquila industry.

Workers at Inexport, a 600-machine factory, formed a union in 1986. Three years later, in the summer of 1989, the management, led by its North American owner, Hank Robbins-Cohen, launched a brutal campaign to crush the union through a combination of massive firings and strong-arm tactics. A month before this assault, over two hundred workers claimed membership in the union, making it one of the largest unions in Guatemala; more significantly, for the first time in the maquila industry, the union and management had just signed a collective bargaining agreement. The union, it appeared, had survived the first two years, the period when most unions crumble, and had moved into a period of relative stability. "We thought the battle was over, that we were moving forward. We had our collective pact, and then everything fell apart," said a union officer.[106]

Robbins-Cohen planned his attack on the union carefully. In early 1989, he hired Edwin Marroquin Porras to be head of personnel, whose harsh practices led the workers, in retrospect, to believe that he was hired precisely to destroy the union. The company also hired new legal counsel known for his violent anti-union tactics. Death threats and violence began when he arrived. "Every time he [the attorney] comes on to the scene—Coca Cola, Bonin Laboratories, and then Inexport—workers begin to suffer violence," commented a U.S. Embassy official. "You can tell that when the death threats start there has been a change in legal counsel."[107] Afterward, Robbins-Cohen proudly told embassy personnel that he had done everything possible to destroy the union.[108]

In March 1989, in violation of both the collective pact and a standing *emplazamiento*, about seventy-four union members were told that they no longer worked at the factory. The next day the workers occupied the factory for two weeks, refusing to leave until Robbins-Cohen agreed to reinstate the illegally discharged workers. The then labor minister, Luis Maldanado Ruiz, intervened, and an agreement was reached between the union and Robbins-Cohen in which about half the workers were to return to work on June 6 and the rest were to resign on account of lack of work. Robbins-Cohen, however, had another plan. On June 6, 1989, he denied entry to those workers whom he had agreed to rehire and proceeded to fire fifty more union members, including the entire executive leadership. The workers were simply informed, "There is no more work for you." Similar illegal discharges were repeated several times over the next month, resulting in more than 150 union members out on the street.

Robbins-Cohen soon converted the factory into an armed fortress. Claiming that the union was a front for communist guerrillas, he hired a dozen uniformed, submachine-gun-toting military policemen to guard the factory. Some of these policemen poured boiling water on a pregnant woman, Maria Elisa Ramirez, who was attempting to enter the factory to speak to Robbins-Cohen. Guards also jeered, intimidated, and struck the few union members remaining in the factory. Other members were isolated in the factory without work, food, or water.

In addition to physical abuse, Robbins-Cohen attempted to initiate a *Solidarismo* association and a second, company-sponsored union. The association, however, had a brief existence, as the directorship of the USG revoked Robbins-Cohen's membership because "he was a terrible manager who treated his workers contrary to the spirit of *Solidarismo*."[109] The government, on the other hand, granted legal recognition to the management-instigated union.

Almost three years later, in May 1992, no union members were working in the factory despite repeated court orders to reinstate the dismissed workers and compensate them with back pay and repeated international protests to the Guatemalan government to enforce these judgments. Because an *emplazamiento* was in force at the time of the dismissals, courts have declared the unauthorized acts illegal. From the first-level labor court to the Constitutional Court, judges have repeatedly ordered the reinstatement and payment of back wages, amounting to several hundred thousand dollars, to the dismissed workers. Yet the workers remain outside the factory. A lawyer for the union sarcastically said: "We are very, very good lawyers. We never lose a case, but who cares, since these are only victories on paper?"[110]

The company has ignored every ruling with impunity and without significant disruption. The former labor minister, Maldanado Ruiz, called the series of events "the worst display of disrespect for workers and the law" he had ever witnessed.[111] Nevertheless, Maldanado Ruiz never sought to enforce the court orders for reinstatement; rather, he proposed revoking Robbins-Cohen's work permit. Commenting on Maldanado Ruiz's proposal, an official of the labor federation to which the Inexport union belonged said: "The Minister [Maldanado Ruiz] told us that he was looking into removing the work permit of Robbins-Cohen, but we simply want him to obey the law. It is one thing to say something and another to practice it. Either the Ministry has acted or it has not. We do not want Robbins-Cohen thrown out of the country, because this will end a precious source of employment. All we want is for him to respect our laws. It is the ministry's main function to make him respect our laws."[112]

The Labor Ministry of the current Serrano administration has tried to ignore the plight of the Inexport workers, referring to it as an unfortunate example of the former regime's incompetence. When the union members from Inexport met with a vice labor minister in early 1991, he tried to persuade the workers to resign from the union and look for new work. To that end, he brought maquila Help Wanted ads from a newspaper for workers to peruse at the meeting. A few months later the union managed to elect a new executive committee composed of workers within the factory. When the factory discovered the existence of the new committee members, they were immediately fired. After three years of struggle, members of the union still meet biweekly. They remain steadfast in their goal: "We would like to dialogue with Mr. Robbins to see if we can return to work."[113]

The Gradual Suffocation of Pindu: Strikes, Merger, and Relocation to Honduras

The small room, once a bedroom and now the meeting salon of a major Guatemalan labor federation, is filled to capacity with Pindu union members. At the meeting all of the seated audience are women, while at the front table sits the temporary directorate, two men and two women. Most of the women are very young, as young as sixteen, while a few others are in their forties. At least two are noticeably pregnant and another tends her young child. They have just arrived from work, which consists of sitting and running a sewing machine for ten or more hours a day. Their green hands and faces are testimony to the green cloth they have assembled that day. The workers, resorting to their sense of irony, call the green dye and dust that stain their skin their "protective" gloves and masks: management has consistently rebuffed all requests for real protective equipment.

The union at Pindu was formed in the summer of 1986, the same time as the one at Inexport. Four years later, having survived countless attempts at union-busting, a merger with another plant, and two costly strikes, the union seems fortunate to exist at all. The impassioned days when workers acted in the belief that "unity could conquer all" have passed. Many sit torpidly, listening to a union organizer describe in racist tones the depravity of their "Chino" ("Chinese," applied to all Asians) owners. As the organizer describes how the Chino has come to Guatemala to exploit and, if left unchallenged, will do just that, most nod all too knowingly. "We used to have enthusiastic rallies and confident confrontations," commented a founding member, "but now we are just barely breathing."[114]

Although the two strikes in 1987 were extremely trying for the union, the workers emerged more united and determined. At this point Pindu's owner decided the game was not worth the trouble and began looking for a swift resolution to the problem. It so happened that a smaller Korean-owned factory, Manufactura Exportación S.A. (Mantexsa), was also suffering union "troubles": at Mantexsa, the Guatemalan supervisors, outraged by the cruelty of their superiors, had started a union drive among the workers. With the assistance of the Korean ambassador, a deal was arranged between the two union-infested factories. The owner of Pindu purchased Mantexsa and renamed it Pindu, then closed down the original Pindu factory, moving the bulk of the operation to his non-union, Honduran plant.

Astutely calculating that most of the union members at Pindu would choose not to transfer to a factory on the other side of the city, the owner and the Korean ambassador believed they could purge most of the original Pindu union. Fulfilling their prediction, only twenty-four (out of more than ninety) members of the original union chose to work at the new location. The Pindu union uneventfully merged with the fledgling Mantexsa union and the soul of the struggle was lost en route. By 1990, only three original members remained.

Approximately one year after this union meeting, workers at Pindu arrived at their factory and found the building locked, empty, and without any sign of management. The workers do not know where the factory or its owners have fled. Some believe the factory has reopened under a different name inside the city. Others assert that the operations were exported to another country, most likely Honduras. After failing to obtain assistance from the Labor Ministry, workers visited the Korean Embassy. There, the ambassador quietly paid the workers their severance pay. The workers, lacking the energy to wage an international campaign against the employer or the brand names, accepted the money and moved on with their lives.

The unions at Pindu and Inexport have shared a similar history and fate. Workers exercised their constitutional right to organize but suffered severe persecution and eventual loss of their employment for their efforts. When asked whether it is possible to organize and sustain a union in a maquila factory, several Inexport executive committee members hesitantly replied: "Of course, we cannot tell workers not to organize since it is the path we have chosen, and we believe it to be the right and just one. However, we can warn them of the persecution they may face. Be prepared. Know what you are getting into because it will likely be a long and difficult path."[115] A federation official was more pessimistic and perhaps more realistic: "There is no law, no judge that will apply the law, and no labor minister to protect the worker. Whatever door the workers try to open, the employers close them. Here the only door that stays opens is the one to discharge."[116]

A Government Conspiracy?

Some union officials consider the abysmal record of union organizing in the maquila industry a poignant example of the overall absence of the right to organize and freedom to associate in Guatemala. The problems of organizing in maquila shops, they argue, demonstrate the weakness and unwillingness of a civilian administration that promised much to workers, but delivered very little. Other labor advocates assert that the case of the maquila industry is the result of a deliberate government decision to sacrifice labor rights for the sake of foreign investment. Knowing that foreign firms find unions distasteful and disruptive, the government, according to this view, deliberately prevents the formation of unions in the maquila industry—the industry which, at the moment, has unquestionably the greatest potential to lure foreign capital. Thus, the government provides even less protection to workers in the maquila industry than in other industries. One labor leader from UNSITRAGUA described this policy: "The maquila industry is a gift to foreign and domestic investors. They are promised no taxes. They are promised unlimited profit repatriation. They are promised an empty labor law and, most importantly, they are promised that there will be no unions. As such, the maquila industry is an especially serious enemy of unions and union rights."[117]

As expected, government officials vehemently deny allegations of a sweetheart deal with investors. When asked to comment on the absence of unions in the maquila, former labor minister Maldanado Ruiz responded, "While it is true that I am the labor minister, I cannot obligate the workers to organize unions or any other type of organization. Under this administration, workers are free to organize. For some reason the workers in this industry still do not have the strong conscience necessary to organize a union."[118] Other officials argued that the industry is too new for a significant union movement and that the young female work force is not prone to organize for cultural reasons: the male-dominated society has relegated women to subservient roles. Although these explanations have some merit, they are inadequate either alone or together to explain the absence of a union in the maquila industry.

The history of the union movement in the maquila industry refutes the argument that the industry is "too new to be unionized." The three most successful union attempts—at Inexport, Pindu, and Transcontinentales—all occurred in 1986 and 1987, during the infancy of the industry. In the subsequent five years, despite numerous attempts, workers have been unable to organize in another factory. This trend suggests that the novelty of the industry has not been a significant factor in the lack of unionized shops.

Further, it is alleged that young women, composing about four-fifths of the maquila labor force, are the "least likely to organize unions because of their docility and lack of experience in the formal work place."[119] Indeed, less than 10 percent of union affiliates are women.[120] But although cultural and political forces place impressive restraints on women workers, there are reasons why the maquila work force may be more likely than others to seek unionization. First, female maquila workers are often less financially vulnerable than their male counterparts. The majority appear to live at home and have not yet begun to raise a family. Loss of employment is not always as grave for a young, single woman as it is for the breadwinner of a family. Second, at this early stage in the industry, employment for experienced operators is relatively easy to obtain. While workers expressed profound fear of losing their jobs, they actually may have a far better chance of acquiring new work in the maquila industry than in other industries. Finally, hundreds, if not thousands, of maquila workers, mostly young women, have attempted to organize. The extent of such organizing makes the notion that the work force is docile or lacks conscience implausible.

Failure of the labor courts, long delays for legal recognition, and the Labor Ministry's delinquent enforcement of the Code are problems that besiege workers in every industry. What makes the maquila workers' experience of unionism unique is that these normal deficiencies seem to have been intensified by a government policy to maintain a union-free industry. Maquila employers as a group possess extraordinary powers, even by Guatemalan standards, to defeat union campaigns.

First, two veteran labor inspectors independently reported that Labor Ministry officials had instructed inspectors not to enforce the Code's provision, Article 13, limiting the proportion of foreign employees in workplaces. Designed to promote technology transfer, Article 13 prohibits employment of more than 10 percent foreign employees in the workplace whose combined salaries may not exceed 15 percent of the total payroll. Considering that dozens of maquila factories, particularly the Korean ones, exceed one and in many cases both of these limits, the article, if enforced, would disrupt the industry. Of this mysterious lapse in enforcement one inspector said: "This article used to be enforced. The Labor Ministry would request inspectors to routinely audit the workers and payrolls as part of an inspection. In the last three years [since 1987], the ministry has stopped requesting these audits, so we don't do them."[121] Another inspector confirmed this directive: "It is frustrating to look at their books and know that the level of foreign personnel and salaries is too high but not be able to act on this information."[122]

Second, the government has apparently stopped validating and monitoring the work permits of foreign employees who work in the maquila industry. According to the Labor Ministry director of statistics, of the 182 foreign employees who were issued authorizations in all sectors for 1990, only two were granted to maquila factories.[123] Yet more than three hundred foreign employees, mostly from the Republic of Korea, are working in maquila factories. The director of statistics attributed the deficient enforcement to an insufficient staff overwhelmed by requests for work permits.[124]

Third, the government's role in the demise of the union at Inexport presents a particularly troubling example of its reluctance to enforce the Code in the maquila industry. As described above, although the union has won at every level of the judicial system, the government has refused to enforce the orders for reinstatement and back pay. Yet the cost of enforcing the orders, in this case, would be minimal. Almost every maquila owner, especially the powerful ones, consider Robbins-Cohen anathema to the industry. "He is a rude, repulsive person. Frankly, I could care less if the government reinstated the workers. The way he treats workers he deserves no better," commented one owner.[125] Robbins-Cohen is the only employer whom the USG and the Chamber of Commerce have rejected for membership. Because of Robbins-Cohen's tarnished reputation, government enforcement of the orders would not likely upset the industry. As an owner observed: "No one will care if Robbins is kicked out. Most will breathe a sigh of relief because of all the bad press he has caused the industry."[126] Despite the tacit approval of the maquila owners, the government has balked. One possible reason is that they fear another Transcontinentales S.A. episode—that the irate North American owner, "chased out of the country by a rabid union," would spread rumors throughout the U.S. garment industry that Guatemala is a land of terror.

Lastly, the Korea ambassador, Key-Sung Cho, has indicated that the Korean and Guatemalan governments have a "special understanding" that unions will not be tolerated in Korean factories. In return, the Korean government promises to invest heavily in the industry. "We know there is a problem with labor unions in Guatemala," Cho explained. "Fortunately, labor unions in maquila factories often belong to the government party's labor federation. [The CGTG is the Christian Democrat-affiliated labor federation.] In the case of trouble between labor unions and our factories, the labor minister and vice president intervene to arrange the problem to meet both our needs."[127] On this pact, Cho later elaborated: "I have maintained close contact with representatives in the CGTG and the Labor Ministry. They understand our predicament quite well, and they are very helpful whenever we have problems."[128]

Since the ambassador arrived in 1988, at least four Korean factories have experienced union-organizing campaigns that achieved *emplazamientos*. None of the campaigns succeeded. The CGTG and Christian Democrat officials have denied complicity with the Korean ambassador. Given that Korea is the major foreign investor in the maquila industry, and the remarkable pattern of union-free Korean shops, the ambassador's matter-of-fact admissions of collusion do not seem far-fetched.

Alone, these anecdotes prove little except that the government has been particularly ineffective in protecting maquila workers. But combined, they build a strong case that the Guatemalan government is conspiring to suppress unionization in the maquila sector. Relatively speaking, unionization in other parts of the private sector have grown at unprecedented rates during the five years of the Christian Democrat administration. The Labor Ministry has given legal recognition to more than a hundred private-sector unions, and many more have reclaimed their vitality between 1986 and 1990, leading the former labor minister to declare, "There is freedom of association and organization in Guatemala."[129] In contrast, unionization in the maquila industry has decreased. These data, combined with the above-cited examples, have led many to the conclusion articulated by a union activist: "At the request of the maquila owners, the government granted the industry a grace period against unions."[130]

Unenforced Law, Vigilante Workers

Ironically, in contradiction to AID's and GEXPRONT's assurances, the maquila sector is anything but free from labor unrest and disruption. In most factories, tension and mistrust lie at the core of the employee-employer relationship and occasionally erupt into overt conflict. A North American owner succinctly explained the phenomenon, from which few owners dissent: "A war exists between the worker and the employer."[131] Similarly, workers generally view owners with fear, suspicion, and sometimes deep hatred. "We are never sure what they [management] are plotting. We view every act of theirs, even if apparently benevolent, with suspicion. They never give us something for nothing," observed a maquila worker.[132]

This "war" manifests itself in a number of ways. Occasionally an embittered employee will sabotage machinery or steal garments; less frequently she will attack a supervisor or manager. The stories of unions at Transcontinentales, Pindu, and Inexport, along with the demoralizing firsthand experience with ineffective officials and institutions, have led some workers to lose faith in the law and its functionaries. These workers, in the words of a union lawyer, "are returning to direct action because it is the only form owners take seriously."[133]

Unable to rely on the Labor Ministry for protection, discontented and wronged workers are turning to this more confrontational, vigilante approach. In the summer of 1990, at Ace Internacional S.A., workers staged a day-long work stoppage to protest the low wages. One enraged supervisor struck a defiant worker. By the end of the day, however, the owner knuckled under to the pressure, granting a Q1-a-day raise. Management at another factory reneged on the payment of the legally required *aguinaldo* bonus of one month's pay. Rather than dashing to the IGT for assistance, the workers gathered at lunchtime and refused to reenter the factory on the day the payment was supposed to be due. According to a worker, "The managers got a water hose and threatened to hose us down if we did not return to work. But we were determined to get paid what was due. Eventually, they came out of the factory and promised that the checks would be ready by the end of the day. We went back to work and got our checks."[134]

7

The Korean Promise of Development

When Ambassador Key-Sung Cho arrived at the Republic of Korea Embassy in Guatemala City in April 1988, six Korean maquila factories were operating there. Within three and one-half years, under Cho's leadership, the number of Korean factories had increased to fifty, one of the largest concentrations of Korean apparel assembly outside Korea. Guatemala rapidly emerged as the hub of Korean investment in Central America and the Caribbean. For Ambassador Cho, this expansion represented the Republic of Korea's commitment to the economic and industrial development of Guatemala and the Central American and Caribbean region. In his words, "We would like to start an economic revolution in Guatemala during my term to demonstrate our model of economic cooperation—industrialization based on Korean cooperation and investment—so that other countries in Latin America might follow."[1]

According to Cho, Korea has evolved from a war-torn, agrarian society, much like contemporary Guatemala, to a self-sufficient, industrialized member of the developed world. The Korean experience, especially in light of the decline of state socialism, he contends, provides the only viable development model for countries in the modern world. Manufacturing and assembly for export have formed the cornerstone of Korea's economic miracle. Beginning with simple garment-assembly shops, Korea has erected a modern infrastructure and cultivated a proficient work force. As the labor force became more skilled, more sophisticated goods, such as electronics, textiles, and computers, were manufactured and exported. The Korean central government also planned and developed heavy industry, resulting in prosperous shipbuilding, auto, and steel trades. In his call for an economic revolution, Cho offers Guatemala the opportunity to replicate Korean's industrialization experience.

Ambassador Cho knows Latin America intimately. In 1961, he began his foreign service career in Chile. Stints in Mexico, Spain, Ecuador, and Peru followed. Between terms abroad, he served as executive director of the American Bureau in the Foreign Ministry in Seoul, where he focused on improving Korea's trade with the Americas. As a culmination of this passion for Latin America, he authored a book on how international organizations should combine their resources to develop export industries in the region.[2]

With this accumulated wisdom and experience, Cho has embarked on a crusade to induce Korean companies to invest in Latin America, particularly Central America and the Caribbean. Few greeted President Reagan's promise to clear barriers in the channels of trade between the United States and the Caribbean Basin with more enthusiasm than Cho. When the United States Congress acted on Reagan's promise and passed the Caribbean Basin Economic Recovery Act (CBERA) in 1983,[3] Cho, then director of the American Bureau, saw an unprecedented opportunity to export the Korean apparel production that was being restrained by U.S. import quotas.

By the mid-1980s, Korea had reached its capacity of garment assembly and export to the U.S. market. For the most part, U.S. quotas on Korean apparel imports and the rapid proliferation of garment-assembly operations in countries with less expensive labor marked the ceiling of domestic Korean apparel production. In response, the Korean government began to seek apparel export platforms. Thus, the CBERA provided a profitable and timely opportunity for Korean firms to assemble in Caribbean countries and import to the United States without restrictive quotas. "When President Reagan announced the CBERA policy, it could not have come at a better moment," Cho explained. "Just as we were looking to expand operations to other regions, Reagan handed us a gift."[4]

Prompted by the CBERA, Cho organized regular meetings between the Korean government and the private sector, principally the Korean Chamber of Commerce, to explain the newfound opportunities and encourage investment in Caribbean and Central American countries.[5] These Cho-sponsored seminars sparked Korean investors' interest in the region's investment possibilities. In 1978, the number of Korean enterprises in the Caribbean and Central America was thirteen; by 1988, there were sixty-eight. Cho's vigorous promotional efforts contributed to this growth. By 1990, more than 130 Korean companies were assembling garments, electronics, and plastic products in the region.[6]

In harmony with this practice of disseminating information, one of Cho's first tasks as ambassador to Guatemala was to translate relevant Guatemalan laws into Korean and circulate bound copies to the Korean garment industry and government agencies. (Significantly, this edition of laws does not contain a translation of the labor code.) Armed with these laws and backed by the determination of Ambassador Cho, the flow of Korean capital into Guatemala's maquila industry began.

The Korean Investment Presence

Maquila industries have flourished in countries throughout the region. Mexico and, more recently, the Dominican Republic, Jamaica, Costa Rica, and even Haiti have experienced dramatic inundations of maquila factories. What is unique in Guatemala's case is that Korean, not U.S., investors are the undisputed leaders of this export-assembly industry. In virtually every other regional industry, U.S. investment stands out as the major source of production and innovation. In Guatemala, on the other hand, U.S. investors are a distant third behind Korean and local investors. According to reliable estimates, Korean factories produce roughly 50 percent of all exported garments, while local entrepreneurs contribute approximately 40 percent. North American investors claim the remaining 10 percent.

The concentration of Korean capital in Guatemala is the highest in the Americas and one of the highest outside Korea. Indeed, Guatemala is home to more than 20 percent of all foreign-located Korean apparel factories.[7] Since April 1988, the date when Ambassador Cho arrived, forty-four Korean factories have begun operation; in 1989 alone, eighteen Korean factories were opened. Presently, fifty apparel-assembly factories are operating in Guatemala.[8] The plants—averaging 375 Guatemalan workers per factory—are more than double the size and far more productive than locally administered ones. Some owners, like those of Ace Internacional S.A. and Mi Kwang S.A., maintain other factories in the region.

A wide range of Korean corporations have opened maquila operations. About three-fourths of the factories are owned by small to medium Korean businesses. Enormous Korean TNCs (or *chaebols*) such as Samsung and Sam Phoong, which own five and three factories respectively, administer at least twelve of the largest and most sophisticated factories. Sam Phoong owns the largest maquila factory (one of the three largest industrial plants in Guatemala), Sam Lucas S.A., which employs nearly one thousand workers. In several instances, the opening of a Korean factory in Guatemala marked the closing of one in Korea. In such cases, entire factories transfer their contents to a Guatemalan warehouse and begin anew.[9]

At least one factory, Modas Americas S.A., has a sister shop in the garment district of Los Angeles.[10] Three first-generation Korean-American brothers own and manage both factories, rotating positions every six months. Contracting work from a regional brand called "Cherokee," the Los Angeles shop assembles the more expensive, intricate work, while the Guatemalan factory assembles the simpler styles. When an owner-brother was asked if there were any noticeable differences between the quality of workers in the factories, he replied that the workers were the same in both shops, because "almost all the workers in our Los Angeles plant are from Central America. If you walked into our [Los Angeles] plant you would think you were in Guatemala."[11]

All Korean maquila factories have a "home" factory in Korea. These home factories provide vital services to the satellite in Guatemala; for example, experienced managers and supervisors come to Guatemala to organize and implement Korean management systems in the new plants. Further, Korean plant managers in Guatemala are usually unconcerned with obtaining contracts, as this task is performed in Korea or the United States where the home factory has long established connections. Free of these burdens that most owners must bear, the management in Korea can concentrate on production.

The Korean Development Model of Economic Cooperation

Beginning in 1962, the Korean government, in collaboration with several large *chaebols* such as Samsung, Lucky-Goldstar, and Daewoo, carefully devised and forcefully executed a series of five-year economic development plans. Unprecedented rates of industrial production and economic prosperity resulted in what many observers have come to call an economic "miracle." With the cooperation of local governments, Korean officials such as Cho believe that the Korean "miracle" can be replicated throughout the developing world. Specifically, the Republic of Korea, led by its dynamic and aggressive ambassador, plans to reproduce this industrial development prototype in Guatemala and then spread it to the rest of the Caribbean and Central America. Guatemala is to become the model—the new Korea, the new Central American Tiger.

The Korean development model stresses cooperation between benefactor and receiver, rejecting out-of-hand the conventional approach of grants and low-interest loans as ultimately deleterious to development. These traditional measures, Ambassador Cho insisted, "simply multiply the problems of dependence and debt for developing countries. For example, if we give a grant to a friendly developing nation, that grant often produces nothing permanent and in the end becomes insignificant, if not harmful, assistance. The deeper problems of underdevelopment remain."[12] True to this principle, monetary assistance from the Republic of Korea to Guatemala is "small and symbolic," comprising less than $100,000. "Instead," said the ambassador, "we help through investments."[13] To reduce dependence and combat the roots of poverty, the Korean development model is founded on the conviction that only direct investment and creation of productive employment foster prosperity and industrialization. This investment, it is argued, begets investment, as profits are reinvested to expand production. Effective economic cooperation, the ambassador said, "promotes investment by means of investment."[14] Thus, instead of schools and cooperatives, the Republic of Korea "donates" factories.

In the short term, this investment, proponents including Ambassador Cho and AID officials argue, provides desperately needed employment and foreign exchange. Already, more than thirty-five thousand people are directly employed in Korean factories around the Caribbean and Central America.[15] Since many of these countries share Guatemala-like problems of under- and unemployment, the creation of jobs is especially welcome. Beyond direct employment, these investments create backward linkages such as transportation, construction, and insurance. Thousands are employed to ensure that the goods are properly handled and managed in the trade circuit. A final advantage is foreign exchange. Korean investments currently export several hundred million dollars'-worth of apparel a year from the region, reducing the severe balance of payments deficit facing each country.

In addition to these short-term benefits, advocates assert that the Korean model holds the promise of long-term industrialization. The transfer of technology from the Korean technicians and managers to the host-country workers, and the subsequent introduction of more sophisticated industries, form the crux of this promise. Experienced Koreans provide the capital and know-how; apprentice Guatemalans provide open minds. A new class of Guatemalan supervisors, workers, and managers weaned on the wisdom acquired from their Korean mentors is the desired outcome. Factories, then, become schools, lifting the collective technological capacity of the local work force. If this technological transfer is repeated on a large enough scale, the increasing skill of this labor force will attract new, more advanced industries.

Since Cho's arrival in 1988, Korean industrialists appear to have systematically established a production structure sufficient to train a significant portion of the native work force. In Cho's first eighteen months or so, a wave of middle-sized, low-cost assembly operations located in the capital. Mimicking local investors, dozens of small and medium-sized Korean companies rented warehouses and imported used machinery. Once these ventures proved secure, larger Korean corporations, including several *chaebols*, increased the scale of investment and deepened the roots of the Korean commitment. Instead of leasing warehouse space, these corporations have been purchasing land outside the capital, constructing multimillion-dollar factories that include living quarters for Korean staff, and importing state-of-the-art machinery. In fact, twelve out of the last fourteen Korean maquila factories have been multimillion dollar ventures.[16] Far surpassing the primitive conditions in most maquila factories, these new structures are among the largest, most modern facilities in all Guatemalan industries. A U.S. maquila owner described these initiatives: "Now, when they [Koreans] build a plant, they build it for more than 500 machines. They build the housing, bring over their own staff. It is a self-contained city. It is beautiful!"[17] By 1991, Korean investors had invested more than $60 million in the Guatemalan maquila industry.[18]

The zenith of this production structure is a Korean-financed and -managed free-trade zone in El Tejar, Chimaltenango—forty-eight kilometers from the Korean Embassy. In this cozy indigenous village, a group of Korean investors has purchased 90,000 square meters of land and plans to construct thirty factories employing some ten thousand local workers to produce a variety of goods ranging from electronics to plastic tubing. The Korean-American promoters of the free-trade zone hope that Lucky-Goldstar will open a television assembly factory. Ambassador Cho sees the El Tejar Free-Trade Zone as a model of a privately administered free-trade zone for the region and the world.

After a certain level and quality of investment has been accomplished in Guatemala, the Korean government intends to proliferate ventures to other parts of the region. Specifically, Honduras, Nicaragua, and El Salvador are part of this long-term vision. Honduras, as part of Ambassador Cho's diplomatic territory, has already expanded from seven to seventeen factories since 1988, including the extension of operations from two factories in Guatemala. Although Korean investments have not yet entered Nicaragua or El Salvador, delegations of prospective investors have visited both nations, and a joint venture with Nicaraguan and Korean investors on a leather project is planned.[19]

Mixed Motives: Altruistic Development or Historical Necessity?

In addition to the Korean Embassy, another state-sponsored agency, the Korean Overseas Trade Promotion Association (KOTRA), maintains an office in Guatemala City. KOTRA was established by the Korean government in 1962 as a nonprofit trade-promotion organization "to encourage the development of the national economy through expanding overseas trade."[20] The KOTRA Guatemala office is the consulting arm of the embassy, acting as a clearinghouse for information and advice for potential Korean investors. As such, KOTRA officials produce economic reports and forecasts; arrange tours for Korean investors; and respond to requests from prospective investors, including giving advice on which locations are union-free. As the KOTRA subdirector explained, "We give the Korean owners advice about everything except how to run their own factories."[21]

When asked why the Korean government and investors had in less than four years invested $60 million in the Guatemalan maquila industry, the director of KOTRA's Guatemala office listed the temperate climate, proximity to the United States, and the cost and availability of qualified labor. Although KOTRA is intimately involved in the cultivation of Korean investment in Guatemala, its director did not mention Ambassador Cho's plan of economic cooperation as a motivating factor. More significantly, none of the reasons offered by either the ambassador or the KOTRA director adequately addresses the historical antecedents that compelled the flood of Korean garment-assembly production to Guatemala.

Economic necessity, more than the desire to stimulate the economies of impoverished nations, motivated the Korean government to export apparel-assembly production to Guatemala. U.S. import quotas, foreign competition, and domestic labor unrest combined in the mid-1980s to halt the growth of Korea's enormous garment-assembly export industry. Faced with this prospect, the Korean government chose to expand assembly operations abroad. Guatemala was selected over other countries as the major export platform in the Caribbean region because its industry was undeveloped, and the two nations enjoyed healthy diplomatic relations.

Since 1962 the textile and apparel industry has been Korea's "single most important contributor to exports, employment, and balance of payments"—accounting for more than $13 billion in exports in 1991 alone. In the early 1980s, growing protectionism in the U.S. textile and apparel industry, along with a waning U.S. dollar and growing foreign competition, began to erode Korea's apparel and textile empire. In 1982, in part to protect its domestic industry, the U.S. government negotiated a series of restrictive apparel quotas with Korea and the other Asian producers; four years later, nearly every category of garments manufactured and assembled in Korea was artificially capped. Since the United States is the largest market for Korean apparel, these quotas caused a fall in Korea's share of U.S. imports.[22] Further, the U.S. dollar began to decline in strength from 1986 onward, heightening awareness of the high costs associated with Southeast Asian assembly. Finally, competition from developing countries, especially China, was chipping away at Korea's clothing dynasty. These countries offered similar financial incentives to investors, but the most important cost—labor—was significantly less.

The Korean labor uprising of 1987 dealt a nearly fatal blow to this industry already weakened by quotas and foreign competition. During this year-long unrest, the Korean apparel industry, the backbone of the economy, became paralyzed by internal strife and rising costs as Korean workers participated in an unprecedented wave of strikes and work stoppages—over three thousand in all.[23] These strikes forced both management and the government to at last heed labor's long-standing demands for higher wages, improved working conditions, and the unimpeded right to organize and collectively bargain. By the end of the year, the Korean government instituted the first state minimum wage, and unions organized more freely. These worker victories increased industrial wages an annual average of 20 percent from 1987 to 1989.[24] As one of the most labor-intensive industries, apparel-assembly production immediately felt the repercussions of this labor unrest and wage increases.[25] (Korean apparel wages—US$1.60 an hour in 1988—are five times as much as those paid Guatemalan maquila workers.)[26] New export platforms were needed. It was, then, no coincidence that Korean factories arrived in droves in the spring of 1988, after a lull of four years from the time when the first Korean factory opened in Guatemala.

Driven to seek new export platforms, the Korean government selected Guatemala as the major production site in the Americas because of mature diplomatic ties and the opportunity to dominate an undeveloped industry. During Guatemala's partial international isolation from 1977 to 1985, the Republic of Korea was one of the few countries, along with Taiwan and Israel, which sustained amiable diplomatic relations. Sharing both an anticommunist ideology and a military-dominated government, Korea empathized with the plight of Guatemala in its battle against guerrilla insurgency. Although there is little known evidence that Korea actually sold weapons or provided other concrete military assistance during this period, it is clear that the Guatemalan government received moral and diplomatic support from the Korean government. Indeed, the opening of the two embassies occurred in 1977, the year in which President Carter cut off economic aid. This growing diplomatic cooperation laid a firm foundation for the Korean investment.

As described in Chapter 2, the Guatemalan maquila industry has been slow to attract foreign investors, especially from the United States. By 1988, U.S. capital had a stronghold in the Dominican Republic, Jamaican, and Costa Rican maquila industries. Guatemala, on the other hand, was barren of foreign investment, and thus offered Korean capital a unique opportunity in the region: to take charge of and lead an industry. Korean investors accepted the challenge and immediately became the foreign leaders of the industry. The Guatemalan government, anxious for foreign investment, welcomed the Korean commitment. "When we came to Guatemala, the industry was unsettled by foreign capital," confirmed the director of KOTRA. "We were the first to take advantage of the benefits of the industry, and the Guatemalan government has been very responsive to our efforts."[27]

Thus, Ambassador Cho's moralistic purpose of "investment as economic cooperation" appears to have been an afterthought. When decisions were made to export production, as one Korean academic noted, "it was to escape the quota, the labor troubles, and rising costs."[28] Guatemala, it seems, provided the most convenient, profitable avenue for this unforeseen expansion.

The Embassy: Korean Central Government in Guatemala

A list of the Korean maquila factories and their phone numbers hangs alone in the receptionist's carrel at the Korean Embassy. These numbers represent the raison d'être of the embassy: to foster the development of Korean investments in Guatemala and the region. With extraordinary precision and control, the embassy acts as headquarters for individual Korean factories and as coordinator of the Korean investment campaign in the Caribbean Basin. As a result, Korean factories, while individually striving to maximize profits, are connected in the grand scheme to establish a Korean production structure in Guatemala.

As the life source of Korean factories, the Korean embassy staff are advocates, spokespersons, mediators, and consultants for individual Korean factories. It is, in the words of a former U.S. Embassy trade attaché, "the self-proclaimed headquarters for all Korean investors."[29] The Korean Embassy micromanages the external, and sometimes the internal, affairs of Korean factories; factories refer every question, concern, or dispute to the embassy for resolution. Korean administrators and supervisors rarely speak directly to Guatemalan officials or strangers before first checking with the embassy. In fact, the role of the embassy is so dominant that few of the administrators arrive in Guatemala with even a rudimentary understanding of Spanish. "Besides the ambassador, they [Korean managers] never speak with anyone outside of the factory," said a U.S. Embassy official. "With the embassy as their voice, they really don't need to learn Spanish."[30]

The embassy acts as a liaison between official Guatemalan agencies and Korean factories. When customs delays a shipment, the Labor Ministry denies a work permit, or a labor inspector arrives unexpectedly, Korean managers routinely contact the embassy for assistance. Experienced in this procedure, Guatemalan labor and union officials have begun to deal directly with the embassy when they have a difficulty with a Korean factory. For example, in August 1991, when the Korean owners of Pindu abandoned the factory and left employees without severance pay and final paychecks, the Labor Ministry advised workers and their union to seek compensation from the Korean Embassy. According to the workers, Ambassador Cho agreed to compensate for a portion of the lost wages.

Embassy personnel also oversee relations among Korean factories. Describing a code of "interdiscipline," Ambassador Cho explained that the embassy "has devised guidelines to deter and resolve disputes" between fellow Korean entrepreneurs. Prior to his arrival, Cho claimed that the handful of Korean factories repeatedly encountered unnecessary, politically messy problems—among themselves and with workers, the Guatemalan government, and even other factories. These disputes, such as the early labor troubles at Pindu, too often became publicly known and "embarrassed the people and government of Korea."[31] In order to avoid such scandals and sustain comity among the factories, the embassy routinely promulgates and enforces an informal code of interdiscipline. "We play an active role in the relations between factories," said the ambassador. "It is very ugly to display publicly disputes among Korean industries, so we are rendering full cooperation with Korean factories for peaceful operation of our factories."[32] The interdisciplinary code in general prohibits certain conduct that disrupts or impedes production and cooperation among factories. Korean factories, for example, may not "steal" Korean technicians or local labor from each other. The essence of the code is that all disputes among Korean factories must be submitted to the embassy for binding resolution.

The Replication of the Three Elements of the Korean Economic "Miracle"

Central government planning is the hallmark of Korea's "economic miracle." As mentioned above, starting in 1963, the government issued and followed, with remarkable determination and precision, a series of "Five-Year Plans." Each plan sought to improve and expand economic growth until national self-sufficiency was achieved. The government assumed the role of the consummate strategist and planner, implementing measures to guide the population on a course of unprecedented economic growth.

In the wake of the Korean War and U.S. military occupation, government planners turned away from the inefficient, faltering import substitution programs. In their place, the planners focused on export-led industrialization. In particular, the plans emphasized the manufacture and export of goods to markets in developed countries. From 1960 to 1966, these efforts resulted in a sevenfold increase in commodity exports.[33] Success was even more impressive over the long term: in 1962, per capita income was US$82 and total exports US$43 million; by 1987, per capita income had risen to US$2,850 and exports were approximately US$47.28 billion.

Central government strategists also planned and facilitated the move of the Korean economy from light to heavy, and now to more technically advanced, industries such as computers. Virtually every facet of this export expansion and diversification was controlled and directed by the centralized authority. As Alice Amsden neatly summarizes, "The state [in Korea] has usurped the domain of the traditional private entrepreneur by making milestone decisions about what, when, and how much to produce."[34]

In essence, the Korean government combined three ingredients to implement the strategy of export-led industrialization: total commitment to economic goals; a refined ability to control and coordinate entrepreneurs and large corporations; and systematic repression and, hence, control of the labor and popular political movements.

First, the government's dedication to nurturing and developing industrial export growth has been a paradigm of conviction and determination. Two scholars describe this effort as an "all out government campaign to expand exports, typified by the constant setting of seemingly unattainable export targets, their attainment, and the setting of even higher targets."[35] The intensity of the commitment is demonstrated by the extraordinary dedication and detailed supervision of high-ranking government officials. President General Park Chung-he, for instance, chaired monthly meetings of cabinet members and private businessmen to review the progress of the export drive for nearly twenty years.[36]

Second, the government has been able to captivate and cultivate the private business sector with a shrewd combination of supportive and restrictive measures. Faced with a paucity of natural resources and national limits on land ownership, Korean entrepreneurs were forced to export. To further encourage and control exports, the Korean government has provided carrots and sticks. Quasi-governmental organizations such as KOTRA furnish institutional support and stability. Cooperation with these institutions is rewarded by more efficient and profitable production. As for the stick, the government has mainly relied an a near monopoly of the banking system, and hence, critical loan capital. As one scholar succinctly states: "When foreign loans need government approval or guarantee, when the stock market plays no significant role, when operating profits are, on the whole, not excessive, and when firms operate with very high debt/equity ratios, their dependence on banks and thus on the Government becomes overwhelming."[37] The threat of termination of credit has become an effective incentive to keep entrepreneurs on the designated path.

The Critical Prong: Worker Control and the Death of Chun Tae Il

Third, and most significant, the central government has practiced an effective system of labor control. Unlike in the case of Korean entrepreneurs, the compliance of Korean workers has been realized exclusively with a stick rather than a carrot.[38] The government has at times authorized the police and the Korean CIA to brutalize and intimidate workers. More subtle has been the state's policy of bestowing upon managers the unrestricted liberty to enforce their own shop rules. As unquestioned patriarch of the factory, the employer has reigned with supreme authority in the workplace. The government's complicity in labor repression has resulted in the consistent squelching of individual and collective dissent. One commentator notes, "Actively or passively, the innovators gave their consent to a subsystem of worker control that inflicted humiliation on the very people who produced the miracle."[39]

Since the early 1960s, workers in the Korean garment-assembly industry have received insufficient compensation for long hours and poor working conditions. The story of Chun Tae Il, a Korean garment worker who sacrificed himself to protest the plight of his coworkers, exemplifies this predicament. Chun Tae Il worked at Seoul's Peace Market, a block-long, four-story garment sweatshop. The twenty thousand, mostly female, workers at Peace Market were confined to tiny sewing cubicles and earned less than a dollar a day for often more than fourteen hours of labor.

In 1970, Chun Tae Il, in front of the gigantic Peace Market, soaked himself with gasoline, lit himself on fire, and burnt to death. The long hours, incessant pressure to produce, confining conditions, and physical abuse had reached intolerable levels for Chun Tae Il, and he could no longer bear to watch young girls suffer. His final words were: "Obey the Labor Standards Act! Don't mistreat young girls!"[40] Although his plea fell on the deaf ears of employers and the autocratic government, it sparked a movement of discontent among workers that would eventually explode in the labor upheavals of 1987. "His flaming body lit up the wretched . . . sweatshop and evoked a groan of anguish and protest from workers everywhere in the country," commented George Ogle.[41]

The Korean Factory System in Guatemala

These same elements—the central government's total commitment to achieve its goals, the economic leverage to oblige private entrepreneurs to cooperate, and a repressive system of worker control—are also evident in the Korean investment campaign in Guatemala. "We want to make the experience of our factories as much like home [Korea] as we possibly can," confirmed a representative from KOTRA.[42] As in

Korea, the Korean Embassy, along with the Korean central government and the Central Bank, has dedicated itself to facilitating and leading their investments to prosperity. The result is the assumption of most entrepreneurial decision making by embassy officials.

The embassy literally holds the purse strings for prospective Korean investors. Through early 1991, the Korean Export-Import Bank had issued over $30 million in subsidized long-term, low-interest (7.5 percent annual) loans to Korean maquila ventures in Guatemala.[43] The embassy is authorized to confirm loan papers and direct the Export-Import Bank to issue loans. As small and medium companies own most of the Korean factories, reliance on loan capital is acute; and the embassy's absolute control over credit ensures obedience from these factories. Further, the political vulnerability of individual Korean factories compounds their dependence on the embassy. Customs officials, labor inspectors, unions, and political instability pose uncertain and potentially dangerous obstacles for Korean owners. The only place these foreigners can find security is in their embassy.

Training Guatemalan *Campesinos* to Work Like Korean Peasants

During Korea's "economic miracle," the central government attained remarkable levels of production and growth through control of both entrepreneur and worker. The means of control over the two, as described above, differed radically. Korean entrepreneurs, at worst, feared loss of credit; whereas Korean workers such as Chun Tae Il continually suffered from "patriarchal, paternalistic and patrimonial systems of labor control."[44] To achieve maximum production in Guatemala, many aspects of these repressive systems of labor control have been imported for the "benefit" of Guatemalan workers and the greater good of Korean factories.

The management system implemented in Korean maquila factories indeed closely resembles the repressive system of labor control found in Korea. The goal of this practice, according to Korean managers and government officials, is to teach Guatemalan workers the "work habits" of Korean workers. The Korean ambassador explained: "They [Guatemalan workers] have their own work habits but we have Korean habits and discipline. For example, Guatemalan workers must learn to show up on time, work as long as necessary, and be obedient to their superiors. The job of Korean technicians is to train Guatemalan workers in Korean habits and discipline. Soon most Guatemalan workers will be working according to our discipline and work habits."[45]

Korean administrators, however, seem to disagree on whether Guatemalan workers can be trained to these work habits. Some argue that Guatemalan workers are inherently inferior to Korean workers. The Korean manager-owner of Booco S.A., comparing the relative merits of Guatemalan and Korean workers, stated: "I have a garment-assembly factory in Korea with less workers but five times the production. Workers in Korea work until ten or midnight without hesitation. Here, all they do is complain."[46] "Korean workers are completely different," confirmed a manager at Sae Han S.A. "They do not talk. They just pay attention to what they are told to do. They are much more intelligent and learn much more quickly."[47]

Other Korean managers believe that Guatemalan workers are salvageable. They often appeal to alleged similarities in heritage and character between Guatemalan *campesinos* and Korean peasants. "The Guatemalan *campesino* is very much like the Korean peasant," said a Korean manager. "They are docile. They work hard. And, they even have short names like our peasants."[48] The director of KOTRA added, "The Indians are really Oriental, almost equal to us. They naturally work well in our factories and under our system of management."[49]

Regardless of the ultimate confidence in this transformative process, the management in Korean maquila factories openly implements a system of labor relations designed to totally control the behavior and actions of workers. The practice is based on a logical and conventional premise: machine operators are only productive while seated and working. Management's task, then, is to keep operators in this productive position for as long as possible. What makes the Korean system distinct is its use of extraordinary physical and psychological means to confine an operator to the productive state. "They never let us stop sewing, not even for a second. They tell us we are there to work. While we are in the factory, nothing else is permitted because productions mean profits," explained an operator.[50]

System of Worker Control

The Korean maquila system of worker control consists of three complementary practices: a brutally enforced discipline code; incessant pressure to produce; and a goal-oriented system of compensation. In Korean factories, the disciplinary code is oral and rigorously enforced through a hierarchial structure of command. Few Korean factories post company rules or explain them to workers. Instead, supervisors, using threats, rebukes, intimidation, and physical abuse, skillfully create an atmosphere of regimentation and fear. A manager at B y D Confecciones S.A. described his factory's policy: "It [the disciplinary policy] is actually quite simple. Workers need only maintain respect for the supervisors and follow the internal regulations." When asked to describe "internal regulations," he replied, "Whatever the supervisor says."[51]

Korean factory discipline sets extreme restrictions on movement and activity. Workers often are forbidden to rise from their seats without permission. As in elementary school, operators in many factories are required to raise their hands before leaving their benches. In particular, access to bathroom facilities is rigidly controlled and breaks limited in number and duration. In some factories, supervisors forbid use of the bathroom during working hours; and in other shops, supervisors carefully keep track of the number of times each worker visits the bathroom. If a worker exceeds the limit, she receives a verbal scolding and her wages may be docked. According to one worker: "You only get one or two minutes, no more. Or they will bang on the bathroom door and tell you to get back to work. Sometimes the supervisor will knock and say 'Too much time' 'Time to work.'"[52]

Disobedience, broadly defined as any divergence from management's dictates, is categorically prohibited in Korean factories. For Korean managers, regimentation depends on total conformity; every command, no matter how trivial, must be followed to sustain the system. When a worker disobeys an order, the entire system is challenged, and hence that behavior cannot be tolerated. A Guatemalan manager at Modas del Este S.A., a Korean factory, explained the rigidity of this policy: "We even lose good workers because of disobedient behavior. If a worker fails to follow a supervisor's command, she will go, no matter how productive she is."[53] "The most common reason for dismissal is disrespect for the company," explained the Korean personnel manager of Mi Kwang S.A. "For example, if they talk back to a supervisor, they are fired. We need people who cooperate; nonconformity is not tolerated."[54] Disagreement with a supervisor—no matter how justified—is cause for immediate dismissal in Korean factories. Workers well understand this fact and choose more often than not to withhold their anger and frustration.

Hierarchy of Enforcement

A hierarchy of Korean management enforces these controls with brutal intensity and dramatic precision. Floor supervisors who monitor and counter infractions represent the initial level of enforcement. Typically, supervisors stalk up and down the lines, overseeing quality of production as well as behavior. "They [the supervisors] are always watching us while we work. Always! They never take their eyes off us," complained a fifteen year-old worker at a Korean factory. "I am the first person in the line so I am the most easily and often watched. I can barely stand it some days."[55]

The second and highest level of enforcement lies with the plant manager. Generally, only when a worker resists and/or refuses to follow the orders of a supervisor or commits an egregious error such as damaging a machine will upper management involve itself in the dispute. Workers spoke with trepidation of being forced into the "office." "Supervisors sometimes grab a worker by the ear and take her to the office, and the next time we see her is outside the factory," reported a worker.[56] In the office, a manager subjects the worker to a tirade of abuse and often coerces her to resign "voluntarily."

Floor supervisors generally respond to worker misconduct with "attention"—a public verbal and/or physical rebuke. If a supervisor catches a worker in a "nonproductive" state, he likely will try to humiliate her in front of her peers. "They do not want you to talk, rise, walk around," explained a nineteen-year-old worker. "They only want you always to be centered at your machine. They will give attention to anyone who does otherwise."[57]

The severity of punishment generally increases with the cost and/or frequency of the offense. If a worker rises one time from her bench or turns to speak to a neighbor, a supervisor may yell at her to return to her proper position. Or, if nearby, the supervisor may place his hands on the worker's shoulders and roughly guide her back into place. Some supervisors routinely rap workers' heads with their hands or knuckles for such "minor" acts of misconduct. The line between these relatively innocuous punishments and more violent and humiliating ones is easily and often breached.

More serious misconduct includes eating at the work station, repeated talking or movement, or a sewing mistake. These acts elicit a more raucous, extended response. Most frequently, supervisors scream at the offender, calling her stupid or slow. In most Korean factories, every day at least one or two operators endure a supervisor's wrath while their peers look on. "When a supervisor yells at a worker, they do it at her worktable," said a worker. "The rest of us just pray that we are not the next one."[58] In some factories, workers reported an almost continual stream of invective. A fifteen-year-old worker fumed, "For every mistake they threaten that you will lose your job, and basically they yell at workers all day long."[59]

During these scoldings, Korean supervisors scream at the workers in either incomprehensible Spanish or Korean. In either language, workers usually comprehend the gist of the message from its tone and volume. "You can tell they [the Korean supervisors] are angry by the tone of their voice," explained a worker. "We do not understand what they are saying but we imagine it is pretty bad because they appear so angry."[60]

Korean supervisors and managers also regularly inflict corporeal punishment on workers. While usually reserved for the most serious offenses, it is not uncommon for supervisors to strike workers physically for routine errors. For example, when caught talking a second or third time, some workers reported that supervisors grabbed and shook their neck or hair. Other supervisors slam a stick down on the worker's hand, or throw pieces of cloth in her face. In Arirang S.A., workers related that when female Korean supervisors yelled at workers they would squeeze the workers' breasts. A young operator described the scene, "Sometimes when the women supervisors are yelling, and they want to make sure you are paying attention, they grab your breasts, hard."[61]

Generally, supervisors slap, punch, and kick a worker when she makes a costly sewing mistake, breaks a machine, or repeatedly talks to her neighbor. The most frequent cause of physical abuse, however, occurs when a worker "talks back" or otherwise shows "disrespect" to a Korean supervisor. One operator described such a situation: "One time a worker in my factory decided that she had suffered enough and yelled back at a Korean [supervisor]. I heard a loud clap and spun around to see her [the worker] holding her face and crying. The supervisor hit her, hit her hard. The whole factory stopped working. Then they yelled at us to start working, and we did."[62]

Faster, Faster, Faster

The second major ingredient of the Korean system of labor control is a relentless pressure to produce. Several workers commented that the only Spanish words Korean supervisors seem to know are "Faster!" "Hurry!" and "Let's go!" The pressure to speed up production is intense and literally nonstop. A Guatemalan administrator in a Korean factory explained his factory's practice: "If somebody is not working as fast as we need, we push, we push, and we push until we get it. . . . For example, if someone says, 'No I cannot make anymore,' we take out our stopwatches and say you can make this amount in such a time, and they have to finish before the designated time. And if they don't, I give them a punishment of some kind, not pay, but usually extra work after hours until they get the same pace as the other people. If the worker never speeds up, she is fired."[63]

Workers again and again recounted that this pressure makes them feel like machines. Explained a female worker at Sam Lucas S.A., "They holler 'Faster, faster!' 'Make haste!' They push us. How can I understand their language? I try to explain that I don't understand their explanations. They just keep yelling, 'Faster, Faster!' but we are human beings, not robots that simply work faster by pushing a button."[64]

The Korean Goal System of Compensation

The final component of the Korean managerial system is its "meta," or goal, system of compensation. Korean factories are the only maquila shops in Guatemala that pay workers per day, not per piece. Rather than depending on the incentive of making each worker an independent contractor with a piece-rate system, Korean factories employ a system of compensation based on group production goals. In addition to a basic daily wage, each line of workers is supposed to receive a bonus according to their level of daily or weekly production. A slate or scoreboard stands at the end of each line, with two numbers on it. The top one refers to the day's goal, and the bottom one indicates the latest count of completed pieces. The uniform practice of this system was confirmed by Ambassador Cho: "With this meta system, they [Guatemalan workers] are working very hard in our industry, as hard as workers in Korea. After six months of training and working, they are almost as productive as the Korean worker."[65]

In theory, the system encourages teamwork and cooperation. Ideally, the workers will grow together as a team and seek to achieve their collective bonuses through mutual cooperation. The greater the production of the line, the greater the compensation for its members. In practice, however, high levels of production are achieved almost in spite of a "team" dynamic of production. The constant humiliation, terror, and pressure for greater output are the critical driving forces. Workers never mentioned the notion or concept of "working together with her line-mates" in order to win a bonus. Instead, when asked what motivated them to increase efficiency, most workers spoke of the incessant pressure to produce and the fear of punishment for failure. "We have this terrible fear of the owner. If we see him, we begin to work harder," said a maquila worker. "I know it doesn't make sense. I wish I could get over this and realize we are all human."[66] Moreover, most Korean administrators, when asked why they use a goal system, provided rationales other than "teamwork." Several asserted that the major reason for the goal system is its ease of accountancy. None spoke of "teamwork" and "cooperation" as purposes of the compensation system.

The absence of worker comments on "teamwork" points to the misuse of this goal system of compensation. Almost always, the production goals set for each line are impossible to achieve within an eight-hour workday. Nevertheless, workers are promised that if they reach the goal, not only will they receive a bonus but they will be allowed to leave early. "Each line has a goal," explained a Korean manager of Modas Americas S.A. "Everyone is working on the same style and will receive a bonus and incentive if production meets the goal. Depending on production, you can even leave early and go home."[67] These goals, however, are rarely, if ever, achieved. A worker at Jobtex S.A. described the demoralizing effect of this system: "They put up these goals, usually 1,000 pieces a day. But we never reach them. The most we ever get to before 5 P.M. is 700 to 800. We spend the next couple of hours closing in on it, and even then sometimes, we leave without achieving it. Sometimes I wonder why they even put the numbers up at all."[68] This system is used to rationalize obligatory overtime. Its promise of financial reward is perverted: workers are forced to work extra hours without any additional compensation, not even for the overtime. The final blow is that even if the goal is reached, since the work was not finished within the allotted time, the bonus is almost always denied.

The real financial incentives are offered and given to the Korean line supervisors. In most shops, the supervisor with the most productive line wins a monetary bonus. This competition intensifies the pressures on the shop floor as the supervisors vie with one another for the money. Like overzealous coaches cheering their players on, supervisors' efforts to speed production escalate near the end of the day, as they try to edge out their colleagues for the daily bonus. This mounting pressure is "unbearable by the end of the day," commented a worker. "You would think their lives were on the line."[69]

The senseless implementation of the goal system of compensation demonstrates Korean management's ultimate confidence in its ability to control and mold workers into productive operators. Monetary incentives found in other maquila factories are unnecessary, and the ideal of cooperation professed in the Korean goal system is forsaken. Instead, it is systemized terror that motivates workers: workers produce in order to avoid punishment rather than to achieve bonuses. The effective implementation of a brutal system of labor control transforms workers, at least for a while, into compliant, efficient assemblers.

Because bonuses are rarely awarded, most workers in Korean maquila factories earn only the government minimum. Some factories pay workers less than the minimum if under age, while in the "training program," or during the two-month probationary period. Labor inspectors described several cases where workers who did not meet the daily goal also were paid less than the minimum wage. According to Korean managers and the embassy, workers are given Q.50, or US$.10, daily raises every six months to one year. Since most workers in Korean factories quit or are dismissed in less than six months, few ever receive this raise. Another reason for management to encourage employee turnover is to avoid paying legally mandated severance pay, which kicks in after one year of employment. Indeed, many workers and labor inspectors reported that Korean factories force workers with nearly a year of experience to resign expressly to elude this cost.

In addition to limiting costs and speeding production, this system of labor control deters unionization. Not surprisingly, employee turnover rates in Korean factories are exceptionally high, ranging between 25 and 40 percent a month. It is unusual to find a worker with more than a few months' experience in the same factory. While most Guatemalan and U.S. managers decried the continual movement of workers among factories as destroying a stable work force and efficient production, Korean managers never shared this opinion. Instead, some admitted that a constantly changing work force deters unions from organizing, since workers are unable to form allegiances. "To some extent, we regret the loss of good workers, but as you can see, there are many more ready and able waiting to take their place," explained a Korean personnel manager. "This turnover, however, has advantages. For example, we will never have a union, because the work force changes every other month."[70]

The Supervisors: Linchpins of the System of Labor Control

The effectiveness of the system of labor control in Korean maquila factories is dependent on the behavior of supervisors who are the day-to-day administrators. Most supervisors are in their early twenties. Some are married and leave their families behind in Korea; the majority, however, are single. About three-fourths of the supervisors are men; nearly all the Korean mechanics are male. According to Korean Embassy statistics, more than three hundred Korean nationals work in Korean factories. Others, including Labor Ministry officials, estimate that at least five hundred Koreans are working in the maquila industry. The most important administrative and managerial positions are staffed by Korean nationals. In more than three-fourths of the Korean factories a sizable portion of the floor supervisors are also Korean citizens. In several of the larger factories, there are as many as fifteen Korean line supervisors.

Labor Ministry officials, however, reported granting work permits to only two Korean nationals in 1990. The Ministry's director of statistics attributed this fact, at least in part, to the ministry's inefficient processing of foreign worker applications. More likely, hundreds of Korean personnel, mainly line supervisors, are working illegally in Guatemala. Most come to Guatemala on a tourist visa, go to work immediately, and stay beyond the legally prescribed limit. According to workers, when labor inspectors visit Korean factories, those supervisors without proper documentation hide until the inspectors depart.

Supervisors are either borrowed from "home" factories in Korea or, less frequently, the embassy acts as the agent, contracting supervisors for a specific factory. In addition, the embassy has assisted some Guatemalan factories to acquire Korean supervisors, who are normally employed for a two-year term, with the option to renew. During the two years, the supervisor lives and works at the factory without returning or, sometimes, even calling home. Transportation costs and room and board are supplied, along with a salary ranging from $800 to $1,200 a month, which is deposited in Korean bank accounts.[71]

Korean supervisors are almost always residents, and sometimes prisoners, of the factory. Factories become little cities. Most eat all their meals and sleep within or nearby its confines. Some supervisors live in tiny one-room apartments inside or adjacent to the factory, while others live communally in a house close to it. This proximity provides constant access to the factory.

Supervisors work extremely hard—frequently more than ninety hours a week. A Guatemalan manager at Modas del Este S.A. commented: "It is frustrating for workers because supervisors want them to work until ten at night. For them [supervisors], working two weeks straight, fifteen to twenty hours a day, is nothing."[72] Although it is explicitly prohibited by the Labor Code, when workers leave for the day, Korean supervisors run machines for several additional hours. These time commitments, the lack of transportation, and dependence on the benevolence of upper management to schedule recreational activities restrict movement and activity for Korean supervisors. Most do little else but work. It is possible for a supervisor to live for two years in Guatemala and never leave the confines of the factory. Under these conditions, most contracted Korean supervisors find a two-year term in Guatemala sufficient. Ambassador Cho admitted as much: "The supervisors suffer a lot in foreign countries and most prefer to return after their tour. Since most are single, they are eager to return to Korea to get married."[73]

Most Korean supervisors begin to work in maquila factories without any formal orientation to Guatemalan society and without the ability to speak Spanish. A few rudimentary phrases, such as "Rapido, rapido," are all that is needed to start. Relevant work jargon is learned on the job. Even after two years in Guatemala, few supervisors speak with even minimal proficiency because most of their time is spent in the factory or socializing with their Korean peers.

The fact that Korean supervisors oversee production without learning the language of their subordinates displays the inhuman simplicity of this system of labor control. In a kind of electric shock treatment, supervisors shake up and startle employees who err or disobey. Tone and intensity of speech, rather than words, differentiate approbation from censure; generally, silence indicates the former, while ranting denotes the latter. "When my supervisor picks up a piece I have just completed, I am filled with anxiety because I am never sure if it will pass his inspection," explained a worker. "If he says nothing, I know I have passed. If he yells, I know I have failed."[74]

In order to facilitate this brutish treatment of Guatemalan workers, Korean supervisors are discouraged from forming relationships with the workers. The high employee turnover alone presents a serious obstacle to even cordial relations between Korean supervisors and Guatemalan workers. In addition to this barrier and the obvious communication difficulties, factory rules and practices discourage relations outside of the workplace. For example, workers and supervisors eat meals and take breaks in different locations. Separate bathrooms also exist for supervisory personnel. In some factories, supervisors and workers never formally meet or exchange names. "I showed up and they gave me a machine. I do not think [the supervisors] know my name," said one worker. "They simply look at you, wave their fingers, and say something I rarely understand."[75]

In sum, Korean supervisors are the linchpins of the system of labor control. Like supervisors in non-Korean factories, they are the commanders of the shop floor, but what distinguishes Korean supervisors from others is the rigor and brutality of their command. Through verbal and physical abuses, they terrorize workers into efficient production. This brutal behavior is psychologically possible because these supervisors are separated culturally, linguistically, and physically from Guatemalan workers. For Korean supervisors, most Guatemalan workers are nothing more than objectified subordinates.

Transfer of Apparel-Assembly Technology or Technology of Terror?

Perhaps the greatest gap between the Republic of Korea's professed desire to assist in the economic development of Guatemala and the reality of Korean assistance is found in the understanding and application of "technology transfer." This phrase, ubiquitous in development literature and in the rhetoric of Korean officials, describes the donors' most profound contribution to the host country. Not only do foreign investors inject capital and employment into faltering economies, they train the native work force in the technology of the particular industry. And, as the local work force increases in skill, the country becomes a self-sustaining export platform and eventually a full manufacturer of more sophisticated industries.

The transfer of technology occurs on the shop floor where employees who gain a valuable new skill can advance to management. In the apparel-assembly industry, this transfer begins with training on the various machines, ranging from single-needle machines to more complex overlock and double-needle machines. Since the garment industry probably has the least technically sophisticated manufacturing process, the most important stage of the progression is the training of supervisors. When factories begin operation, foreign supervisors manage the shop floor. Ideally, the more experienced, competent operators gradually become floor supervisors, responsible for a group, or line, of operators. The mission of the foreign supervisors is to eliminate their own roles, eventually leaving the factory in the competent hands of the less expensive native workers.

As described above, the Korean ambassador has advocated technology transfer as essential to the industrialization of Guatemala. He points to Korea's thirty years of experience in the apparel industry and offers to share this wisdom with the people of Guatemala. "We expect to lead Guatemalans from simple operators to supervisors, and eventually Guatemalan-run factories will be as efficient and productive as our factories in Korea," explained Ambassador Cho. "It is only a matter of time."[76]

Despite Cho's confidence, beyond an introduction to the time discipline and relatively low technical skills of sewing machines, few workers in Korean factories acquire additional skills or managerial experience. Since production and efficiency is achieved through fear and humiliation, most workers' experience in Korean maquila factories is miserable and dehumanizing, a fact demonstrated by the high worker turnover rate. "What do we learn?" asked a worker in a Korean factory. "We learn to sit without moving or talking; we learn to hold in our anger; we learn to hate; and if we are lucky, we learn how to pretend we are busy so we can sneak rests."[77]

Further, whatever skills the Korean factories impart to Guatemalan workers are often learned under duress. Workers reported that some of the most frustrating moments occur when they are learning a new style or how to operate a machine. According to workers, training is almost always too rapid and too abrupt. "Everyone who is human commits errors, and we are not experts at first. We learn little by little. When you try to explain that you do not understand the operation, they do not listen. They only continue to yell. How are we supposed to learn in this atmosphere?" asked an operator.[78] The worker is caught in a bind. If she asks the supervisor to repeat the lesson, the supervisor will become hostile, humiliating her in front of her peers. If she begins to apply the newly learned stitch, she may follow the instructions correctly. However, the consequences of misapplication may be traumatic. First, she will likely draw the "attention" of a supervisor. Her cries that she never understood the technique will not be heard. If the pieces are reparable, she will probably mend them during voluntary overtime, late into the evening. If the pieces are beyond repair, she will likely have the cost of the cloth deducted from her salary—that is, only if she is not discharged instantly. Technology transfer, ironically, has become a source of extreme agony and anxiety for many Guatemalan workers.

Perhaps the most significant indictment of the overall failure of widespread transfer of skills is that Guatemalan supervisors do not appear to be replacing Korean ones in

Korean factories. According to Korean Embassy figures, the ratio of Korean to Guatemalan personnel per factory has remained virtually constant for more than two years. Further, four out of the first five Korean factories in Guatemala still have at least eight Korean managers and supervisors.

This continuing presence of Korean supervisors is attributable to deep mistrust of Guatemalan employees on the part of Korean management and to the fact that few Guatemalans desire the position. While Ambassador Cho says he wants Guatemalan supervisors in Korean factories, most Korean factories do not appear to share this sentiment. One Guatemalan administrator in a Korean-owned shop stated: "The Korean managers do not trust Guatemalan workers enough to let them supervise other workers. They hired me to work with customs and shipping, but they would not hire a Guatemalan to oversee the floor. That job is too important, and they say Guatemalans are not capable of doing it."[79]

A common complaint of Korean managers is that "capable" Guatemalan line and quality control supervisors are scarce. They tend, as one Korean manager explained, to be "too lenient and understanding with the workers. Guatemalans do not yet have the commitment to be supervisors. Production falls. They never last very long here. To be successful, they need to be tougher, more demanding."[80]

Another reason for the lack of Guatemalan supervisory personnel is the fact that most workers find the position objectionable and unattractive. "Who would want to be a supervisor? All they do is yell and punish," remarked an operator. "And the hours they work! It would be impossible to care for my children and work."[81] In the cases where Guatemalans do supervise in Korean factories, workers reported that they either become as oppressive as their Korean mentors or simply do not last. "We have a few Guatemalans who are supervisors, but they are as bad as the Koreans. It is as if they suddenly became Korean citizens," said a worker. "I guess the raise is worth it. But they no longer are friends of the workers."[82]

The extent of the transfer of productive knowledge and skills in Korean factories is difficult to document, especially in the short term. Based on current trends, however, the technology of terror practiced in Korean factories is not accomplishing the goals of the transfer of production technology. In short, workers loathe and learn little from the system, and local supervisors are not rapidly supplanting Korean ones. Despite this despair, Korean factories are the most productive in Guatemala. Yet it is difficult to see how these trends will provide a springboard for industrialization. Like Korean workers such as Chun Tae Il, Guatemalan workers may be forced to endure for the greater good. But if the workers have any say in the decision, they will certainly select a different path.

Guatemalan Reactions to the Korean Model: Worker Rage and Owner Jealousy

The combination of experienced supervisors and a repressive system of labor control has made Korean factories the most productive in Guatemala, but this success contains a major failure in public relations. Virtually every worker believes that these factories are the most dreadful in the maquila industry. Likewise, Guatemalan maquila owners express disdain for what they call the inhuman practices and isolationist behavior of their Korean counterparts. Since it is desperate for both foreign investment and jobs, the government has tended to overlook the abuse, usually with deliberate ignorance. More recently, however, prompted by U.S. Embassy officials and international pressure from unions and labor rights advocates, representatives of the Guatemalan government have joined in the criticism of Korean factories.

Naturally, Guatemalan workers condemn the practices of Korean management. The Korean ambassador, sensitive to criticism that his factories mistreat workers, blamed the discord on superficial differences in cultures, which in time will subside. "There is no great difficulty between Korean and Guatemalan workers because the personal character of the two peoples is very similar," he contended. "Of course, they have the language barrier but they can communicate very easily. Sometimes there are small misunderstandings, but these are very rare. Soon there will be none."[83] While it is possible this harmony may one day emerge, the contempt for Korean administrators is growing with every worker who is humiliated by a Korean supervisor.

The most common reaction of workers inside the factory to the Korean system of labor control is frustration and humiliation. Workers regularly weep when challenged by an enraged supervisor, an unattainable production goal, or other trying situation. "The only thing we can do is cry, and that is something we do often. If we argue, we lose our jobs. Instead, we choose to cry," explained a worker at Welly's S.A.[84] "Sometimes people are hit in the face by the supervisors," affirmed a worker at Korgua S.A. "They continue to work, but they cry. There is so much humiliation in this place. All we can do is weep."[85]

A telling example of the strained relations between Korean management and Guatemalan workers surfaced during an interview with a Korean manager at the factory Ace Internacional S.A. The manager claimed that the worker behavior which most troubled his staff was the excessive time they spent in factory bathrooms. He attributed these frequent, extended visits to irresponsible behavior and laziness, adding, "I don't understand why they would want to use them [the bathrooms] anyway. They smell so bad. I am disgusted by them."[86] A Guatemalan supervisor at the factory provided a different explanation for this "odd" behavior. "Workers use the bathrooms as a refuge. After a Korean supervisor scolds and humiliates a worker, she runs to the bathroom to cry and regain her composure."[87]

Weeping, however, is not the only response to this system of labor control. Several workers reported instances in which workers burst out laughing while being yelled at. "One time he [the supervisor] had lost complete control. He was raving up and down," said the worker. "I had no idea why, and I could not help laughing."[88] Other workers have defended themselves against pugilistic supervisors, blocking a hand and sometimes striking back. Still others have tried to protest collectively against the abysmal labor conditions. The most common response, however, is to resign. One worker summed up the reaction: "They demand so much for so little that we have no choice but to quit. Most of us simply cannot take the abusive atmosphere for more than a few months."[89]

Owners: Jealous Ridicule

A visit to a GEXPRONT-sponsored workshop or conference might lead an outsider to believe that Guatemalan entrepreneurs control most maquila production, because invariably almost all of the attendees will be Guatemalan. An important consequence of the Korean structure of production in which the embassy is the headquarters is that Korean factories, aside from purchasing some local components, are isolated from the other entrepreneurs and institutions of the maquila industry and the rest of the Guatemalan economy. A Korean shipping company has even been created so that Korean factories can transport their shipments independently. Officials of GEXPRONT are annoyed and frustrated by the fact that fewer than ten Korean factories pay dues, and that of these only one or two actually participate in events.[90] GEXPRONT's 1991 maquila promotion brochure, in its description of foreign investment, mysteriously omitted any mention of the Korean presence—a fact flaunted in the previous edition.

Because interaction between Guatemalan and Korean managers is rare, unfettered jealousy and rumors have festered within the Guatemalan business community. The most frequently voiced complaint, perhaps ironically, is that Korean management abuses and exploits Guatemalan workers. Ilse Patricia Ponce De Husmann, an owner of a maquila with over ten years experience in the apparel industry, asserted: "They [the Koreans] are hurting workers. Their mentality is different—work, work, work, and mistreat the workers to get them to work. They will learn that you cannot treat people in Guatemala the way they treat people in the Orient."[91] Still other Guatemalan entrepreneurs are disturbed by the ultimate secrecy and isolation in which the

Koreans do business. "It is as if they lived in their own separate world," commented a Guatemalan investor.[92]

Despite such sentiments, a handful of Guatemalan owners welcome the Koreans as their mentors. Confident in Ambassador Cho's promise, they believe that Korea will impart its experience in garment production to the Guatemalan industry. An owner expressed this positive view: "The Korean presence is most definitely good for the country. They came to Guatemala with all the uncertainties and invested their capital. We should applaud them for this effort and try to learn from their vast knowledge of the industry."[93]

For their part, Korean administrators are ambivalent toward native investors. Their lack of contact with GEXPRONT, along with the cultural and language barriers, has distanced most Korean owners from Guatemalans. Ambassador Cho does not see local entrepreneurs as competitors; instead, in his view, the smaller, less productive Guatemalan shops are pupils gradually learning from the larger, parent Korean factories. He explained, "We are transferring our know-how to Guatemalan enterprises, so as soon as they catch up with our level of industry we would like them to take over. We then will move on to new industries."[94]

Most Guatemalan owners, however, reject the offer to be pupils; they want to be leaders. This ambition, it seems, is the real cause of the opposition against Korean owners: Guatemalan entrepreneurs are jealous and covetous of the Korean domination of the maquila industry. Korean firms, with ample capital and extensive experience, in only a few years have become the major force in the industry. The well-founded belief that Korean investors have come to exploit the quota-free status of the Guatemalan industry exacerbates this tension. The president of VESTEX, Marco Antonio Rosalez, agreed, saying: "There is not a good reception for Koreans here. They are simply not welcome. They are famous already and do not have to come here to further spread this fame. It is our turn."[95] A representative of Comercializadora BBT Panamericana S.A. succinctly affirmed, "Koreans are no good, because they are taking the opportunity from Guatemalan businessmen."[96]

The Guatemalan Government: An Uneasy Alliance, Crumbling?

In July 1990, the Guatemalan government, in a well-publicized ceremony, awarded the Order of Quetzal, the highest civilian honor, to Hyun-Hwak Shim, a former prime minister of the Republic of Korea and current president of Samsung. The medal was presented in honor of, and in gratitude to, the Republic of Korea's "valiant contribution" to the economic and political development of Guatemala.[97]

Korea's sole "contribution" to the country's economic development of Guatemala has been dozens of garment maquila factories. In the last two years, Samsung alone has begun five of the largest maquila operations in Guatemala. And Samsung is not finished; the primary purpose of the former prime minister's visit was to survey future investment possibilities.

Less than a month after this ceremony the then chairman of the Labor Commission of the Guatemalan Congress confided: "The Labor Minister has admitted to us that his office cannot control the maquila industry. This country has become a paradise for Korean labor practices. We cannot tolerate it much longer."[98] Yet former labor minister Luís Maldanado Ruiz refused to comment publicly on the mounting outcry against Korean managers and supervisors, merely referring to Korean labor practices as "distinct."[99] In fact, up to the end of its term, the Christian Democrat administration remained silent about the well-known harsh treatment of workers in Korean factories. In light of this lack of official government criticism and action, many unionists and some Labor Ministry representatives speculate that the Korean and Guatemalan governments made a secret pact, in which Korea promised massive investment in exchange for guarantees against government and labor disruption.

The motives for such a pact are self-evident. Guatemala, like many of its neighbors, is in desperate economic straits—so desperate that the government does not believe it has the privilege to select who can and cannot invest in Guatemala. "The facts are simple. We need jobs, foreign exchange, and capital," explained a representative from the Economy Ministry. "We are not in a position to discriminate against investors. If the Koreans or the North Americans want to invest, we have no leverage to refuse or negotiate their offers."[100] As evidence, the Economy Ministry has never rejected the application or revoked the license of any maquila factory.

While no direct evidence of a conspiracy between Guatemala and Korea was offered, proponents of this theory provide some circumstantial evidence. First, though the Korean Embassy and plant management complained about immigration problems, they actually enjoyed exceptional freedom to employ their own nationals. No improperly documented Korean employee has been deported to Korea. Moreover, as described in Chapter 6, the Labor Ministry appears to have suspended enforcement of Article 13 of the Labor Code, which places specific limits on the percentage of foreign employees and salaries.[101] As a result, hundreds of Korean managers and supervisors have worked freely and illegally in the country.

Further, Ambassador Cho asserted that he had a "special relationship" with the Christian Democrat vice president Jorge Carpio Nicole and the Christian Democrat-sponsored labor federation CGTG (General Confederation of Guatemalan Workers).

Though the CGTG and Christian Democrat officials vehemently denied the allegation, Cho claimed that several labor disputes in Korean factories were "arranged very well" with the help of CGTG, the labor minister, and, in at least one case, the vice president. In each instance, a union failed to materialize.[102]

Whatever the level of collaboration between the former Christian Democrat government and the Korean Embassy, this alliance may be crumbling. In March 1991, as one of its first acts, the newly elected Congress formed a committee to investigate and recommend ways to counter deplorable labor conditions and wages in maquila factories. More significantly, the labor minister, Social Democrat Mario Solorzano—the only left-of-center member of the new rightist government—has begun a highly publicized crusade against the labor abuse in Korean-managed maquila factories. In its first months of office, the Labor Ministry issued a report concluding that the Korean maquila factories were guilty of egregious labor abuses and called for new labor legislation directed specifically at eliminating these violations.

Most unionists and labor rights advocates, however, question the sincerity of this newfound criticism of the maquila. They are quick to point out that throughout the new government's assault against Korean companies no mention has been made of labor violations, especially the forced labor, inadequate health and safety conditions, and paltry wages prevalent in Guatemalan and North American factories. Also forgotten is the dramatic exploitation of *campesinos* on Guatemalan plantations, where wages are often less and the toil much more difficult than in the maquila factories. In fact, the government has issued more rhetoric than it has made actual changes. Most poignant is the fact that the new administration, like its predecessor, has assisted maquila companies in their opposition to unionization, most recently refusing, without explanation, to process the application of workers at Phillips-Van Heusen factories for a union.[103] The Guatemalan Human Rights Office also found the Labor Ministry negligent in its investigation of the maquila industry, including covering up abuses.[104]

The matter of the Korean maquila factories is, in the words of one political analyst, "the perfect political issue."[105] The abuse is flagrant. The victims are young women and minors. The abusers are recently arrived foreign intruders (who happen not to be North American); and, most important, they are intruding on the turf of wealthy Guatemalans. Thus far, except for the Korean ambassador, no one has defended the Korean industry against this criticism. Most elements of the private-business sector want the Korean investment to stall so that the Koreans will not swallow up the entire industry. "The government comes off as the courageous hero, rebuking the foreign invaders and saving the young women," commented a Guatemalan journalist. "To make things perfect, the private sector is applauding its efforts."[106]

An unanswered question is whether the Guatemalan government can afford a breach with Korean entrepreneurs. Up to now, action has been limited to public criticism. What measures will the executive or Congress take to correct the abuses? It is doubtful that they will jeopardize the financial welfare of other maquila owners. Increased vigilance on the part of the labor inspection may disrupt other factories. Even if the government were successful in pressuring Korean factories to curb their harsh treatment of Guatemalan personnel, the effects on future Korean and other foreign investment might be detrimental. The legacy of the fleeing Transcontinentales still looms large in the minds of U.S. investors. And, in the end, the new regime, like its predecessor, cannot afford to lose this critical influx of jobs and capital.

The U.S. Giant Waits Its Turn

The U.S. State Department and AID officials are loath to admit that their efforts to spur maquila investment have benefited Korean entrepreneurs rather than U.S. ones. Yet that is exactly what has occurred. Over the last six years, AID has skillfully directed the construction of a stable export apparatus. However, the main foreign investors who have taken advantage of this structure have been from Korea. U.S. investors at whom the structure was principally aimed have yet to arrive. This leaves U.S. officials in a uncomfortable position: they consider the Guatemalan maquila industry a successful "pet project," but would much prefer that U.S. companies led the industrial expansion.

Resolution of this quandary appears to be surfacing. Little by little, U.S. officials are joining Guatemalan critics in condemning Korean investment. As late as March 1989, the U.S. Embassy was publicly ambivalent toward Korean factories. An unclassified memo reported that "[t]he Koreans also provide clean, well-lighted working conditions and a variety of non-cash benefits ranging from sports programs to housing improvements." On labor practices, the memo continued, "Management is openly seeking to develop a spirit of worker identification with the company and to discourage union organizing."[107] Yet a little more than a year later, in early 1990, the U.S. Embassy was a leader, albeit silent, in encouraging official outcry of the Guatemalan government against the same factories. United States Ambassador Thomas Stroock prompted Guatemalan congressmen to initiate the commission to investigate abuses in Korean factories. Asserting that the abuses of Guatemalan workers is a "very, very serious problem in Korean factories," the U.S. Embassy labor attaché also aided the new Labor Ministry's quest to reveal Korean factory abuses.[108]

Considering the U.S. State Department's recent "discovery" of Korean labor abuses, the motive for condemnation appears to be opportunistic. The mounting pressure against Korean investors could move them out, leaving a hole for U.S. investors to fill. In a different tone, Ambassador Cho is now calling for cooperation between the United States and the Republic of Korea "to resolve the problems of Guatemala and the Caribbean." If it were to follow the Korean economic/industrial development model of investment rather than loans and credit, Cho claimed, "the United States would reduce its economic and military assistance to these countries."[109]

From all accounts, the U.S. State Department has not been receptive to this offer of cooperation. More likely, the State Department wants U.S. investors to displace Koreans in order to open up proven venues for U.S. capital. Alvaro Colom, the premier maquila consultant, concurred: "I think U.S. investment will be motivated if some Korean companies leave the country. In particular, the U.S. government would be pleased. They do not like this type of treatment and would like to see U.S. investors who treat workers correctly take root in the industry."[110]

"The *chinos* treat the workers very badly," said a young worker.[111] Traditionally, Asian immigrants to Guatemala and Central America themselves have suffered discrimination, isolation, and sometimes physical abuse. The word *chino* is frequently used pejoratively to describe all Asians. The arrival of the Korean model of investment has added fuel to this bigotry. From union halls to GEXPRONT meeting rooms, Koreans are decried as inhuman and unethical managers. "They [the Koreans] ought to return to their own country and abuse their own people. We don't want and we don't need them," declared an enraged Guatemalan manager.[112] In particular, Ambassador Cho has been the object of a series of ad hominem attacks from the media and government. The frustrated ambassador lamented: "I just don't know what to do. They refuse to see the value in our work. What can we do to make them understand?"[113] Fortunately, the plain-clothes guards outside the Korean Embassy have not been provoked into firing their automatic submachine guns. The potential for an explosion of racial hatred, however, is very real.

8 Conclusion: Reconciling the Demands of Capital and the Needs of Labor

Emilio's Opportunity

The maquila industry has offered "Emilio," a young Guatemalan entrepreneur, the chance of a lifetime. After graduating from a private university in the United States, Emilio worked as an engineer for a Guatemalan computer company. "I might still be at that job, staring at computer screens, if this opportunity had not come along," he confided.[1] When he was only twenty-three years old, Emilio and a financial partner opened a thirty-machine maquila factory. In the beginning the shop survived by contracting excess work from larger factories. Within three years the plant was negotiating directly with U.S. labels, and production had increased tenfold. This rapid and lucrative expansion reveals only a fragment of Emilio's vision. He and his partner have purchased a second building which, when filled with workers and machines, will double production capacity.

When asked what was his best experience in the industry, Emilio exclaimed, "Profits!" He and his partner enjoy a 40 percent profit margin on sales, most of which is deposited in U.S. bank accounts. Emilio believes that all participants in the maquila industry, if they work hard enough, can enjoy similar material benefits. "We are providing opportunities these people [the workers] never knew were possible," he explained. "[The maquila industry] will help these people buy televisions and bring them into the modern era."[2]

For Emilio, prosperity, however, requires dedication and collaboration. He works hard, at least ten to twelve hours a day, six days a week. Expecting his employees to approach their jobs with equal devotion, he demands that operators work as long as he deems necessary: "If they [the workers] refuse to work overtime, they will not work here." Emilio considers union activity the antithesis of this requisite collaboration, a sign of outright disloyalty. As a consequence, suspected organizers and troublemakers are routinely discharged.

Pleased by the government's dedication to the maquila industry, Emilio stated: "The government for the first time in my life has done something good—they opened up an opportunity for people who could use it. This is the beginning of a revolution, from sewing to computers. We are the new Korea!"[3]

Maria's Predicament

Only thirteen years old, "Maria" works at Sung Sil S.A., a five-hundred-machine shop owned by Samsung, a Korean TNC. Sung Sil is located in a recently constructed maquila factory park ten miles outside of Guatemala City. Maria lives with her two brothers, her parents, and her grandmother in a two-room shack on a dirt road near the modern factory. She does not attend school and cannot read. But Maria can sew—for eleven hours a day, six days a week she sews. When management requires, she works until 3:00 A.M., and then rises four hours later to begin again.

The compensation and conditions at Maria's factory are not commensurate with the restraints on her freedom. Maria rarely enjoys her paltry earnings, which total slightly more than US$1 a day, because the income is used to pay family debts. "My paychecks are their paychecks," she said, pointing to her family.[4] Finding the pressure to produce demoralizing and physically exhausting, Maria articulated her powerlessness: "They [the supervisors] never let up on us, always pushing for more. Sometimes I just can't take it, and I break down and cry. I mean, I am so young. Will I have to do this the rest of my life? Isn't there something we can do?"[5]

Living on the brink of survival, Maria has few options: if she refuses to work extra hours or demands a raise, management will fire her, and her family will sink deeper into poverty; if she says nothing, she will endure physical and psychological abuse. Like most of her coworkers, Maria has opted for the latter, suffering in silence.

Explaining Away the Vicious Side: Central American Jaguar

Emilio's experience of exhilaration and exploration and Maria's experience of poverty and imprisonment exemplify the divergent accounts of the maquila industry in Guatemala. Many AID and Guatemalan government officials and entrepreneurs hail the maquila as the most important and productive economic phenomenon in the last three decades. To them, the maquila industry presents a unique opportunity offered by "development capitalism": participating in a free market, entrepreneurs with minimal capital can simultaneously enjoy healthy profits and contribute jobs and technology critical to the economic development of their country. Specifically, entrepreneurs like Emilio and their financial supporters believe that maquilazation— industrialization through increasingly sophisticated assembly industries—is the most practical vehicle for industrial development. By far the fastest-growing sector in the economy, the industry appears to be living up to its proponents' expectations; in 1991, more than fifty thousand were employed and several hundred million dollars'-worth of assembled garments were exported.

As this study documents, however, these figures and Emilio's success are only one side of the story. Interviews with workers and labor inspectors and visits to factories reveal an industry prospering from the toil and suffering of Maria and other poor children and young women. Factory conditions and compensation are drastically inadequate: obligatory overtime, restrictions on movement, and incessant pressure to produce transform shops into work camps. Fundamental human rights such as the freedom of association and the prohibition against forced labor are virtually absent inside factory walls. Individual and collective efforts to improve these brutal conditions have repeatedly failed. Lost employment and violent suppression are the only consistent results.

Those proponents of maquilazation who acknowledge the existence of this vicious, dehumanizing side of the maquila industry claim that worker suffering and restraints on freedom are the necessary, but temporary, evils—the "growing pains"—of a country attempting to break out of the cyclical poverty of a preindustrial, economically unbalanced society. They assert that the maquila industry, despite its present harshness, offers eventual prosperity to all participants, a possibility unknown in the traditional agro-export economy. A GEXPRONT official described this opportunity: "The maquila industry is unlike the traditional bases of this economy—coffee, sugar, and bananas—where wealth is limited to the production of the land and the price of the market. There is only so much land, and it is already divided. The yearly migrants who harvest will never enjoy this wealth. On the other hand, the maquila industry will continue to multiply. The employment is limitless, as is the wealth. And unlike the coffee *finca*, the worker can and will share in this prosperity."[6]

Such advocates argue that the industry provides both a short- and a long-term response to Guatemala's endemic poverty. In the short term, the maquila strategy offers, at the very least, employment and supplementary household income. Considering the existing acute poverty and widespread under- and unemployment, jobs—of whatever quality—are precious.

Over the long term, if maquilazation is implemented correctly, proponents contend that it presents an unprecedented opportunity to industrialize Guatemala. Espousing a "ladder" model of development, they assert that industrialization will occur through a series of increasingly sophisticated and capital-intensive export-assembly operations. Relatively unsophisticated garment-assembly production initiates the scheme, with textiles, lightweight electronics, appliances, and more sophisticated manufacturing, such as computers, to follow.

Maquila strategists readily concede that sacrifice and austerity on the part of the workers is necessary for long-term success. In particular, employees at the start will endure primitive factory conditions and some restrictions on freedom. "Certainly, we will have to sacrifice in the beginning. Sewing is not an easy job, but, then again, neither is harvesting sugarcane," said a GEXPRONT official, who himself had never cut cane or operated a sewing machine. "But we must be patient. This tremendous growth is a hint of things to come. Soon we shall have electronics [factories] and before long workers will see the results of their efforts."[7] Indeed, most promoters claim that workers control their own destinies. Labor, gradually accumulating mastery and skill, is the fuel of this expansion and will enjoy progressively improved benefits so long as it is obedient to the demands of capital. The sooner workers become proficient and efficient, the quicker their anguish will end. "Workers must understand that this industry depends on their cooperation," said an AID official. "In fact, this kind of industrialization will only progress if the worker works with, not against, management."[8]

The experiences of the newly industrialized countries of Southeast Asia—South Korea, Taiwan, Hong Kong, and Singapore—provide the paradigmatic examples for this ladder development model. Over the last three decades, the Asian Tigers, so this historical view proposes, embarked on this strategy with simple garment-assembly operations, in a few decades achieving astounding levels of industrialization and self-sufficiency. This notion that Guatemala can become the next Asian tiger is a core belief of the maquila promoters and has led some AID officials to begin calling Guatemala the "Central American Jaguar."

Short-term Solution: Alleviation or Perpetuation of Hunger?

"If you go out into the countryside and ask the people what they want, they always say a maquila factory or nontraditional exports," claimed an AID official.[9] Few

Guatemalans, workers or managers, argue with this depiction, but most think the peasants' longing for maquila factories demonstrates the depth of their economic misery rather than the attractiveness of the industry. A labor leader described the opening of a maquila factory near his town: "A large [maquila] factory opened near my village. Before it arrived, the situation was very difficult. In fact, it was so bad that people regularly ate chilies to hold off the hunger. With the factory there was a certain level of alleviation, of improvement. The population responded with great enthusiasm because at least now there were jobs. But how else could they react? The desperation of the people necessitates taking jobs that earn little money, because a job, no matter how miserable, is better than eating chilies."[10] For workers, unions, and some U.S. and Guatemalan government officials, the reaction of these villagers captures Maria's and other workers' predicament: while the conditions and compensation may be inhuman, for thousands the maquila industry provides a necessary, albeit brief and insufficient, respite from hunger.

Although the maquila industry contributes an important source of income to many households, its precise impact on poverty is difficult to evaluate. The creation of fifty thousand maquila jobs has not reduced under- and unemployment because the maquila industry does not employ the male workers who compose most of the unemployed. Instead, the maquila industry employs almost exclusively girls and young women who entered the formal sector for the first time when they accepted positions in the factories. Many were neither working nor seeking employment prior to the advent of the maquila industry.

More significantly, the very economic restructuring that AID and the World Bank believe necessary to lure maquila investors—specifically, the devaluation of the local currency and the removal of price controls—has cut the real income and purchasing power of most Guatemalans, notwithstanding nontraditional exporters and the landed oligarchy. These measures have impelled many young girls and women, who otherwise would not have, to join the economically active population to supplement household income. Forced to work by these maquila incentive measures, the maquila worker earns a less than subsistence wage that effectively serves to bond her to the factory. According to a 1991 study, a family of four requires almost eight times the government set minimum wage—which in all but a handful of factories is the maximum wage—to meet subsistence needs.[11] Describing the compensation, one unionist at Pindu said: "The [maquila worker's] salary is a superexploitation. The maquila worker works for such a small amount that it is almost useless to her. As such, the maquila is a new name for the free work that occurred in another time in the history of humankind. This is a modern example of slavery."[12]

Long-term Miracle: Central American Jaguar?

Guatemala is not the first country to attempt to follow in the footsteps of the Asian Tigers. During the 1980s in countries throughout Central America and the Caribbean, AID development experts made favorable comparisons to the possible replication of the economic "miracles" of Southeast Asia.[13] After more than a decade of experimentation in the region, this rhetoric has failed to spawn any genuine industrial development in the region, much less a newly industrialized country. Political turmoil and unreliable utilities and services in Jamaica, the Dominican Republic, and Haiti have proven formidable barriers to maquilazation. In these nations, maquila-sector development has stalled: apparel and other sewing operations such as sporting goods dominate, with a sprinkling of light-weight electronics-assembly operations. Even Costa Rica, with its more educated work force and stable political situation, is locked in this apprentice stage of apparel and electronic assembly.

Like its neighbors, Guatemala is not in a political or economic position to duplicate the Asian model of development. In addition to the fundamental question of whether development experiences are historically and geographically transferable, the obvious fact that the international market can sustain only a few "Korean miracles," and the complexities inherent in a heterogeneous population such as that found in Guatemala, the lack of a powerful central government in itself precludes the possibility of repeating the experience of the Asian Tigers.

The role played by the central governments in the Asian economic successes cannot be overstated. In the Korean experience, the most frequently mentioned model for Guatemala, an authoritarian central government, much like those in state socialist economies, methodically planned and systematically achieved production goals. Rather than being manipulated by the private sector, the Korean government dictated the economic agenda and wielded financial and police power to "protect the interests of local firms as well as to regulate foreign participation."[14] "[I]t could be argued that the Korean model," concluded an AID study, "if it demonstrates anything, shows that government intervention in the private sector has been as profound, pervasive, and all encompassing as in many socialist countries. A *laissez-faire* economy it is not."[15]

Even during military dictatorships, however, the Guatemalan central government has consistently been an impotent actor in matters of economic reform and development; the Guatemalan landed oligarchy is and has been the major economic player.[16] A historic, pervasive mistrust between the Guatemalan private-business sector and government, in most instances, impedes substantial cooperation or partnership. Thus, although private-sector, Guatemalan government, and AID officials all have embraced the maquila strategy, the division of responsibilities is clear: the government passes the laws, the private sector implements them, and AID supervises and sustains the process.

Specifically, without the leadership of a strong central government, the improvements in infrastructure and education necessary to foster industrial development will not occur. The second smallest public sector and one of the lightest tax bases in the world, combined with widespread government corruption, makes for an ineffectual and inefficient central government.[17] One consequence is the government's inability to maintain, much less improve, its infrastructure. Ports, road, and airports are literally crumbling.

More important, expenditures on public education are woefully inadequate. Few maquila workers have graduated from elementary school, much less high school; most, as a result, are illiterate.[18] Apparel and light-electronics assembly does not require a literate work force. But more sophisticated industries do demand a more adaptable and educated labor force. Korea's economic miracle was only possible because of a simultaneous miracle in public education. Education, as one study states, played "a critical role in the modernization of Korea; it did this primarily by assisting a strong government with 'modernizing' policies to impose its will upon the nation."[19] As a result of the government's emphasis on education, literacy in Korea leaped from 22 percent of the adult population in 1950 to 95 percent in 1974.[20] In contrast, the Guatemalan education system only reaches a small portion of the population—far less than in other developing nations. An AID study of forty developing nations found that the countries spend, on average, 3.5 percent of their Gross Domestic Product (GDP) on education; Guatemala, by comparison, spends 1.18 percent of its GDP educating its populace.[21] Out of 3.5 million Guatemalan children between five and eighteen, only 1.5 million are enrolled in school.[22]

Without radical educational initiatives, which can only be accomplished through increased public revenues, new factories may arrive but will find a dearth of qualified personnel. Already, management in many maquila shops complains of a lack of skilled local supervisors and middle managers. As factories sprout up in rural areas where schools are even more scarce and Spanish is the second language for the majority of the population, these problems will become more acute.

Acknowledging these obstacles, some promoters believe that the private sector, in turn, is capable of implementing all elements, including infrastructure and education, of the development of a Central American Jaguar. While the business class may possess the raw political might to guide and implement this growth, it lacks the consensus and the will to carry it out. Intransigent opposition to any form of wealth redistribution, widespread lack of support from the nation's landed oligarchy, and simple greed all frustrate any realistic hope for unilateral, private-sector-led industrialization.

Unless the government acquires the muscle or cooperation to guide and nurture the industry efficiently, Guatemala's maquilazation will not follow the path of the Asian Tigers. It is not a matter of vision, but of will. All the essential parties—the government, the private sector, and AID—want the maquila industry to prosper and thrive. The major impediment is the central government's incapacity to control development and allocate resources.

Nontraditional Exports Alone: A Superficial Solution

A final difficulty with the maquila strategy specifically, and the nontraditional export strategy of development generally, is their predominance in the development plans of AID and hence in the economic charter of the Guatemalan government and private sector. The U.S. government has designated nontraditional exports (and the economic restructuring necessary to stimulate their growth) as the exclusive means of economic development for Guatemala. Many development experts readily concede that nontraditional exports, including the maquila industry, can probably be vital components of an effective development strategy in the modern international division of labor and production—but not alone.[23] Serious development strategies cannot ignore the fundamental wealth and political inequalities perpetuated by a disparity in ownership of the sources of wealth, particularly land, that surpasses every country in the region. Without additional reforms aimed at alleviating this underlying problem, the maquila strategy remains a superficial response to deep-seated poverty.

Since the CIA-directed coup in 1954, Guatemalan economic policy-making and implementation have been dependent on U.S. economic and technical aid. The effective interruption of this economic aid from 1977 to 1985, combined with domestic strife and a regional recession, destroyed the Guatemalan economy, leaving it in the worst condition in over thirty years. The 1986 election of a civilian government induced the Reagan administration to renew the U.S. commitment to economic development in Guatemala. Almost immediately, a fully-staffed AID mission was reinstalled, and economic assistance was restored, increasing from $5 million in 1984 to $150 million in 1987.[24]

From the first days of its return, AID's plans for Guatemala were identical to those for other countries in the region: to prepare the country for competition in the world market and create a haven for U.S. direct investment. At AID's prompting, the new regime immediately targeted the import substitution development structures of the 1960s and 1970s for demolition. Tariffs were removed, price controls lifted, and the currency devalued. The runaway inflation and spiraling cost of living caused by these initiatives were accepted as part of the initiation to the world market.

These policy changes set up the centerpiece of this strategy: the reintroduction and the promotion of nontraditional exports. In the early 1970s, U.S. development experts, faced with the demise of the Alliance for Progress—particularly its emphasis on tax and agrarian reform—selected by default nontraditional exports as the new development policy. In essence, that policy was a reaction to the failure of Alliance redistribution efforts. The actual implementation of this strategy, however, was interrupted by President Carter's aid cutoff in 1977. Reinvigorated with the return of AID a decade later, nontraditional export production spread to the fields and factories. Traditional crops such as corn and beans gave way to blueberries, cauliflower, and tulips—products more desired in Western markets. In the industrial sector, scores of garment maquila factories opened and began assembling cheap garments for large North American department stores.

With the imprimatur of AID and the carrot of U.S. economic aid, the Guatemalan government adopted the nontraditional strategy as the path to national prosperity. "Nontraditional exports," confirmed a high-level Economy Ministry official, "will be the means of social and economic development for Guatemala for the twenty-first century."[25]

Thus, the nontraditional export model emerged as an alternative, not a complement, to remedy economic disparity in Guatemala. It focuses on a more equal distribution of future wealth, not on redistribution of present sources of wealth. In particular, this new strategy avoids redistribution of land—Guatemala's most valued but least shared resource. Byron Morales, a union leader at UNSITRAGUA, explained the superficial nature of this scheme: "Basically, there is a tremendous need for employment in Guatemala. The [maquila] industry gives a partial answer to this problem. But we need deep answers to our deep-rooted problems. . . . The real answer to unemployment must begin with the redistribution of our most important asset: land."[26]

For decades, Morales and other progressive forces have contended that although land reform would not eliminate poverty, it would provide thousands of families with a stable income and slow the massive migration to the urban areas. Because land is the foundation of the indigenous culture, agrarian reform would also enhance the long-trampled-upon rights of the indigenous people who account for at least half the population. Most important, substantial land redistribution would lessen the disparity of wealth between rich and poor, increase political stability, reduce dependence on food imports, and build the internal market—prerequisites of any viable development strategy. Nevertheless, AID officials today denigrate this solution as a failed relic.

However, as one journalist noted: "It is not that land reform has been tried and failed [in Guatemala]. It is that the proponents of land reform have been tried and killed."[27]

Ironically, the development experiences of the Asian Tigers—the very models cherished by these AID experts—clearly demonstrate that nontraditional export production was a necessary, but not sufficient, cause of their economic prosperity. For instance, prior to embarking on their economic miracle, Korea and Taiwan underwent major agrarian reform programs, easing the disparity of wealth. One AID study concluded of the Korean land reform: "Korea demonstrates that land reform is likely to be the single most important criterion for overall equitable distribution of a heavily populated, land-poor developing society."[28] Furthermore, Korean national industries, such as steel and shipbuilding, were successful only because the government protected their development with rigid tariff barriers, precisely the trade practice that the nontraditional export strategy seeks to eliminate in Guatemala.

For centuries, inexpensive labor combined with arable land has been Guatemala's comparative advantage in the world market. Since the Spanish conquest, control over labor through decree and coercion has enabled the agro-export sector and its proprietors to flourish. Today, labor controlled by force has given way to labor controlled by hunger. Most Guatemalans, particularly the indigenous population, continue to live in extreme poverty. Tens of thousands die from hunger-related diseases each year, and more than half the economically active population lack consistent employment. This desperate situation has perpetuated an enormous pool of cheap labor. For many maquila investors, this comparative advantage of labor offsets domestic strife and an inadequate infrastructure. When asked why he chose to invest in Guatemala, one investor responded sarcastically: "Labor, and labor alone. I certainly did not come here for my personal safety."[29]

The vitality of the Guatemalan maquila industry, then, depends mainly on the attractiveness of the labor force. If workers succeed in unionizing and/or winning wage increases, Guatemala's comparative advantage weakens. Already five factories have relocated because of union activity. What benefits the maquila industry brings to Guatemala can only last as long as investors find the atmosphere congenial to investment. If the country does not develop other comparative advantages, such as a modern infrastructure or a literate work force, the health of the maquila industry will continue to rest precariously on the lowness of wages and the docility of the work force.

An Industry That Will Accommodate Emilio's Demands and Maria's Needs

Without significant distributive reforms, the maquila industry will probably expand, but production will be limited to apparel, and possibly a handful of light-electronics factories. These apprentice industries, however, need not be deleterious to workers. Unjust compensation and brutal working conditions result from avaricious investors and an incompetent, and possibly complicitous, government, not the nature of the production. Non- and weak enforcement of outdated and toothless labor laws enables factories to operate without restraints. In a few plants, spontaneous and organized worker uprisings have provoked and produced divergent, more humane, practices. Ironically, most maquila workers seem to enjoy the work; some even find it fulfilling; but all detest the treatment, hours, and wages. "I like to create. I like to sew," said a worker. "It is the constant harassment and pressure to produce that make me feel like quitting at the end of each day."[30]

Even in its deplorable state, one should not trivialize the economic contribution of the maquila industry to tens of thousands of Guatemalan households. Without this supplemental income, these families would endure greater hardships. Most workers choose this extra income over the deprivation of physical and emotional well-being. While workers move from factory to factory, hoping for improvement, few appear to drop out of the maquila labor force altogether. Alternative solutions do not exist, but they could. "The maquila industry is thriving on the grave necessity of Guatemalans," explained a maquila worker. "There is the need for bread, for another tortilla for the children, but this can be eliminated in more ethical, humane ways. These conditions in maquila factories are unacceptable at any moment in history. With the maquila we are perpetuating the exploitation, the core of the problem."[31]

An ideal apparel and light-electronics maquila industry would provide a safe, healthy, and dignified working environment, the unimpeded right to organize, a just wage for workers, *and* adequate profits for entrepreneurs. Such an arrangement would satisfy the demands of capital and the needs of labor. Emilio and his financial backer's primary objective is profits. Their profit margin, if accurate, is extraordinary by any objective measure. A 40 percent margin on sales, or even half that amount, well exceeds the threshold for prudent investment. Explained one AID official, "Guatemalans know it would be foolish to invest in anything that returns less than what they would receive if they left their money in U.S. bank accounts and money-market funds. Generally, the return must exceed 10 percent. Today, even the most sloppily run maquila factory meets this requirement. Few, if any, factories close because of financial difficulties."[32] Whether or not entrepreneurs would be completely satisfied with less profits is uncertain; but if the receipts exceed the U.S. bank account interest rate, the threshold for investment has been met.

A humane maquila industry would ameliorate much of Maria's anxiety and agony.

In a more perfect world, a thirteen-year-old girl would be in school, not a factory, but the indigence endured by most Guatemalans dictates another order. Maria must work to assist her family's survival. The maquila industry is not wholly responsible for, nor can it alone alter, this predicament. Maria could work in a factory that permitted, and perhaps paid for, evening literacy classes; that permitted work breaks in the morning and afternoon to prevent cumulative trauma disorders; that implemented a fair piece-rate scale; that respected the workers' right to organize and collectively bargain.

The more difficult question is not whether this ideal industry, or even one approaching it, is theoretically possible, but whether it is feasible in contemporary Guatemala. Realization of this ideal industry would require overcoming an enormous, possibly insurmountable, obstacle: the absence of a strong organization to uphold and protect minimal working conditions and the freedom to associate in the factories. The government or labor unions are the most logical candidates to improve and sustain equitable factory conditions. Under the current circumstances, however, the Labor Code and its system of enforcement are almost farcical. Only radical modernization, restructuring, and reallocation of resources can mold this inept apparatus into an effective guardian of worker rights.

U.S. Government and Worker Rights in the Maquila Industry

Because the United States represents the largest market and, to a great extent, dictates the conditions of development, achievement of even minimal success in the endeavor to improve labor's plight is dependent on U.S. involvement. The impact of U.S. foreign and trade policy on Guatemala is enormous. The United States is Guatemala's largest trading partner, supplying 40 percent of imports and receiving 32 percent of exports.[33] In particular, U.S. markets receive more than 95 percent of Guatemalan apparel-assembly exports. Beyond economic dependence, the Guatemalan military, the nation's major political force, has deep links with the U.S. military.

The U.S. government therefore possesses the economic and political leverage and power to compel and carry out vast improvements in the Guatemalan maquila industry. On the one hand, it can make access to its market conditional on the protection of minimal worker rights. On the other hand, U.S. economic assistance and expertise are capable of erecting a structure to protect these rights.

One of the most obvious ways to use this influence is to make the issuance of apparel quotas and the availability of Guatemalan-assembled goods for duty-free entry programs dependent on the state of the rights of maquila workers. The Generalized

System of Preferences[34] and the Caribbean Basin Economic Recovery Act,[35] trade statutes that provide duty-free entry for goods imported from specified developing nations, contain such worker rights provisions.[36] Under this system, if a recipient country is not "taking steps" to afford fundamental, internationally recognized worker rights—which include the freedom of association, the right to organize and bargain collectively, the prohibition on the use of any form of forced or compulsory labor, a minimum age for the employment of children, and acceptable conditions of work with respect to minimum wages, hours of work, and occupational safety and health—the executive is required to suspend tariff benefits to that program.

While much controversy surrounds the efficacy of these worker rights provisions,[37] a similar program specific to apparel-assembly industries, it seems, would be easier to formulate and carry out than these more wide-reaching trade schemes. Already when the U.S. government negotiates an apparel quota with an importing nation, a multisector committee composed of government, private-sector, and labor representatives visits the importing country and meets with its representatives several times to discuss the contents of the agreement. On visits to the importing nation, U.S. members of this negotiating team could easily investigate the state of worker rights in the apparel-assembly industry. Since in many countries, including Guatemala, the apparel-assembly industry is clustered around urban areas or is located in geographically confined zones, inspection of these facilities, as well as interviews with workers and labor representatives, are manageable tasks.

Furthermore, the United States could mandate that the importing nation allow union representatives from all significant labor federations, and perhaps members of women's rights organizations, to participate in the negotiations to ensure that the rights of workers will be aired at the negotiating table. Finally, since the quota is variable and negotiated at regular intervals, the U.S. negotiators possess substantial latitude to vary the amount according to the progress or regression of the nation's protection of labor rights in the industry. In a similar manner, for non-quota items, the U.S. government could devise a scheme making the use of the only tariff reduction program that benefits apparel imports, HTS 9802.00.80 and HTS 9802.00.60 (previously known as Item 807 and Super 807, respectively), conditional on the status of labor rights.

If such a review of Guatemalan factories were undertaken today, quotas (Guatemala only has two) would likely be reduced and access to HTS 9802.00.80 duty-free programs suspended. The litany of failed union-organizing drives and destroyed unions in the industry plainly demonstrates the absence of the right to associate, organize, and collectively bargain in the industry. The case of the organizing efforts in the Phillips-Van Heusen factories, in which the government has failed to process the prospective union's application within the legally mandated thirty days, thereby halting the organizing effort, is simply the most recent example of this deficiency. Virtually every factory practices forced labor in the form of obligatory overtime, sometimes forcibly keeping workers locked in the factory overnight. While Guatemala has a minimum age for employment of children on the books, it is widely disregarded, and children as young as six years old labor in maquila factories, particularly those in the rural areas. The minimum wage of the maquila industry is far below a living wage, and violations of basic health and safety precautions such as insufficient exits can be found in nearly every factory. Overall, the Guatemalan maquila industry fails to respect these internationally recognized labor rights and thus would be ineligible for the benefits provided by U.S. trade laws.

Complementing this threat of sanctions, the U.S. government has the capability to improve the rights of maquila workers in Guatemala by reallocating its financial and technical resources. Just as it has GEXPRONT, the AID mission could develop, modernize, and sustain the Labor Ministry. For one million dollars, slightly more than 1 percent of the total U.S. economic assistance to Guatemala, AID could pay for salaries, training, and transportation for one hundred additional labor inspectors, as well as construct offices in the areas where most of the maquila factories are located. When such a possibility was presented to a high-ranking AID official, he stated: "We want to work with many different government agencies to make them less bureaucratic and more efficient. The Labor Ministry is included in these plans."[38] To my knowledge, AID's sole assistance has been an arbitration training retreat for labor inspectors. Moreover, as the official indicated, heretofore AID has concentrated on decreasing government intervention, to unencumber the market. For example, AID, as well as other international assistance agencies, has urged the privatization and streamlining of government-owned services and industries. Increased intervention and oversight by labor inspectors contradict this grand strategy of reducing government interference in nontraditional export production.

The Private Sector

The chances of worker rights being respected in the maquila industry are also dependent on the will of the private business community, which historically has viewed government intervention with disdain. The fact that Guatemala was the last country in the hemisphere to institute an income tax, and still has one of the lowest rates (personal income tax accounts for only 3.4 percent of all tax income, and of course maquila investors are exempt from all taxes),[39] indicates the depth of the private sector's unwillingness to part with profits and its distrust of government spending. Although the rise of nontraditional exports, to some extent, has created a new class of dynamic young entrepreneurs, thus far their absolute rejection of government intervention matches that of the landed oligarchy. Few private business persons deviate from this stance. Economy vice minister and premier maquila industry consultant Alvaro Colom is one who has articulated a different approach, recognizing that progress is dependent on sacrifice by all participants. He said: "We must increase the tax base if we want development. It is crazy here. We pay nothing, but we cannot keep going in this direction as we have for the last five hundred years, especially if we want the maquila industry to lift the country into the modern age."[40]

Colom's comment pinpoints the essential problem of the private sector: its refusal to sacrifice profits and control—whether through taxes, cooperation with the Labor Ministry, or voluntary internal improvements—continues to undermine any hope for long-term development. In fact, this obstinacy may well lead to the dissolution of the industry. Under present conditions, the maquila industry's impact on economic development will diminish as long as the cost of living outstrips maquila worker wages. Further, a generation of female workers will probably either end up disabled with long-term stress disorders or one day explode into a mass labor rebellion similar to the 1987 Korean uprising. These scenarios promise a stalled, if not crippled, maquila industry.

Improved working conditions, on the other hand, might actually increase profits over the long run. At present, an operator cannot survive on the compensation, and no human being should be subjected to the indignities found in most factories. "Improvement," in this context, signifies bringing conditions up to minimal levels of fairness and dignity. Improved conditions and wages throughout the industry might relieve growing antagonism toward management and lessen the pressure and strain on workers. Employees' allegiance to factories would grow, and this would most likely improve efficiency and productivity. Already, there is a clear and obvious correlation between the working conditions and turnover rates: the better the conditions, the lower the rate of worker turnover. Most importantly, according to managers at these few factories, profits are bountiful. A living wage would of course also spur the growth of the internal market, an event which all agree is necessary for long-term economic development.

Inevitable Departure, Maybe Not

Yet many investors and consultants contend, and this study in part confirms, that since maquila investors chose Guatemala because of its abundant, inexpensive labor force, any modification of this attraction might deter future investors as well as instigate a mass withdrawal of maquila capital. "If labor costs rise or if unions form," argued a maquila owner, "many of us might just leave."[41] The concern over maquila flight is very real and ought not to be discounted, especially considering the transient nature of the garment-assembly industry.

Nonetheless, several factors militate against an inevitable exodus of maquila capital. Unlike the case with other industries in the region, Guatemalan capitalists control almost half the production. The prospect of flight is less likely for these entrepreneurs as long as the "U.S. bank account" threshold is exceeded. Since most of these local capitalists are small and only familiar with Guatemala, they are less inclined than a major foreign TNC would be to relocate to an unknown venue. The impact of U.S. pressure on these new entrepreneurs must not be underestimated. AID has established GEXPRONT and groomed many of its entrepreneurs. As a consequence, most of the key private-sector officials in the industry enjoy friendly relations with AID officials. If AID dedicated substantial resources to the Labor Ministry, enlarging and modernizing the staff while educating employers about the necessity for labor rights and the dire consequences of noncompliance, it is possible that conditions might rise to the bare minimum.

Korean investors, who represent the major source of foreign capital, are also unlikely to flee. The Korean government has dedicated significant resources to construct an export platform in Guatemala. Because the Korean factories arrived under the direction of this government, it is unlikely that they will leave independently of government encouragement. The recent flurry of Guatemalan government attacks on the abuses in Korean factories illustrates the substantial roots of the Korean investment structure. Rather than calling for a withdrawal of capital, Ambassador Cho publicly apologized for abuses in Korean factories and promised to help deport any supervisors who are found to be abusing workers. Although the Korean ambassador's remarks served more to ameliorate deteriorating public relations than to convey an actual promise of improvements, the incident exemplifies the high level of Korean commitment to the region.

Furthermore, over the last two years Korean investments have increased in capital intensity, making a mass exodus of Korean capital less likely. Unlike those in the rest of the industry, Korean investors have purchased land and constructed modern factories and housing facilities for staff. The massive Korean free-trade zone presently under construction exemplifies this trend toward more permanent enterprises. The threshold to incite an investor who merely rents space to move is considerably lower than that for one who has invested several million dollars to construct a factory. Moreover, Korean factories do not have many options. Production cannot return to Korea, and alternatives in the region are not significantly more attractive. Only Costa Rica and Mexico offer a more qualified work force and a sounder infrastructure, but the cost is higher wages and more quotas. The Dominican Republic, Haiti, and Jamaica have similar political difficulties and slightly more expensive wages. It is conceivable that if the U.S. government supported improved conditions, the Korean investment structure would remain because of the depth of its commitment and a lack of regional alternatives.

In sum, in its present state the maquila industry, while temporarily supplementing thousands of families' income, represents a superficial answer to Guatemala's poverty and massive disparity in wealth. Unless underlying problems of land and wealth distribution are addressed, the maquila industry will never assemble more sophisticated goods than apparel and light electronics. Under present labor conditions and compensation, even this apprentice maquila industry may be doomed. If steps are not taken immediately to improve working conditions industry-wide, massive worker discontent may be inevitable. What it will take for AID and the Guatemalan private-business sector to recognize that the long-term health and profitability of the maquila industry are dependent on improved working conditions and wages and protected labor rights is unknown. It might just take widespread worker revolt. Or it might take a prudent AID or U.S. Embassy official who recognizes the dangers inherent in the maquila industry's present path to persuade the private sector to accept the necessity of improving working conditions, compensation, and union rights.

Methodology

I conducted more than three hundred interviews with three basic categories of people: workers; owners, managers, and investors; and other persons who possessed special knowledge of or interest in the industry.

Workers

I interviewed approximately 225 direct production operators with experience in more than eighty different factories between May and September 1990, and in March 1991 and March 1992. Of this pool, 71 of the interviews consisted of intensive narratives, while 116 were informal interviews. Intensive interviews comprised systematic inquiries based on a standard list of questions, which included specific factual questions on background and working conditions, as well as general ones designed to encourage longer narratives. Informal interviews were much briefer and consisted of a short set of specific questions and a few general questions on working conditions. I conducted most intensive interviews at the homes of the workers or in small restaurants. In contrast, informal interviews took place at bus stops, the General Inspectorate of Labor offices, or other public locations.

As might be expected, intensive interviews with workers were difficult to obtain. Many were understandably fearful of my motives and intentions. In order to allay this fear, I never asked for the worker's full name and tried, as best I could, to convey my intention of keeping the conversations confidential. Gradually, I gained the confidence of several workers in different communities, who introduced me to their friends, and so on.

Informal interviews, on the other hand, were easy to obtain because workers congregate in the same places—bus stops, food stands—every day. I visited these locations regularly and interviewed workers. Another location that yielded numerous interviews were the General Inspectorate of Labor offices in Guatemala City. There, maquila workers arrive almost daily to submit complaints and generally were very willing to speak about their experiences.

Of the eighty factories represented, interviewed workers provided information about 23 Korean-owned, 7 North American-owned, and 50 Guatemalan-owned factories. Thus, I obtained the workers' perceptions from approximately 50 percent of Korean factories, 70 percent of North American factories, and 35 percent of Guatemalan factories.

Of the eighty factories represented, 35 had less than 99 machines, representing about 25 percent; 27 had between 100 and 249 machines, representing about 50 percent; 11 had between 250 and 499 machines, representing about 33 percent; 7 had more than 500 machines, representing about 50 percent.

Management

I interviewed approximately fifty-four investors, owners, and managers from fifty-two factories between May and September 1990, and in March 1991 and March 1992. All of the interviewees worked in the factory; most were present in the workplace every day. Most of the interviews were conducted inside factories and consisted of a set of questions (see Questionnaires). Most managers provided a tour of the factory during the course of the interview. Only one manager allowed an unsupervised inspection of the factory.

I interviewed 15 managers from Korean-owned factories, representing approximately 33 percent of Korean factories; 31 from Guatemalan-owned factories, representing about 28 percent of these factories; 6 from North American-owned factories, representing about 60 percent of these factories. The size of the factories was as follows: 19 had less than 99 machines, representing approximately 16 percent; 17 had between 100 and 249 machines, representing about 40 percent; 11 had between 250 and 499 machines, representing about 33 percent; 4 had more than 500 machines, representing about 25 percent.

Other Interested Parties

In addition to workers and management representatives, I interviewed more than sixty persons who either worked in, had specific information about, or promoted the maquila industry. I conducted intensive interviews, sometimes extending over several sittings, with labor inspectors and other Labor Ministry officials, Economy Ministry officials, maquila consultants, AID officials, GEXPRONT and VESTEX representatives, U.S. and Korean embassy personnel, and U.S. Department of Commerce representatives.

Questionnaires

I. Owners/Management

A. Personal and factory background

—Name, nationality, educational background, and position.
—How did you become involved in the industry? Explain.
—Previous experience in the apparel-assembly industry.
—What is the company's source of capital?
—Date factory opened.

B. Plant Operation

—Number, type, age, and origin of sewing machines when first opened? Now?
—Cutting room in the factory? Size and capacity?
—Number, gender, average age of line employees?
—Number, gender, average age, and national origin of supervisory and administrative personnel?
—Does factory train apprentices? How many?
—What are daily hours of operation? Is there overtime? Is it obligatory or voluntary? Does the factory operate overnight?
—Daily hours of work for management?
—How often do you or other management personnel travel to the United States on business?

—How are workers paid, per piece or per day? What is the rationale for this system?

—What is the average salary for line workers? for supervisors? Are bonuses awarded? Explain. Are there any other incentive or benefit programs for workers?

—Is there a union or a *solidarismo* association at the factory? Why or why not?

—From where does the cloth arrive? Is it precut? Which types of apparel does the factory assemble?

—Do accidents occur in the factory? How many in the last six months? What is the procedure for caring for injured or ill employees? Does the factory have a first-aid kit or other medical supplies? Does the company employ a physician or other medical personnel?

—How does management solicit new workers? What documentation or other proof is required of prospective employees? Are they given certain tests, such as sewing or literacy? Are workers without sewing experience hired?

—What are the most common reasons for disciplining and discharging workers? What is the discipline procedure? How many employees were disciplined and/or discharged in the last six months?

—What is the employee turnover rate per month? What reasons do employees give for resigning?

—What is the procedure for hiring and treating pregnant employees?

—Does the factory maintain a quality-control section? What happens to an employee who makes a mistake on a garment?

—How does the company obtain contracts or orders? Is this easy or diffcult? Explain. Does a factory representative attend trade shows in the United States or elsewhere?

—For which labels does the company produce? Does the factory consistently work with particular brands of clothing? What is the relationship between the factory and clothing companies in the United States?

—Does the factory own or rent the building? What is/was the rental/purchase cost?

—Why was this location selected?

—What is the capital investment per worker?

—What is the company's profit margin?

—How many garments are produced weekly? What is the potential production capacity?

C. Perceptions of the Industry

—Evaluate the quantity and quality of support the maquila industry and this factory in particular receives from the Guatemalan government? From GEXPRONT? From the United States government and embassy?
—What is your relationship with other maquila owners in Guatemala? Is there substantial competition among owners for business?
—What do you think about the growth of Korean-financed and -managed maquila factories?
—Evaluate the dependability and responsibility of the plant's supervisory personnel and line workers. What are your most pressing personnel problems? Describe the relationship between workers and management at the factory.
—Does the political situation in Guatemala affect your business? Explain.
—How often do Labor or IGSS inspectors visit the factory? What do they do? Are they corrupt?
—Why has the maquila industry exploded in Guatemala? Has the industry reached a saturation point or is there more room for growth? What does the future hold for the Guatemalan maquila industry?
—What benefits does Guatemala receive from the industry?
—Evaluate the adequacy of the infrastructure, transportation, and customs.
—What is your best experience in the maquila industry? Your worst experience?

II. Workers

A. Personal background

—Age. [If under sixteen] Do you have work permit?
—Marital status. [If married] Does spouse work? Where?
—Do you have children? Who cares for them during work?
—Do you live at home?
—Other employment experience.
—How far away from the factory do you live? How long does it take you to go to and from work? How much do you spend on transportation each day?

B. Factory Experience

—Name and address of factory.
—Tenure at factory.

—Name and national origin of owner/manager.
—Type of clothing assembled?
—Brand names. Do they change frequently?
—What kind of cloth? Does it arrive precut?
—What is your position?
—Number, gender, and age of workers.
—When you applied for work, what were you required to bring, to do, or to sign?
—Is there a training program? How long does it last? How much are workers paid?
—What tools do you bring to work? Who supplies the tools? What happens when you lose or break a tool or machine?
—How does the factory pay, per piece or per day? How much do you earn in an average day, week, and month? Does it pay on time?
—If per piece, is there a minimum you must produce? What happens when you do not produce the minimum?
—What are the hours of work? Is there overtime? Is it obligatory or voluntary? Do you ever work overnight? When you work overtime, does the factory provide the necessary services, such as food and place to sleep? What happens if you refuse to or cannot work overnight?
—Do you receive a paid vacation and aguinaldo each year?
—Do you receive information about the salaries and discounts, such as IGSS and other expenses? Is this information written or verbal?
—If a person makes many pieces in an hour and earns more than the minimum, does the management pay the wage or reduce the per-piece cost?

C. Normal Day

—What do you do in a normal day?
—What kind of machine do you operate?
—Do you enjoy your work? Explain.
—How many and when do you take breaks? How long do they last?
—Is there a cafeteria in the factory? Describe. Where do you eat lunch?
—Do pregnant employees receive the required leaves? Do they receive the lactation benefit?
—What is the procedure for rising to use the bathroom? To get water?

D. Workplace Safety

—Do you pay the IGSS? Do you have an IGSS identification card?

—Have you attended the IGSS for treatment? Explain what occurred.

—What is the factory's policy for using the services of the IGSS?

—Have you had any accidents on the job? What happened? How was this treated?

—Have other people had accidents in the factory? Explain what happened and how their injury was treated.

—What are the most common accidents?

—Are there a first-aid kit, medical supplies, or medical personnel in the factory?

—Have you or other workers ever passed out from fatigue or heat exhaustion? Explain.

E. Workplace Health

—Do you have or have you ever had any injuries? What kind? When? Treatment?

—Have you suffered headaches? Stomachaches? Eye problems? Skin irritation? Wrist pain? Back pain? Throat irritation? Difficulty breathing? Other? How often?

—How are these illnesses treated? Explain.

—Have you ever taken time off to recover? Explain.

—What is the factory's policy on workers who become ill? Can they return? Under what circumstances?

F. Factory Design

—Are there windows in the factory? Are they open or closed during the day? Explain.

—Are there fans? How big are they and how many?

—Of what are the walls and ceilings composed?

—Describe the temperature in the factory during the day? Evening?

—Is there enough space between the machines to move safely?

—How many bathrooms for women and men? Are they functioning, supplied, and clean?

—How many doors are there?

—Are they usually open or closed during work hours? If closed, who has the key to open them?
—Are there fire extinguishers? If so, do you know how to use them?
—Have any fires started in the factory? When? What happened?

G. Labor Relations

—How many supervisors? What is their nationality and gender? Do they speak Spanish?
—What is the disposition of the supervisors? Explain.
—Do the supervisors yell or hit workers? For what reasons?
—What penalties does the factory impose on workers?
—What happens when a worker mars a garment, breaks a machine, disobeys a supervisor?
—Are there sexual abuse problems in the factory? Explain.
—Are there discharges? How often? For what reasons? For illness? Absenteeism and tardiness? Pregnancy? Poor work quality or slow production speed? Demands for higher wages? Organizing a union? Describe any incidents.
—Do you feel that your job is secure? Explain.
—Is there a union or *solidarismo* association in the factory?
—Is it possible to organize one in your factory?
—Describe the relations between workers and management. Explain.
—Do labor inspectors visit the factory? How often and what happens? Explain.
—Why do you think the maquila industry has become so popular in Guatemala?

Acronyms

AID	United States Agency for International Development
CBERA	Caribbean Basin Economic Recovery Act
CBI	Caribbean Basin Initiative
CGTG	Confederación General de Trabajadores de Guatemala (General Confederation of Guatemalan Workers)
CIA	Central Intelligence Agency
CTDs	cumulative trauma disorders
CUSG	Confederación de Unidad Sindical de Guatemala (Confederation of Guatemalan Trade-Union Unity)
FUNTEC	Fundación Tecnológico (Technological Foundation)
GAL	Guaranteed Access Level
GDP	gross domestic product
GEXPRONT	Gremial de Exportadores de Productos No Tradicionales de Guatemala (Nontraditional Products Exporters Association)
GSP	Generalized System of Preferences
GUATEXPRO	Centro Nacional de la Promoción de las Exportaciónes (National Center of the Promotion of Exports)

HTS	Harmonized Tariff Schedule
IGSS	Instituto Guatemalteco de Seguridad Social (Guatemalan Social Security Institute)
IGT	Inspección General de Trabajo (General Inspectorate of Labor)
INE	Instituto Nacional de Estadística (National Institute of Statistics)
INTECAP	Instituto Técnico de Capacitación (Vocational Training Institute)
KOTRA	Korean Overseas Trade Promotion Association
MAS	Movimiento de Acción Solidaria (Social Action Movement)
NGO	nongovernment organization
PRES	Plan de Reordenamiento Económico y Social (National Social and Economic Reordering Plan)
PVH	Phillips-Van Heusen
ROCAP	Regional Office of AID for Central America and Panama
S.A.	Sociedad Anónima (Incorporated)
SGS	Société Générale de Surveillance S.A.
TNC	transnational corporation
UNSITRAGUA	Unión Sindical de Trabajadores de Guatemala (Trade-Union Unity of Guatemalan Workers)
USG	Unión Solidarista Guatemalteca (Guatemalan Solidarity Union)
VESTEX	Comisión de la Industria de Vestuario y Textiles (Apparel Manufacturers Exporters Commission)
ZOLIC	Zona Libre de Industria y Comércio (Free Zone of Industry and Commerce)

Notes

Notes to Preface

1 Author interview, March 1992.

2 German Press Agency Study, *Central America Report*, March 8, 1991.

3 Author interview, March 1992.

Notes to Chapter 1

1 *Maquila* reportedly is derived from the word used in colonial times to refer to the portion of flour that the miller kept for himself after grinding a farmer's corn. In the modern context, the "miller" is the worker of the developing countries; the "corn" is the pre-cut cloth or electronic components provided by large foreign corporations; and the "ground corn" is the finished product, i.e., the assembled garment or television set. The worker, the modern miller, keeps a *maquila*, the wages for her labor; and the corporation imports the components into the developing nation and exports the assembled goods for sale in a developed country, most often the United States. In Guatemala, *maquila* refers exclusively to garment-assembly production. Throughout this study, the term *maquila* will be used rather than drawback, maquiladora, or outsourcing.

2 Author interview, June 1990.

3 Even more remote villages, such as El Tejar in the Department of Chimaltenango, located an hour from the capital, await the impact on their way of life of a 90,000-square-meter Korean Free Trade Zone, aimed to employ over 10,000 people in thirty maquila factories.

4 Author interview, March 1992.

5 Author interview, July 1991.

6 Author interview, March 1991.

7 Author interview with vice ministers of labor, March 1991. The ministry also assigned a vice minister, a former social worker, to work full-time on improving working conditions and lessening exploitation of female workers in the maquila industry.

8 "Investigación explotación humana en la maquila," *Diario de Centro America*, Guatemala, March 21, 1991, p. 2.

9 According to ACAN-EFE, *Central America Report*, June 6, 1990.

10 Author interview, August 1990.

11 Author interview, July 1990.

12 Both the United States and Guatemala have adopted legislation to expedite the assembly of U.S.-manufactured cloth in Guatemala. These laws reduce or suspend tariffs on components designated for assembly and on the final, assembled product. Significantly, the Caribbean Basin Initiative (CBI) excludes apparel from duty-free entry (See Chapter 2, pp. 24–25). Hence, the only duty-reduction program available for apparel manufactured abroad and imported into the United States is the Harmonized Tariff Schedule (HTS) 9802.00.80, formerly referred to as 807. HTS 9802.00.80 provides reduced duties for articles composed of U.S.-made components that are wholly or partially assembled abroad and subsequently returned as a finished good. U.S. customs duties for such goods, otherwise payable at the normal duty rate, are assessed only on the value added to the goods as a result of assembly or the labor costs incurred outside the United States. Duty is not assessed on the value of the exported and reimported U.S. content.

In 1986, President Reagan instituted an additional program as part of the Caribbean Basin Initiative, HTS 9802.00.8010, formerly known as Super 807 or 807–A, which guarantees virtually unlimited levels of access for apparel assembled from U.S.-made and U.S.-cut fabric in Caribbean and Central American nations. Eligible countries receive guaranteed access levels (GALs) on specified categories of clothing through bilateral agreements with the United States. Generally, countries negotiate for a GAL after the United States has placed a quota on an apparel category, as the GAL effectively allows for unlimited importation of qualified goods, regardless of quota. In Guatemala, shortly after the United States placed quotas on Category 347/348, men's and women's cotton pants, the government negotiated GALs for these categories.

The Guatemalan Congress passed parallel legislation, Decree 29–89, which suspends import duties on incoming components and export duties on the assembled product.

For specific application of these programs in Guatemala, see Chapter 2, pp. 17–18.

13 For an excellent, clear analysis of the nature of the emerging global factory, see Rachel Kamel, *The Global Factory: Analysis and Action for a New Economic Era* (Philadelphia: American Friends Service Committee, 1990).

14 Joseph Grunwald and Kenneth Flamm, *The Global Factory: Foreign Assembly in International Trade* (Washington, D.C.: The Brookings Institution, 1985), p. 8.

15 Carmen Diana Deere et al., *In the Shadows of the Sun: Caribbean Development and U.S. Policy* (Boulder, Colo.: Westview Press, 1990), p. 4.

16 Jim Handy, *Gift of the Devil: History of Guatemala* (London: South End Press, 1984), p. 21.

17 W. George Lovell, *Conquest and Survival in Colonial Guatemala: A Historical Geography of the Cuchumatan Highlands, 1500–1821* (Montreal: McGill-Queens University Press, 1985), p. 119.

18 According to Eric Wolf, two-thirds of the population were killed between 1519 and 1610. Eric Wolf, *Sons of the Shaking Earth* (Chicago: University of Chicago Press, 1959), p. 31.

19 1990 Health Commission of the National Dialogue Report, cited in *El Gráfico*, August 3, 1990.

Notes to Chapter 2

1 See Americas Watch, *Guatemala: A Nation of Prisoners* (New York: Americas Watch, 1984), and Amnesty International, *Guatemala: A Human Rights Record* (New York: Amnesty International, 1987).

2 Over the last thirty years hunger and military repression have been interrelated problems, in part because food has become a crucial weapon in the military's "pacification" campaign. The army has aggressively pursued a policy of exploiting the widespread starvation in rural areas, dispensing food in exchange for pledges of support. See James Painter, *Guatemala—False Hope, False Freedom: The Rich, the Poor, and the Christian Democrats* (London: Catholic Institute for International Relations, 1987), pp. 24–26.

3 Hank Frundt, "To Buy the World a Coke," *Latin American Perspectives* (Summer 1987), p. 398.

4 *Notas para el Estudio Economico de America Latina y El Caribe, 1985: Guatemala,* United Nations Economic Commission for Latin American and the Caribbean, June 13, 1986, freely translated in *Central America Report*, October 10, 1986.

5 *Inforpress*, October 30, 1986, in Painter, *Guatemala—False Hope, False Freedom*, p. 105.

6 *Business Latin America*, August 4, 1986.

7 Author interview, July 1990.

8 "National Social and Economic Reordering Plan," cited in *Central America Report*, August 6, 1986.

9 Decree 367–86 (1986).

10 "National Social and Economic Reordering Plan," cited in *Central American Report*, August 6, 1986.

11 Quoted in Carroll Rios de Rodriquez, "Investing in Guatemala," *Viva*, Supplement, 1989.

12 The five laws were: Decree 443 (1966); Decree 30–79 (1979); Decree 80–82 (1982); Decree 21–84 (1984); Decree 29–89 (1989).

13 Decree 29–89, Articles 16, 17, and 18, p. 9.

14 *Prensa Libre*, August 18, 1990.

15 Author interview, July 1990.

16 According to Decree 29–89, each applicant must submit an application outlining his project to the Industrial Policy Office in the Economy Ministry prior to establishing the business. Production may begin the very day the application is submitted. The process has become an uncontested rubber stamp, as the ministry has yet to reject an application.

17 GEXPRONT, "Guatemala: A Manufacturing Tradition," 1992, p. 1.

18 Author interview with AID official, July 1990.

19 Author interview, July 1990.

20 John Dombrowski *et al.*, *Area Handbook for Guatemala* (Washington, D.C.: Government Printing Office, 1970), p. 221.

21 *Central America Report*, September 5 and December 9, 1986.

22 The new government is attempting to alter these traditionally hostile and divisive private sector–government relations. The Serrano administration is composed largely of ex-private-sector officials. As mentioned, the Economy Ministry is staffed by ex-nontraditional export promoters. Likewise, the finance minister and Central Bank president are "well-known proponents of the free-market systems, and will surely be promoting that model" (*Central America Report*, January 11, 1991). In effect, the private sector has been recruited to guide the new government. It remains to be seen whether this will actually be the case.

Serrano's predecessor, Vinicio Cerezo, also loaded the government with prominent members of the business community, which led some observers to predict new heights of government–business cooperation (See *Business Latin America*, January 20, 1986). However, this cooperation was never achieved.

23 In 1966, the Guatemalan Congress passed Decree 443, which was the first law directed to lure investment in assembly–export operations.

24 For a more thorough discussion of the Alliance for Progress and its impact on Guatemala, see James P. Dunkerly, *Power in the Isthmus: A Political History of Modern Central America* (London: Verso, 1988).

25 Jerome Levinson and Juan de Onis, *The Alliance That Lost Its Way: A Critical Report on the Alliance for Progress* (New York: Quadrangle Books, 1970), pp. 203–4. See also Stuart K. Tucker, "Trade Unshackled: Assessing the Value of the CBI," in *Central American Recovery and Development: Task Force Report to the International Commission for Central American Recovery and Development*, ed. William Ascher and Ann Hubbard (Durham and London: Duke University Press, 1989).

26 Gary W. Wynia, *Politics and Planners: Economic Development Policy in Central America* (Madison: University of Wisconsin Press, 1972), p. 91.

27 Handy, *Gift of the Devil*, p. 193.

28 *New York Times*, November 14, 1966.

29 Susanne Jonas and David Tobis, eds., *Guatemala* (Berkeley, Calif.: NACLA, 1974), p. 105.

30 Handy, *Gift of the Devil*, p. 194.

31 Jonas and Tobis, *Guatemala*, p. 106.

32 Ibid., p. 107.

33 Ibid., p. 111.

34 Ibid., p. 110.

35 Ibid., p. 111.

36 General Carlos Arana Osorio, *Informe al Honorable Congreso de la Republica, Tercer Año de Gobierno*, Guatemala, June 1973, p. 84.

37 AID memo, "Export Development," p. 3, cited in Jonas and Tobis, *Guatemala*, p. 111.

38 Address before the Organization of American States on February 24, 1982, *Department of State Bulletin* 82 (April 1982): 3.

39 David R. Ross, "The Caribbean Basin Initiative: Threat or Promise?" in *The Central American Crisis: Sources of Conflict and the Failure of the United States Policy*, ed. Kenneth M. Coleman and George C. Herring (Wilmington, Del.: Scholarly Resources, 1985), p. 153. In terms of a "trade" bill, many observers contend that what was omitted from the final proposal is more significant than what eventually survived congressional editing. A 10 percent tax credit for U.S. businesses investing in the region was replaced by a narrow provision permitting U.S. businessmen to deduct expenses for attending trade conventions in the Caribbean region from their taxes. Further, the inclusion of apparel on the eligible duty-free imports was struck down; this meant that the fastest-growing export item in the region was still subject to "normal" import duties. (Recognizing this omission, President Reagan in 1986 added an unlimited category of quota, called Guaranteed Access Limits, which effectively removed quotas from garments assembled in the CBI countries made of U.S. manufactured and cut cloth. Nevertheless, this category failed to reduce the tariff on the value-added portion of the imported garment item, giving little incentive for domestic production of components. Lacking a significant tax incentive and apparel on the tariff-free list, the CBI in its final form had more symbolic import than real impact.

In addition, 87 percent of the items on the CBI eligible list already possessed duty-free import status from the Generalized System of Preferences (GSP), a separate trade regime that also reduces tariffs on many designated goods imported from developing countries. A few, mainly insignificant, items not covered under the GSP are eligible for duty-free status under the CBI. Hence, the centerpiece of the CBI, the duty-free-access provision, is little more than a spurious enticement, in reality granting the region minuscule trade and market access. It comes as no surprise, then, that as a result of these factors the CBI has had a minimal effect on trade in the region. Apparel assembly has seen enormous growth, but this falls outside the scope of the CBI. See Stuart K. Tucker, "Trade Unshackled: Assessing the Value of the CBI," in *Central American Recovery and Development: Task Force Report to the International Commission for Central American Recovery and Development*, ed. William Ascher and Ann Hubbard (Durham and London: Duke University Press, 1989), p. 357. See also Wilfred Whittingham, "The United States Government's Caribbean Basin Initiative," in *CEPAL Review*, no. 39 (December 1989), pp.73–92.

40 Author interview, August 1990.

41 Author interview, June 1990.

42 U.S. Department of Commerce, "Foreign Economic Trends and Their Implications for the United States: Guatemala," February 1990.

43 SRI International, "National Export Plan for Guatemala: 'Guatemala mil millones'—final report," prepared for U.S. Agency for International Development/Guatemala, January 1990.

44 See Chapter 3, pp. 57–60.

45 AID's attempts to groom the Guatemalan private sector go well beyond GEXPRONT, which is probably their most successful project. The list of AID development programs that seek to assist the private sector include Agribusiness Development, Private Sector Development Coordination, Private Enterprise Development, Private Sector Education Initiatives, Micro-Enterprise Development, Micro-Enterprise Promotion, and Entrepreneurial Development. Tom Barry, *Guatemala: A Country Guide* (Albuquerque, N.Mex.: The Inter-Hemispheric Education Resource Center, 1989), p. 133.

46 *Prensa Libre*, August 26, 1990. The remaining Q5 million was obtained from other international organizations and annual dues from its members.

47 Author interview, March 1991.

48 Author interview, August 1990.

49 Author interview, March 1991.

50 Ibid.

51 The 1991 Apparel Show, however, failed to live up to expectations. Only fourteen maquila factories purchased tables at the show, none of which was Korean-owned.

52 Author interview, July 1990.

53 Philip Karp, "Guatemala," in *Struggle Against Dependence: Nontraditional Export Growth in Central America and the Caribbean*, ed. Eva Paus (Boulder, Colo.: Westview Press, 1988), p. 75.

54 Author interview, March 1991.

55 Author interview, July 1990.

56 Author interview, March 1991.

57 Ibid.

58 Author interview, July 1990.

59 U.S. Department of Commerce, "Foreign Economic Trends and Their Implications for the United States," February 1990, p. 2.

60 Three major sources of maquila information exist: the Guatemalan government, the Guatemalan private business community, and the U.S. government. Guatemalan government agencies possess the best vantage points to gather and calculate data on exports, employment, etc. However, these sources tend, almost inherently, to be extremely unreliable. For example, the two government agencies that publish this data, the Bank of Guatemala and "One-Stop-to-Export" in the Economy Ministry, consistently publish different export and import data. Apparently, the bank receives its figures from customs, which is notoriously inefficient and unprofessional. "One-Stop," on the other hand, merely tallies the export licenses that it issues. The amounts and values of these licenses, however, are frequently manipulated by exporters.

GEXPRONT is the main Guatemalan private-sector agency that publishes data on maquila exports. This organization regularly distributes promotional material with charts and graphs documenting maquila growth. Often these numbers lack citations. According to GEXPRONT officials, the information is generally culled from various sources. The association's unique data supply is its intimate connection with owners. Using this source, GEXPRONT periodically surveys proprietors about their operations. Unfortunately, usually less than 50 percent (and no Koreans) respond to these surveys. Further, there is no means to verify the responses.

U.S. government entities are the third, and most accurate, source of information. Up to now, AID has not published a study of the industry. The most reliable source of export data is the U.S. Department of Commerce, which compiles import and export quantities by product. Since the U.S. receives almost all of the production from Guatemalan maquila factories, this information provides a reasonable estimate of the overall growth of the maquila industry.

61 This is according to the U.S. Department of Commerce. The department classifies textiles and apparel as one category. Since only apparel is assembled in maquila factories, imports of textiles must be deducted from this total. According to GEXPRONT and the Bank of Guatemala, textile exports to the United States, most of which come from small artisan workshops, are relatively insignificant, amounting to about US$5–7 million annually.

62 *Central America Report*, Feb. 23, 1990.

63 In 1991, the gross value of exports for apparel, coffee, and sugar totaled $349.6 million, $328.2 million, and $143.2 million, respectively. *Central America Report*, February 7, 1991.

64 Ibid.

65 Peter Steele, *The Caribbean Clothing Industry: The U.S. and Far East Connections*, Special Report No. 1147 (London: The Economist Intelligence Unit, October 1988), p. 1.

66 Honduras and Panama also exported more clothing than Guatemala in 1985 (ibid., p. 68).

67 Total regional production for 1991 was $2,560.9 million. Interview with Tom Wilde, U.S. Department of Commerce, March 12, 1992.

68 In fact, it appears that apparel assembly in Jamaica, Costa Rica, and Haiti is stagnating.

69 In 1991, textile and apparel imports to the United States from the Dominican Republic and Costa Rica were $912.3 million and $450.0 million, respectively. Interview with Tom Wilde, U.S. Department of Commerce, March 1992.

70 Author interview, July 1990.

71 Author interview, June 1990.

72 Author interview, July 1990.

73 From the Industrial Policy Office in the Economy Ministry, March 1991. Applications for both laws, Decree 24–84 and Decree 29–89, are submitted for approval to the Industrial Policy Office. This office keeps rather complete records of the names of companies and dates of application and authorization. This list, however, only includes those operations which receive the benefits of the law directly. Hence, sub-maquila factories, those which subcontract work from maquila factories, generally are not registered with the office unless they also export directly. As far as I know, no reliable quantified data exist about the number, location, and size of sub-maquila factories.

74 Like export data, reliable employment statistics are extremely difficult to acquire and verify. Most estimates range between 45,000 and 50,000 workers employed directly in maquila factories. The Guatemalan Institute of Social Security, or IGSS, is required to produce annual reports on the workers they serve, theoretically all employed persons in Guatemala. However, since IGSS officials themselves estimate that less than one-fourth of all employees are covered under state social security benefits, these figures are, at best, rough estimates. A second source, the National Institute of Statistics (INE), also publishes employment data based on a yearly national census. These reports are considered more reliable than IGSS, though again the survey is based on an extremely limited sample. In both cases, however, maquila workers are not distinguished as an independent classification.

The most reliable bearer of statistics is the Korean Embassy, which, for its own purposes, maintains exact records of the number of local and Korean employees in factories. As of March 1992, some fifty apparel assembly factories employed nearly 19,000 local employees. By most estimates, Korean factories are much more productive than their Guatemalan and U.S. counterparts and, as proof, produce nearly 50 percent of the assembled garments for export. This means that between 26,000 and 31,000 workers assemble the remaining half of the apparel value. (It also must be noted that a small portion of the Korean production is subcontracted to smaller maquilas.)

75 Estimate of Edgar Garzaro, VESTEX director of statistics. These include dozens of five-to-twenty machine shops located in San Pedro, Sacatepequez, a small

village located twenty kilometers outside of the capital. The exact number of tiny shops and homes which contract from larger factories is unknown.

76 Instituto Nacional de Estadística, *Encuesta Nacional Sociodemográfica, 1989: Empleo —Total Republica*, vol. 2 (June 1990), p. 45. These results are derived from a survey done in 1988, thus making my calculations less precise. At that time the maquila industry accounted for about 20,000 workers, or about 5 percent of the industrial manufacturing work force.

77 Ibid., p. 112. About 85 percent of the production and employment of maquila assembly occurs in factories inside the boundaries of the capital. As described above, the main industrial area in Guatemala City, Zone 12, is home to over forty factories. In the past two years an increasing number of factories have migrated from the city to take advantage of cheaper and more abundant labor.

78 Eva Paus, "A Critical Look at Nontraditional Export Demand: The Caribbean Basin Initiative," in *Struggle Against Dependence: Nontraditional Export Growth in Central America and the Caribbean*, ed. Eva Paus (Boulder, Colo.: Westview Press, 1988), p. 205.

79 General Accounting Office, *Caribbean Basin Initiative: Impact on Selected Countries*, Report to the Chairman, Subcommittee on Western Hemisphere and Peace Corps Affairs, Committee on Foreign Relations (Washington, D.C.: U.S. Senate, 1988), p. 18, and Steele, *Caribbean Clothing Industry*, p. 51. In addition, a U.S. Department of Commerce survey of 1989 and 1990 apparel and textile exports from the Caribbean Basin found that 84 percent of these exports qualified for HTS 9802.00.80 and 9802.00.60 programs. U.S. International Trade Commission, *Annual Report on the Impact of the Caribbean Basin Economic Recovery Act on U.S. Industries and Consumers—Sixth Report 1990*, USITC Publication 2432, September 1991.

80 Author interview, July 1990.

81 This estimate is based on factories paying $3 in wages, benefits, and other expenses six days a week for 50,000 employees, with a 25 percent profit margin. The $3 figure comes from GEXPRONT's 1990 promotional brochure, "A Manufacturing Country by Tradition," and is probably a third greater than the actual cost per worker.

82 Ventanilla Unica para las Exportaciónes, Ministerio de Economía, "Exportaciones Mensuales de Maquila Durante el Año de 1990."

83 See footnote 63 above.

84 U.S. Department of Commerce, Cost Profile on Men's 65/35 Polyester–Cotton Dress Shirts, 1988.

85 GEXPRONT brochures list only three domestic textile companies in addition to Liztex, and one of these primarily manufactures apparel and blankets made from Guatemala's distinctive indigenous cloth.

86 Author interview with U.S. representative of Liztex, April 1991.

87 The region-wide average of apparel imports under HTS 9802.00.80 programs, as mentioned in footnote 79, is approximately 84 percent. Since the U.S. Department of Commerce categorizes textiles and apparel together, the actual amount of apparel imports qualifying for this duty-reduction program is probably somewhat higher. In addition, according to U.S. customs statistics between 1985 and 1989, more than 66 percent of apparel imported from Guatemala qualifies for Item 807 programs. U.S. Department of Commerce, "U.S. Apparel and 807 Apparel Imports from CBI for 1986–1989" (undated).

88 Estimates from AID officials, Korean ambassador, March 1992, and Megatex S.A. representatives, August 1991.

89 See Steele, *Caribbean Clothing Industry*, p. 58.

90 See Chapter 1, note 12, for a description of these duty-free programs.

91 Author interview, March 1991.

Notes to Chapter 3

1 Author interview, August 1990.

2 Author interview, June 1990.

3 SRI International, "National Export Plan for Guatemala: 'Guatemala mil millones'—final report," prepared for U.S. Agency for International Development/Guatemala, January 1990, p. 1.

4 See Chap. 5, pp. 84–85.

5 *Central America Report*, January 29, 1988.

6 *Central America Report*, May 10, 1991.

7 Richard Rothstein, *Keeping Jobs in Fashion: Alternatives to the Euthanasia of the U.S. Apparel Industry* (Washington, D.C.: Economic Policy Institute, 1989), pp. 29–32.

8 Author interview, July 1990.

9 Megatex S.A., "General Bases to Establish a Garment Assembly Industry in Guatemala," March 1990.

10 For instance, the Dominican Republic has experienced seemingly irreversible setbacks, at least in reputation, because of its notoriously unreliable electricity supply.

11 According to U.S. Department of Commerce 1990 data, Guatemala's electric rates were US$.03 per kilowatt hour, ranking better than any other country in the region. In 1991, however, the reliability of the electrical supply was shaken, as a drought upset the hydroelectrical system that provides most electricity. Rationing and unpredictable shutdowns wreaked havoc in the industry. See Rhonda Yearly, "The Lights Go Out in Guatemala," *Report on Guatemala*, 12, issue 4 (Winter 1991): 12.

12 U.S. Department of Commerce Data, 1990; Megatex S.A., 1990; author survey of fifty-four employers.

13 Author interview, June 1990.

14 See *Bobbin Magazine*, November 1991.

15 *Bobbin Magazine*, May 1990.

16 Rothstein, *Keeping Jobs in Fashion*, p. 31. The average wage for U.S. apparel workers was $6.10 in 1988, plus an additional $1,001 a year in benefits.

17 These estimates comport with profit margins in the Jamaica apparel maquila industry. Emerson Young of JAMPRO, Jamaica's private-sector, nontraditional-export promotion organization, claimed that profits ranged between 10 and 40 percent in the Jamaican maquila industry. Author interview, March 1992.

18 Kenneth Flamm and Joseph Grunwald, *The Global Factory: Foreign Assembly in International Trade* (New York: The Brookings Institution, 1985), p. 226.

19 Based on author interviews with workers, management, and other interested persons (see Methodology). In addition, a survey of sixty maquila factories in November 1989 found that more than 70 percent of the workers were women, 65 percent of whom were unmarried. Facultad Latinoamericana de Ciencias

Sociales (FLACSO), "El Desarrollo de la Industria de la Maquila en Guatemala: Estudio de Casos de la Ocupación de la Mano de Obra Femenina," December 1990, pp. 57–58.

20 INE, *Empleo*, 1989, p. 19.

21 See Norma Chinchilla, "Industrialization, Monopoly, Capitalism, and Women's Work in Guatemala," *Signs: Journal of Women in Culture and Society* 3, no. 1 (Autumn 1977): 38–56.

22 Author interview, June 1990.

23 INE, *Empleo*, 1989, p. 25.

24 In this study, more than three out of four interviewed employers complained of a lack of skilled, or qualified, workers. In addition, a University of San Carlos study, based on surveys from management of forty-two maquila factories in June 1989, found that over three-fifths of the surveyed employers complained of a lack of qualified workers. Luis Everardo Estrada Vasquez and Francisco Leonel Santizo Gonzales, "La Industria Maquiladora en Guatemala: Perspectivas y Efectos Económicos y Sociales," University of San Carlos, Guatemala, Department of Economics, November 1989.

25 Author interview, July 1990.

26 Survey of three major newspapers in July 1990.

27 Author interview, July 1990.

28 Author interview, March 1991.

29 Author interview, July 1990.

30 Based on survey of employers and their representatives (see Methodology).

31 Author interview, June 1990.

32 Ibid.

33 Author interview, July 1990.

34 Author interview, March 1991.

35 Author interview, July 1990.

36 A GEXPRONT undated, unpublished memo, "Quiet Revolution in Guatemala," articulated this explanation: "The impact of this job creation [by the maquila industry] can be seen in many areas. Domestic help is much more difficult to obtain in Guatemala City, and upper- and middle-class families have to pay

higher salaries and provide better working and living conditions if they want to secure and retain domestic help." In a similar situation, many wealthy Costa Rican families have been recruiting domestic workers in Guatemala because the growth of the maquila industry in Costa Rica has been swallowing up the young, unmarried women.

37 Author interview, July 1990.

38 Author interview, March 1991.

39 See Susan Tiano, "Maquiladora Women: A New Category of Workers?" in *Women Workers and Global Restructuring*, Kathryn Ward, ed. (Ithaca, N.Y.: ILR Press, 1990), and Maria Kelly-Fernandez, *For We Are Sold, I and My People: Women and Industry in Mexico's Frontier* (Albany, N.Y.: SUNY Press, 1983), for excellent discussions about the origins and impact of female maquiladora workers in Mexican export zones.

40 See Chapter 2, pp. 14–15, for an account of the depression of the 1980s.

41 *El Gráfico*, December 14, 1991.

42 Author interview, July 1990.

43 Author interview, March 1991.

44 Author interview, June 1991.

45 Author interview, March 1991.

46 Steele, *Caribbean Clothing Industry*, p. 79.

47 Leslie Sklair, *Assembly for Development: The Maquila Industry in Mexico and the United States* (London: Unwin Hyman, 1988).

48 In Chapter 7, the operation and design of Korean factories is described and analyzed in detail.

49 Korean embassy figures and VESTEX estimates, March 1992.

50 A smattering of other foreign investors, including Israeli and German, accounts for production in eight to ten other shops.

51 Author interview, August 1991.

52 Although this is an explicit goal, as described above, the most significant incentive toward this end, a major tax break for investment in the region, was removed in Congress prior to passage.

53 Inexport is also the factory with the most controversial labor dispute in the industry. It has come to symbolize the trials and suffering of workers who attempt to organize a union in a maquila factory (see Chapter 6).

54 Author interview, June 1990.

55 "Maquila de Sacatepequez, un ejemplo de desarrollo," *Crónica*, December 15, 1989. Following the lead of PVH, Liz Claiborne is working with AID to pay indigenous peasants living deep in the highlands of Quiche, a region in northwest Guatemala enmeshed for decades in the civil war between the military and guerrilla insurgents, to knit sweaters. Claiborne will provide the tools and yarn and compensate on a per-piece basis. The goal of the project is to reduce poverty and political strife in the area.

56 Author interview, July 1990.

57 Ibid.

58 David Tobis, "The Alliance for Progress: Development Program for the United States," *Monthly Review*, January 1968.

59 U.S. Department of Commerce, "Report for Guatemala Required under the 1988 Trade Act," 1988.

60 Author interview, August 1990.

61 Author interview, July 1990.

62 *Central America Report*, April 25, 1990.

63 An AID study from the period reported that U.S. investment accounted for 11 percent of the total direct investment but only 1 percent of the labor force; the national average of people employed per $100,000 of total assets was 658, as compared to fifty-eight for U.S. capital. Phil Church, "Foreign Investment: The Operation of U.S. Direct Investment in Guatemala" (unclassified U.S. AID document, CERP D Guatemala A–107, June 16, 1972, pp. 4–5), cited in Jonas and Tobis, *Guatemala*, p. 133, n. 14.

64 Jonas and Tobis, *Guatemala*, p. 167.

65 Repeated attempts to speak with Play Knit executives have been unsuccessful.

66 Author interview, August 1990.

67 Author interview, July 1990.

68 Author interview with a worker who participated in the negotiations of the settlement, August 1990.

69 Chapter 7 contains a detailed discussion of Korean investment in the industry.

70 Author interview, March 1991.

71 Handy, *Gift of the Devil*, p. 77.

72 Author interview, July 1990.

73 Ibid.

74 GEXPRONT unpublished memo, "Quiet Revolution in Guatemala," Summer 1990.

75 Author interview, July 1990.

76 Ibid.

77 This label, though meant to be disparaging, contains some truth. Although the Jewish community is extremely small (around a few thousand people), at least ten factories are owned by Jewish entrepreneurs; one is even named Haifa, after the third-largest city in Israel. Several other factories are managed by descendants of Middle Eastern nationalities.

78 Author interview, July 1990.

79 See Dunkerly, *Power in the Isthmus*, p. 466.

80 Author interview, March 1991.

81 Author interview, July 1990.

82 Study from San Carlos University (see note 24 above).

83 Author interview, June 1990.

84 Author interview, July 1990.

Notes to Chapter 4

1 Author interview, July 1990.

2 Ibid.

3 Ibid.

4 Ibid.

5 Ibid.

6 Ibid.

7 Author interview, August 1990.

8 Author interview, July 1990.

9 Author interview, June 1990.

10 Author interview, August 1991.

11 Decree 1441, June 1961.

12 Instituto Guatemalteco de Seguridad Social, "Reglamento General Sobre Hygiene y Seguridad en el Trabajo," January 1, 1958.

13 The IGSS is actually a quasi-governmental agency founded on October 30, 1946. Authorized by law, Decree 295–46, and recognized in the 1986 Constitution, Article 71, the agency is supported through mandatory employer and employee contributions. The institution devises its own budget and operates largely independently of government supervision.

14 Labor Code, Article 197, p. 46.

15 Code, Article 198, p. 47.

16 Code, Article 203, p. 47.

17 Regulations, Article 11, p. 3.

18 A innovative health and safety promotion and prevention pilot program, with the assistance of the Italian government, was implemented in the early 1980s in the department of Escuintla near the Pacific coast. This project employs over fifty inspectors. Outside of this region, fourteen inspectors are responsible for the rest of the country.

19 Author interview, July 1990. The lack of reliable transportation for most inspectors further diminishes their effectiveness. Although the Social Security Law requires that each inspector have access to a vehicle, in most regions, particularly outside the capital, safety inspectors are fortunate to have use of a car once or twice a week, leaving them to rely on inefficient public transportation for other inspections.

20 Author interview, August 1990.

21 Author interview, July 1990.

22 Ibid.

23 Author interview, March 1991.

24 Author interview, July 1990.

25 Author, interview, August 1990.

26 Author interview, July 1990.

27 Author interview, June 1990.

28 In the collective IGSS administrative memory, the last time an inspector was prosecuted for corruption was some five years ago; when details of this incident were requested, officials declined to comment.

29 Author interview, July 1990.

30 In Regulations, see Title I, Chapter 5, Article 13, p. 4, and in the Code see Article 281, pp. 63–64.

31 A common tactic in Korean maquila factories is to feign no understanding of Spanish, thus making communication between inspectors and management impossible.

32 In an effort to combat breast cancer, IGSS began a program in 1990 in which a mobile unit of medical professionals visited various factories, offering mammograms and instructions on how to check for the cancer. Logically, the unit focused on maquila factories because of the large concentration of women workers. Unfortunately, according to IGSS officials, the program was least effective at these locations because factories frequently denied their workers access to the doctors.

33 Author interview, July 1990.

34 Regulations, Title VII, p. 24.

35 Author interview, March 1991.

36 Author interview, July 1990.

37 Ibid.

38 Ibid.

39 Ibid.

40 The descriptions and findings in this section are derived from a combination of interviews with workers and labor inspectors, and from visits to the interior of fifty-two factories and to the exterior of ninety others. In all, I have drawn my conclusions from specific data on more than one hundred and fifty factories.

41 About twelve investors, almost all Korean, have constructed their own factories. In these instances, the buildings are designed and constructed to house garment-assembly factories. When a company invests in land and a building, the facilities tend to be more modern and humane in order to maximize efficiency and production. These investors practice a more sophisticated management strategy in which the physical atmosphere—e.g., the lights, temperature, machinery, etc.—are considered critical factors in achieving maximum output. They realize that poor or uneven lighting, cramped space, and insufficient ventilation can prevent workers from reaching maximum levels of efficiency. These investors seem to share the belief that capital invested to improve physical conditions means increased production and profit in the long term. In contrast, the inferior physical conditions of the warehouse–factories demonstrate, to a large extent, the crude, short-sighted desire to maximize immediate profits which saturates the industry. Most entrepreneurs are unwilling to invest in more expensive lighting, electrical, or ventilation systems because of the potential loss of short-term profits.

42 Megatex S.A., "General Bases to Establish a Garment Assembly Industry in Guatemala," March 1990, p. 4.

43 Author interview, July 1990.

44 Author interview, August 1990.

45 Author interview, May 1990.

46 Author interview, July 1991.

47 Not one factory which I visited or received physical information about contained windows of adequate size and number to permit a significant flow of air.

48 Author interview, August 1990.

49 Author interview, July 1990.

50 Regulations, Title IV, Chapter I, Article 97, p. 21.

51 Author interview, July 1990.

52 Author interview, August 1990.

53 Ibid.

54 Regulations, Title IV, Chapter 6, p. 23.

55 Advocates of the industry point to the tremendous growth of independent food stands outside of factories as a unexpected benefit of the industry. AID claims that over a thousand "entrepreneurs" are employed in these stands.

56 Regulations, Title II, Chapter I, Article 18, p. 5.

57 This arrangement is convenient and practical for management. Among other advantages, the management can decide whether or not to allow a person to view the floor.

58 Author interview, July 1990.

59 Author interview, June 1990.

60 Ibid.

61 Author interview, July 1990.

62 The older machines arrive from either the United States or South Korea; some actually come directly from a recently dissolved factory abroad, in which everything is moved except the four walls, the roof, and, of course, the workers.

63 In at least one factory, the wooden chairs and tables are constructed in a small wood shop in a patio area outside the plant. I do not know the source of this simple furniture for the rest of the factories, but I assume it is locally produced.

64 Author interview, May 1990.

65 Ibid.

66 Ibid.

67 Author interview, August 1990.

68 Author interview, March 1991.

69 An International Ladies Garment Workers Union study of New York City garment workers revealed that more than one-sixth of the 1,000 respondents reported CTD symptoms (*Los Angeles Times*, June 11, 1989). The number of CTDs reported by U.S. workers increased from 22,000 in 1981 to 150,000 in 1989 (*Los Angeles Times*, March 29, 1991).

70 Author interview, March 1991.

71 Author interview, June 1990.

72 Author interview, August 1990.

73 Author interview, July 1990.

74 Author interviews, July and August 1990.

75 Author interview, June 1990.

76 Author interview, July 1990.

77 Author interview, June 1990.

78 Ibid.

79 Author interview, August 1991.

80 Author interview, June 1990.

81 Author interview, March 1991.

Notes to Chapter 5

1 Author interview, July 1990.

2 In Guatemalan labor law, severance pay is understood to include compensation for pregnancy and maternity leave.

3 Author interview, July 1990.

4 Ibid.

5 Ibid.

6 Author interview, March 1991.

7 IGT archives, Guatemala City, Summer 1990.

8 Author interview, March 1991.

9 Instituto Nacional de Estadística, "Empleo," p. 113. In 1988, there were slightly more than 700,000 economically active persons employed in Guatemala City. Two years later, according to INE officials, this number had increased to nearly 800,000. Using this rough number, maquila workers compose approximately 7 percent of all workers.

10 An analysis of complaints, as inspectors were quick to point out, is of limited value. They are allegations, and the inspectors' intervention and successful mediation does not necessarily imply evidence of actual employer wrongdoing. Further, since workers on most occasions only request the services of the IGT after they are dismissed, this survey might be the best indicator of the high turnover in maquila factories.

11 Code, Article 103, p. 29.

12 Constitution, Art. 102(b) and (c), pp. 16–17.

13 Author interview, July 1990.

14 Code, Article 129, p. 35.

15 Government Decree 1230–87, 1987; conversions are based on a Q5 to US$1 exchange rate.

16 Decree 65–389, 1965.

17 Author interview, July 1990.

18 Ibid.

19 *Central America Report*, May 25, 1990.

20 Author interview, March 1991. This figure was provided without substantiation.

21 Author interview, August 1990.

22 Author interview, June 1990.

23 Author interview, March 1991.

24 A more detailed discussion of the day-rate compensation system practiced in Korean factories can be found in Chapter 7, pp. 154–56.

25 Code, Articles 96 to 98, p. 28.

26 Author interview, July 1990.

27 Ibid.

28 Ibid.

29 Author interview, March 1992.

30 Ibid.

31 Author interview, June 1990.

32 Author interview, August 1990.

33 Author interview, June 1990.

34 Author interview, August 1990.

35 Author interview, July 1991.

36 Ibid.

37 Ibid.

38 Ibid.

39 Author interview, March 1991.

40 Code, Article 200, p. 46.

41 Author interview, July 1990.

42 Ibid.

43 Estimates from both workers and employers which ranged from 10 percent to over 50 percent.

44 Code, Article 150, p. 38.

45 Instituto Nacional de Estadística, "Encuesta Nacional Socio-Demográfica 1986–87—Empleo—Total Republica" (1988), 2:107, 164; quoted in James A. Goldston, *Shattered Hope: Guatemalan Workers and the Promise of Democracy* (Boulder, Colo.: Westview Press, 1979), p. 89.

46 Code, Article 153, p. 39.

47 Megatex S.A., "General Bases to Establish a Garment Assembly Industry in Guatemala," March 1990, p. 5.

48 Author interview, March 1991.

49 Author interview, August 1990.

50 Author interview, July 1990.

51 Author interview, August 1990.

52 Ibid.

53 Ibid.

54 Author interview, June 1990.

55 Author interview, July 1990.

56 Code, Article 76, p. 21.

57 Code, Article 82, p. 24.

58 See Chapter 5, pp. 81–83.

59 Author interview, July 1990.

60 This arbitrary grant of vacation time, of course, is a violation of the Code. All workers have the right, after one year of work, to two weeks' paid vacation according to their choice. Code, Article 130, p. 35.

61 Author interview, July 1990.

62 Author interview, June 1990.

63 Author interview, March 1991.

64 Author interview, July 1990.

65 Author interview, August 1990.

66 Ibid.

67 Ibid.

68 Author interview, July 1990.

69 Ibid.

70 Ibid.

71 See Chapter 7 for a more detailed discussion of the "Korean" system of management, which I call a "technology of terror."

72 Author interview, June 1990.

73 Author interview, June 1990.

74 Author interview, March 1991.

75 Author interview, July 1990.

76 Author interview, August 1990.

77 Author interview, July 1990.

Notes to Chapter 6

1 The government estimates that 8 percent of the private- and public-sector work force is unionized. Most unions contend that the actual percentage of workers in active unions is closer to 3 or 4 percent, and one leader from UNSITRAGUA claimed that less than 2 percent of the labor force belonged to functioning unions.

2 Mario Lopez Larrave, *Breve Historia del Movimiento Sindical Guatemalteco*, 2d ed. (1979), p. 31.

3 Ibid., p. 54.

4 See Henry J. Frundt, *Refreshing Pauses: Coca Cola and Human Rights in Guatemala* (New York: Praeger, 1987), for a thorough account of the union's year-long occupation of the Coca Cola bottling plant.

5 Anna Eisner, "Guatemala Unions: Testing the Waters," *Report on the Americas*, July/August 1986, p. 7.

6 Ibid.

7 See Amnesty International, "Guatemala: Trade Unionists and Political Activists Targeted under the New Government," June 1991.

8 Guatemala Human Rights Commisssion/USA, "Guatemala Labor Update," January 1992. Even the notoriously cautious U.S. State Department Human Rights Report noted in 1989 that some unionists "quit and went abroad as a result of threats." "U.S. State Department Human Rights Report: Guatemala 1989," February 1990.

9 Author interview, November 1990.

10 GEXPRONT, "Guatemala: A Manufacturing Country by Tradition," 1992, p. 1.

11 Author interviews, July and August 1990.

12 See Chapter 4, pp. 63–65.

13 Author interview, June 1990.

14 Department of Commerce, "Investment Climate Statement: Guatemala" (May 31, 1990), p. 16.

15 Constitution, Article 102(r), p. 19.

16 Goldston, *Shattered Hope*, p. 94. See pp. 93–96 for a thorough description of the complexities of obtaining legal status and recognition as a union.

17 Although not yet a problem in most maquila factories, many employers have manipulated the "twenty-person" minimum to avert union drives. A management facing a union campaign will divide its company into smaller legal entities, each consisting of less than twenty persons, thus preventing the formation of a union.

18 Code, Article 217, p. 49.

19 Cited in U.S. Department of Labor, "Guatemala," 1988–89, p. 6.

20 Author interview, June 1990.

21 Ibid.

22 This revised Labor Code was supervised by International Labor Organization experts but never even reached the floor of the Congress for a vote.

23 Author interview, August 1990.

24 Author interview, July 1990.

25 Ibid.

26 Ibid.

27 Ibid.

28 Author interview, June 1990.

29 Ibid.

30 Author interview, July 1990.

31 Author interview, June 1990.

32 Author interview, March 1992.

33 Author interview, July 1990.

34 Author interview, August 1990.

35 Author interview, July 1990.

36 Ibid.

37 Author interview, August 1990.

38 Author interview, June 1990.

39 Author interview, July 1990.

40 Ibid.

41 Author interview, August 1990.

42 Author interview, July 1990.

43 Ibid.

44 Author interview, March 1991.

45 Letter from Pamela N. Hootkin, Vice President, Treasurer, and Secretary of Phillips-Van Heusen, to Keith Phelps, December 24, 1991.

46 Letter from Lawrence Phillips to Stephen Coats, Director, U.S./Guatemala Labor Education Project, May 14, 1991.

47 Author interview, March 1991.

48 Ibid.

49 Author interview, March 1991.

50 Letter from Lawrence Phillips to Stephen Coats, May 14, 1991.

51 Author interview, March 1991.

52 The U.S. Ambassador, Thomas F. Stroock, in a February 12, 1992, letter to Bruce Klatsky, president of PVH, dismissed allegations of bribes as "street rumors." He also wrote, "Based on my personal observations and conversations, it can be categorically asserted that we have never had any shred of evidence presented to us indicating that workers in your plants are mistreated." The ambassador later admitted that neither he nor any of his staff had investigated the allegations.

53 Cited in Steve Coats, "Made in Guatemala: Union Busting in the *Maquiladoras*," *Multinational Monitor*, November 1991, p. 25.

54 Author interview, August 1990.

55 Author interview, June 1990.

56 Ibid.

57 Author interview, July 1990.

58 Ibid.

59 Ibid.

60 Author interview, June 1990.

61 Author interview, July 1990.

62 Author interview, August 1990.

63 Workers have formed ad hoc committees and obtained an *emplazamiento* in the following factories: Transcontinentales S.A. (1986); Pindu S.A. (1986); Internacionales de Exportaciones S.A. (1986, 1991); Koram S.A. (1988); Diseños Panamericanos S.A. (1988); Dong San S.A. (1989); Mantex S.A. (1989); Camisas Modernas S.A. (1989, 1990, 1991); Tradema S.A. (1990); Mikwang S.A. (1990, 1991); Booco S.A. (1990); Confecciones Unidas S.A. (1991); Sportex S.A. (1992).

64 Author interview, March 1991.

65 Author interview with four executive committee members of the Inexport union, June 1990.

66 *Emplazamiento* issued February 11, 1990.

67 Author interview, July 1990.

68 Author interview, August 1990.

69 Ibid.

70 Author interview, July 1990.

71 *Emplazamiento* issued on May 11, 1990.

72 Author interview with an organizer of the union campaign in Booco, July 1990.

73 Author interview, July 1990.

74 At Diseños Panamericanos S.A., a Korean supervisor threatened a worker named Rosa Delmi Recinos on August 29, 1988, telling her he would kill anyone who joined a union. The worker filed a complaint with the Criminal Court, and the supervisor fled to Korea soon after this incident.

75 Author interview, June 1990.

76 The factories that have transferred part or all of an operation to another location, either in Guatemala or to another country, due to union organizing are the following: Transcontinentales S.A., 1987 (after union formed, entire operation was transported out of the country); Diseños Panamericanos S.A., 1989 (in response to a union drive, the factory shut down and moved to another location outside the city); Booco S.A., 1989 (after defeating a union movement through bribes and intimidation, the owner closed the factory, returned to Korea for several months, and then reopened a new factory under the same name in Guatemala City); Dong San S.A., 1989 (after the factory was enjoined for the second time, it closed down operations in ZOLIC and moved to Zone 13 in Guatemala City); Pindu S.A., 1988 and 1991 (unable to defeat a fledgling union, the factory first moved most of its operations to Honduras and consolidated with another smaller factory, then, three years later, shut down Guatemalan operations altogether).

77 A fuller description of the events at Transcontinentales S.A. can be found in Chapter 3, pp. 53–55.

78 Author interview with the CGTG official who assisted workers of Diseños Panamericanos S.A. to organize, June 1990.

79 Author interview, July 1990.

80 Ibid.

81 Author interview, August 1990.

82 Ibid.

83 Ibid.

84 Ibid.

85 Author interview, June 1990.

86 Author interview, July 1990.

87 Curtin Winsor, Jr., "Solidarismo: The Dawn of Popular Capitalism?" undated manuscript.

88 Author interview, July 1990.

89 Curtin Winsor, Jr., "The Solidarista Movement: Labor Economics for Democracy," *The Washington Quarterly* (Fall 1986), p. 177.

90 Author interview, July 1990.

91 The association at the main Pepsi bottling factory in Guatemala City, for instance, reportedly is investigating the creation of a trucking company.

92 U.S. Department of Labor, "Guatemala," Foreign Labor Trends, 1988–89, p. 6.

93 Ciencia y tecnología para Guatemala, "The Trade Union Movement in Guatemala (1986–1988): Part 1," Mexico City, May 1990, p. 11.

94 Author interview, August 1990.

95 Ciencia y tecnología para Guatemala, "The Trade Union Movement in Guatemala (1986–1988): Part 1."

96 Author interview, August 1990.

97 Author interview, June 1990.

98 Author interview, July 1990.

99 A USG list of *Solidarismo* associations dated June 1990 reveals that only 170 businesses, rather than the 300-plus official figure, had associations. The list includes three maquila factories that no longer maintain an association; for an unknown reason, it also contains two listings for each business which, if counted separately, would add up to more than 350 associations. When asked about this duplication of listings, Joseph Recinos commented: "It is probably true that some associations drop away. We shall redo our list" (August 1990).

100 The factories where associations had been initiated are: Fábrica Navarra y Confecciónes Rivas S.A.; Confecciónes Ideales S.A.; Manufacturas Best S.A.; Confecciónes Iberoamericanas S.A.; Cortex S.A.; Koram S.A., B y D Confecciónes

S.A., Mantex S.A., Pindu S.A., Inexport S.A.; Cardiz S.A.; and Camisas Modernas S.A.

101 These factories are: Koram S.A., B y D Confecciónes S.A., Mantex S.A., Pindu S.A., Inexport S.A., Confecciónes Iberoamericanos S.A., and Camisas Modernas S.A.

102 Author interview, July 1990.

103 Author interview, June 1990.

104 Author interview, July 1990.

105 Author interview, June 1990.

106 Ibid.

107 Author interview, July 1990.

108 Author interviews, July and August 1990.

109 Author interview with Joseph Recino, cofounder of USG, June 1990.

110 Author interview, September 1990.

111 Author interview, August 1990.

112 Ibid.

113 Author interview, March 1991.

114 Author interview, August 1990.

115 Author interview, June 1990.

116 Author interview, August 1990.

117 Ibid.

118 Ibid.

119 Author interview with labor inspector, March 1991.

120 Labor Ministry, Department of Statistics, "List of Inscribed Unions," March 1991.

121 Author interviews, July and August 1990.

122 Author interview, July 1990.

123 Author interview, March 1991.

124 Ibid.

125 Author interview, August 1990.

126 Author interview, July 1990.

127 Author interview, August 1990.

128 Author interview, March 1991.

129 Author interview, July 1990.

130 Ibid.

131 Author interview, June 1990.

132 Author interview, July 1990.

133 Author interview, March 1991.

134 Author interview, July 1990.

Notes to Chapter 7

1 Author interview, August 1990.

2 Key-Sung Cho, *Organismos Interamericanos: Sus Antecedentes, Estructuras, Funciónes y Perspectivas* (Quito, Ecuador, 1984).

3 A discussion of the contents and limitations of the CBERA can be found in Chapter 2, pp. 24–25.

4 Author interview, August 1990.

5 The meetings included representatives from the Korean Foreign Ministry, the Commerce and Industry Ministry, the Chamber of Commerce, and the Chamber of Small and Medium Industry, as well as assorted private companies.

6 As of May 1992, there were fifty Korean factories in Guatemala. The Dominican Republic has twenty-nine plants; Costa Rica, eighteen; Jamaica, eleven; Honduras, seven; and the remainder are spread out mostly among Caribbean islands.

7 *Korea Trade and Business*, October 1991, p. 7.

8 Of the fifty Korean factories, six are owned by dual citizens of the U.S.A. and Korea. Another two Korean-owned factories manufacture plastic tubing.

9 Author interview with Ambassador Cho, August 1990.

10 Another factory, B y D Confecciónes S.A., opened in Guatemala after closing its doors in New York City. The owner cited higher wages and immigration problems as the main reasons for relocating in Guatemala.

11 Author interview, June 1990.

12 Author interview, August 1990.

13 Ibid.

14 Author interview with Ambassador Cho, August 1990.

15 Author interview with Ambassador Cho, March 1991.

16 Author interview with Korean ambassador, March 1992.

17 Author interview, May 1990.

18 Korean Embassy, March 1992.

19 Author interview, March 1991.

20 Korea Trade Promotion Corporation, *KOTRA, 1990*.

21 Author interview, July 1990.

22 Steele, *Caribbean Clothing Industry*, p. 26.

23 *Far Eastern Economic Review*, March 24, 1988.

24 *Business Korea*, April 1989, p. 30.

25 Since 1987 Korean textile and apparel factories have had great difficulty finding young workers who are willing to work at wages said to be bearable for manufacturers. See *Korean Trade and Business*, November 1991, p. 43.

26 Japan Textile Information Center, *Apparel Handbook*, 1988.

27 Author interview, July 1990.

28 Author interview, November 1990.

29 Author interview, August 1990.

30 Author interview, July 1990.

31 Author interview, August 1990.

32 Ibid.

33 David C. Cole and Princeton N. Lyman, *Korean Development: The Interplay of Politics and Economics* (Cambridge, Mass.: Harvard University Press, 1971), p. 201.

34 Alice H. Amsden, *Asia's Next Giant: South Korea and Late Industrialization* (New York: Oxford University Press, 1989), p. 112.

35 Cole and Lyman, *Korean Development*, p. 19.

36 Gilsbert van Liemt, *Bridging the Gap: Four Newly Industrialized Countries and the Changing International Division of Labor* (Geneva: International Labor Office, 1988), p. 61.

37 Ibid, p. 60.

38 For a more thorough discussion of this repressive system of worker control, see George E. Ogle, *South Korea: Dissent within the Economic Miracle* (London: Zed Books, 1990).

39 Ibid., p. 47.

40 Ibid., p. 73.

41 Ibid.

42 Author interview, July 1990.

43 Ambassador Cho, March 1991.

44 Frederic C. Deyo, *Beneath the Miracle: Labor Subordination in the New Asian Industrialism* (Berkeley: University of California Press, 1989), p. 8.

45 Author interview, August 1990.

46 Author interview, July 1990.

47 Ibid.

48 Author interview, August 1990.

49 Ibid.

50 Author interview, July 1990.

51 Author interview, August 1990.

52 Author interview, June 1990.

53 Author interview, March 1991.

54 Author interview, August 1990.

55 Author interview, June 1990.

56 Author interview, August 1990.

57 Author interview, July 1990.

58 Author interview, March 1991.

59 Author interview, July 1990.

60 Author interview, May 1990.

61 Ibid.

62 Author interview, August 1990.

63 Author interview, June 1990.

64 Author interview, July 1990.

65 Author interview, August 1990.

66 Ibid.

67 Author interview, June 1990.

68 Author interview, July 1990.

69 Author interview, August 1990.

70 Author interview, March 1991.

71 In contrast, Guatemalan supervisors in Korean factories earn between $100 and $200 a month.

72 Author interview, March 1991.

73 Ibid.

74 Author interview, July 1990.

75 Author interview, March 1991.

76 Ibid.

77 Author interview, July 1990.

78 Author interview, September 1990.

79 Author interview, March 1991.

80 Author interview, July 1990.

81 Ibid.

82 Author interview, March 1991.

83 Author interview, August 1991.

84 Author interview, July 1990.

85 Ibid.

86 Author interview, June 1990.

87 Ibid.

88 Author interview, July 1990.

89 Author interview, June 1990.

90 Author interview with Gary Garzaro, VESTEX director of statistics, August 1990.

91 Author interview, July 1990.

92 Author interview, June 1990.

93 Author interview, July 1990.

94 Author interview, August 1990.

95 Ibid.

96 Author interview, June 1990.

97 *El Gráfico*, July 27, 1990.

98 Author interview, August 1990.

99 Ibid.

100 Ibid.

101 See Chapter 6, pp. 133–34.

102 See ibid., pp. 115–16.

103 See ibid., pp. 110–13.

104 *La Hora*, April 22, 1991.

105 Author interview with Guatemalan reporter who requested anonymity, March 1991.

106 Author interview, March 1991.

107 Unclassified memo from U.S. Embassy to U.S. State Department, No. 002809, March 1989.

108 Author interview, March 1991.

109 Author interview, August 1990.

110 Author interview, July 1990.

111 Ibid.

112 Ibid.

113 Author interview, March 1991.

Notes to Chapter 8: Conclusion

1 Author interview, July 1990.

2 Ibid.

3 Ibid.

4 Author interview, March 1991.

5 Ibid.

6 Ibid.

7 Author interview, July 1990.

8 Ibid.

9 Ibid.

10 Author interview, August 1991.

11 German Press Agency Report, *Central America Report*, March 8, 1991.

12 Author interview, July 1990.

13 From the beginning of GEXPRONT, Korea was seen as the paradigmatic example of the development formula. As early as 1986, GEXPRONT officials were referring to Korea as the most appropriate example of the possibility represented by the introduction of new markets and the development of nontraditional products. See *Central America Report*, December 19, 1986, pp. 385–87. See *Report on the Americas* 23, no. 5 (February 1990): 14–26 for an excellent analysis of recent AID expectations for economic development in Jamaica.

14 Barbara Stallings, "The Role of Foreign Capital in Economic Development," in Gary Gereffi and Donald Wyman, eds., *Manufacturing Miracles: Paths of Industrialization in Latin America and East Asia*, 1990, p. 77. See also Alice Amsted, *Asia's Next Giant*, pp. 79–113.

15 David I. Steinberg, "Foreign Aid and the Development of the Republic of Korea: The Effectiveness of Concessional Assistance," AID Special Study No. 42, U.S. AID, October 1985, p. 8.

16 One of the few traits Guatemala shares with the newly industrialized countries of Southeast Asia is a politically repressed labor force. In both situations, the government leaves labor relations to employers, occasionally supplementing this iron fist with the police, military, and sanctioned death squads.

17 U.S. Department of Commerce, "Foreign Economic Trends and Their Implications for the United States: Guatemala," February 1990, p. 7.

18 Over half of the Guatemalan adult population cannot read or write, making the work force the least literate in the region. This percentage is higher for women, who, of course, compose most of the maquila work force: 58 percent of adult women and 75 percent of indigenous women are illiterate. Only one in a hundred women makes it to college, and barely one in two thousand graduates. UNICEF, *Análisis de Situación del Niño y la Mujer*, Guatemala, August 1991.

19 Noel F. McGinn et al., *Education and Development in Korea* (Cambridge, Mass.: Harvard University Press, 1980), p. 241. See also Gilbert Brown, *Korean Pricing Policies and Economic Development in the 1960s* (Baltimore: Johns Hopkins Press, 1974), p. 13.

20 Brown, *Korean Pricing Policies*, p. 13.

21 *Central America Report*, May 24, 1991.

22 Ibid., February 2, 1990. In the last thirty years, Guatemala has spent only 1.6 percent of its GDP on public education.

23 See, for example, Paus, *Struggle Against Independence*, p. 3.

24 Carmen Diane Deere et al., *In the Shadows of the Sun: Caribbean Development Alternatives and U.S. Policy* (Boulder, Colo.: Westview Press, 1990), p. 173. Data taken from U.S. government sources.

25 Author interview, July 1991.

26 Author interview, August 1990.

27 Author interview, March 1992.

28 Steinberg, "Foreign Aid and the Development of the Republic of Korea," p. 89.

29 Author interview, July 1990.

30 Author interview, March 1991.

31 Author interview, August 1991.

32 Author interview, July 1991.

33 U.S. Department of Commerce, "Investment Climate Study," May 31, 1990.

34 19 U.S.C.A. §2461 et seq.

35 19 U.S.C.A. §2701 et seq.

36 See Bruce H. Turnbull, *Worker Rights under the U.S. Trade Laws* (New York: Lawyers Committee for Human Rights, 1989), for an explication and discussion of the worker rights provisions in these and other statutes.

37 Many labor and human rights advocates and U.S. unions contend that these provisions are applied more with regard to political considerations than the actual conditions of labor rights. For example, in Central America, the U.S. government removed the GSP privileges from Nicaragua soon after the Sandinista Revolution. El Salvador and Guatemala, nations with far worse records of labor rights violations, have never lost access to these benefits.

For a more complete analysis of worker rights provisions in trade legislation, see Terry Collingsworth, "American Labor Policy and the International Economy: Clarifying Policies and Interests," *Boston College Law Review* 31, no. 1 (December 1989): 31–102, and U.S. Department of Labor, Bureau of International Labor Affairs, *Labor Standards and Development in the Global Economy*, 1990.

38 Author interview, March 1991.

39 *Central America Report*, April 12, 1991.

40 Author interview, August 1990.

41 Author interview, March 1991.

Index